Courage
to Think Differently

Written and Edited by
George S. Johnson

Additional copies are available from Bang Printing, Brainerd, MN 1-800-328-0450 or Perryg@bangprinting.com or Amazon.com. Or contact the Author at georgesjohnson@gmail.com. Liberal discounts are offered for multiple copies. Invoice will be sent with the books.

Book and Cover design by Lora Westberg

Cover art by Rodolfo Arrelano, from the peasant paintings of Solentiname, used by permission.

Courage to Think Differently
About Issues that Really Matter

ISBN 987-0-9703028-1-6

WHAT OTHERS ARE SAYING

An important book for American Christians today, put together by one of our prophetic voices.

Marcus Borg, author of Meeting Jesus Again for the First Time

Ashley Montagu believed that "there are millions of Christians in the world but few followers of Jesus." With selections from several contemporary prophets, Johnson hopes to move us to follow Jesus and stand with him by thinking and acting to alleviate poverty, oppression and war. Read, think, act!!

Lowell Erdahl, Bishop Emeritus, St. Paul Area Synod, ELCA

Einstein has said that you cannot solve a problem by using the same mindset that created it. Thinking differently has become a survival imperative. That is why this book is important.

Vandana Shiva, author, scientist, environmentalist, New Delhi

Following Jesus can be a lonely and scary passion. We don't seem to be able to look to our churches. At their best they fail to provide courage to think differently and at their worst they become cheerleaders for dominance and oppression. Johnson's book provides a unique perspective. I highly recommend it.

Hans Kraus, entrepreneur and business CEO

It is a matter of not fitting in, embodying alternatives, and thinking differently as Johnson and the authors whose voices are brought together here argue.

Joerg Rieger, professor of Theology, Perkins School of Theology, Dallas

Each time I have had contact with George Johnson over the years I have found a kindred spirit. Grounded in scripture and good theology, George has found the freedom to think and act in ways that challenge my own thought and action. In this book he continues to do this for every reader.

Herbert W. Chilstrom, Former Presiding Bishop of the ELCA

I rejoice in George Johnson's courage to write and edit a book which addresses many of the issues that politicians and religious leaders are afraid to tackle. He has assembled a "who's who" of prophetic and scholarly voices who probe root causes of injustice in the world.

David Ellingson, professor, environmental leader, Trinity College

Johnson's book arrives at an opportune moment. We are living in an unsustainable global situation. God is calling us to think differently. This book is an excellent tool so that we as Christians can make a difference.

Elsa Tamez, author, professor of Biblical theology in Costa Rica

This book is a gold mine and powerfully useful for parishes, schools, universities, seminaries and training church rostered leaders.

Janet Hansted, pastor of Holy Trinity Church, Thousand Oaks, CA

Courage to Think Differently presents bold thoughts in a compelling way.

Anita Coleman (from India), Presbyterian wife, mother, author

If you were going on a journey and could take only ten books what would you take? This book would be a very good choice with 35 powerful essays. Johnson's book is a valuable resource for people who feel very alone, longing for a different kind of church and world.

Barbara K Lundblad, Professor of Preaching, Union Seminary

George's insightful reflections challenge us to find the courage to look at deeper questions that don't have easy answers.

David Beckmann, President of Bread for the World

As a business person and former publisher I was very pleased to see this new publication by George Johnson . . . The list of authors is stellar. Thank you, George, for the courage to challenge us.

John Yackel, Past president and CEO of (AGS) American Guidance Service

I find my sense of gratitude for this book rising steadily page by page. George Johnson draws on his lifetime of work for justice. In the pages of this book it becomes clear that thinking differently can actually open the way for genuine transformation in life.

**Paul R. Sponheim
Professor Emeritus, Luther Seminary, St Paul, MN**

This book is a choir of voices that are not often heard in the church today. I have used this book with boards of directors and congregational councils to reflect on the radical call of the gospel.

**David Nagler
Pastor of Christ Lutheran Church, San Diego, CA**

Courage
to Think Differently

Written and Edited by
George S. Johnson

TABLE OF CONTENTS

TABLE OF CONTENTS

If you want more information on the authors look them up on the internet.

SPECIAL THANKS

I first want to acknowledge and express appreciation to my wife, Vivian, who has been an encourager and supporter for me in the work that has resulted in this book. She kept asking me, "George, darling, when are you going to work on your book? But don't forget it's Thursday, your night to make dinner."

When Vivian and I were pastors in residence at El Camino Pines Bible Camp last summer we invited a group of friends to come to camp for a Day of Conversation about *Courage to Think Differently*. It was a very helpful discussion. Among those who participated were:

Jane Affonso, David Gist, Hank Kraus, Gloria Kinsler, Erin Armstrong, Janet Hansted, David Nagler, Ross Kinsler, Steve Beckham, Lara Janssen, Ron Nelson, Alexa Salvatierra, Glen Egertson, Vivian Johnson, Dan Rift, Aaron Tidwell and George Johnson.

I have received insightful editorial and computer services from a number of people: Alyssa Stanford, Lora Westberg, Gerri Slabough, Joy Wright, Vivian Johnson and Dean Whitten. I am deeply in debt to them. They have been great.

Self-publishing involves a great deal of preliminary work and up-front money. I invited a few friends who are active in social justice ministry to consider investing in this book project. Their sacrifice and commitment have helped to bring this book to fruition and make it possible to lower the price. Please offer a prayer of thanks for them.

I want to thank Adventure Publications, Bang Printing, Irvine United Congregational Church, the many permissions people, and the artists who have helped in the process of producing a book like this.

I know some of the authors in this book personally. Their books are all appreciated. They have a special place in my library. One struggle I have had is deciding which articles and authors to include. There are so many others that I would have loved to include. I apologize for leaving them out. A sincere thanks to all who have shared their hearts and minds . . . and experiences in this book. Thank you for passing its message along.

Dedicated To:

**The memory of all those who lost their lives because they
had the courage to think differently and took a stand with the poor
and oppressed. We honor them by continuing the struggle.**

*We have this treasure in earthen vessels . . .
We are afflicted in every way, but not crushed;
Perplexed, but not driven to despair;
Persecuted, but not forsaken;
Struck down, but not destroyed.*

*Always carrying in the body the death of Jesus
So that the life of Jesus may be made visible . . .
So death is at work in us, but life in you.*

II Corinthians 4

A neglected beatitude
*Blessed are those who are persecuted for justice sake,
For theirs is the kingdom of heaven.
Blessed are you when people revile you,
And persecute you
And utter all kinds of evil against you
falsely on my account.*

A rabbi from Nazareth, Matthew 5

George Johnson is one tenacious guy! His tenacity is in the service of his passion for the truth and claim of the Gospel. That combination of tenacity and passion has resulted in this book that is a rich resource for missional thinking about the church in the midst of our society. Johnson sees clearly that the Gospel in its central intention is not about the saving of souls, as in much traditional piety. It is about the rule of God in the world and the ways in which that rule impinges upon matters of economics and politics. Johnson has not only recruited the writers for this book and secured the necessary permissions, but he has also himself authored a number of pieces in the book that bear witness and make connections.

Johnson has taken as his lead text the parable in Luke 16:19-31 concerning the rich man and Lazarus, the management of resources in this age, and prospects for the age to come. Johnson and his companions in this book know several things about this parable. They know that it occurs only in Luke, the gospel that begins with the revolutionary Song of Mary (Luke 1:46-55) and ends in the preaching of the apostles in the Book of Acts that confounds the Roman Empire (Acts 3:17-26; 24:10-21). `All the way from the Song of Mary to the preaching of the apostles, this testimony challenges the empire and thinks differently about the themes of the empire, that is, power and money. For these commentators, it is no venturesome move from the Roman Empire to the empire of the United States that now, in its exploitative greed and violence, must be called into question by the same song, the same parable, and the same preaching.

Johnson and his colleagues can see that this parable, perhaps an epitome of the Lucan rendering of the good news, provides a basis for class analysis that brings to light the deep tension between the haves and the have-nots. They know, moreover, that while the poor man gets Abraham and all of the gifts of the unconditional presence of God, the rich man gets only Moses and the Torah. That is, the rich man gets only the commands of covenant concerning the neighbor, nothing more. That juxtaposition of the two traditions, Abraham and Moses, assigned respectively to the poor man and the rich man, is counter-intuitive amid our common social practice. In our usual world the haves characteristically enjoy God's free gifts while the have-nots are subject to stringent requirements. It turns out, however, that the stringent requirements imposed upon the have-nots are not those of the covenantal God, but of the "pyramid club" of wealth and power that is designed to keep the have-nots in "their place" and in their role as cheap labor. Thus the parable provides a ground for summoning the haves to Torah obedience. That obedience entails not only attending to a list of commandments, but in casting one's life in a performance of the commands of neighborly justice as those commands well up in the midst of the rough and tumble of the political economy.

Focus on the song, the parable, and the preaching shows that the Gospel of Luke does not flinch from class analysis. Thus already Mary can attest to the lowly and the rich:

> **He has brought down the powerful from their thrones, and lifted up the lowly; he has filled the hungry with good things, and has sent the rich away empty.**
>
> *Luke 1:52-53*

Such a distinction provides categories through which to think differently the gospel. Our usual way is to imagine that we are all – haves and have-nots – equal before God's throne of mercy. This tradition, however, specializes in inequality and places a heavy burden upon the haves.

The intent of the present book is that we should think, that is, that we should not settle for the repeated mantras of our society, but that we should probe and reflect, and critique and hope in ways that construe the world differently. The book is a call for venturesome imagination.

But the test is not merely to think. It is to think "Christianly," to think with reference to the narrative of Jesus with his summons, "Follow me." That summons characteristically is to depart the categories of the empire and to walk an alternative walk that culminates in a confrontation with the authorities of the empire (as in the book of Acts). In such a frame of reference, of course, there is no dimension of our common life that is not construed differently when it is taken in such away.

To "think Christianly" is a deep departure from the habits of our society both to think at all, and to think differently. Our society is organized to discourage thinking. Our reliance upon technological solutions to human problems, our preoccupation with consumer goods, our engagement with professional sports that are all about money, power, and virility, our saturation of militarism, and our systemic violation of Sabbath all contribute to the thoughtlessness that makes for consenting conformity to the ideology of the empire. Susan Thistlethwaite describes this condition as being "anesthetized," or I might say, narcoticized. Either way, a refusal or inability to think means that we forfeit the freedom and shun the responsibility that properly belongs to adherents of the gospel. Thus the book is an invitation to break the spell of dominant culture.

But of course such thinking is no intellectual pass-time. It is rather thinking that morphs to action, so that the book is indeed about *praxis*, about thinking coming to practical possibility that is performed in concrete ways.

In order to provide a rich variety of thinkers and in order to reflect on how the gospel impinges upon the several dimensions of our common life, Johnson has recruited a remarkable cast of characters that includes many of our most courageous activist thinkers who are at work on a variety of fronts. This cast of characters will provide important entry points into the hard work now facing those who care in obedient ways. Or it will serve as a stimulus and confirmation for those who have already begun their journey to thinking action. Among the voices offered here, Harry Emerson Fosdick is the senior member. Coming from an earlier generation, Fosdick attests to the "divinity of Jesus" by seeing that "God is love," and Jesus embodies that love in radical ways. And of course in such a collection it is inevitable that Martin Luther King should be front and center in his chiding "good people" who remain passive amid the emergency. What emerges in this collection is an awareness that the gospel pertains to every public question among us concerning the economy, the environment, race, war, and every justice issue imaginable. The voices represented here have, over time, been bold in their thinking and wise in making connections that refuse to let society float off into selfish, violent greed or to permit the gospel to be caricatured as an enterprise about "saving souls."

These essays reflect a sense of urgency. They do so because we now live in a predatory society in which the poor, weak, and marginal are profoundly at risk along with the environment at risk. In a society that is largely deregulated, the powerful can, as they will, prey upon and exploit the vulnerable. But these essays are characteristically acts of hope. These writers are fully convinced that another way to arrange public power in indeed possible. That "other way" requires courage, the courage to withstand commonly accepted assumptions and conclusions, and to run the risk of alternatives. The courage required is the kind to which Jesus called his disciples with his "follow me." And before him, it was the courage of Moses summoning his people to depart Pharaoh's predatory system.

It is easy enough in our society to conclude that the claims of the gospel are fanciful, outmoded, and irrelevant to our social condition. This book, however, invites us to pause in amazement to ponder the question concerning the gospel, "What if it is true?" What if the gospel tells the truth about society under the rule of God? If true – and surely true – many things become possible as alternative. And many things we take for granted become unacceptable in light of the gospel. This is a welcome book that summons us. It is welcome because many of us stand alongside the rich man in the parable who wanted a messenger sent to warn his five brothers (Luke 16:27-28). This book just might be that messenger with a warning . . . to which attention must be paid.

Walter Brueggemann
Columbia Theological Seminary
July 25, 2012

This volume speaks at a pivotal moment in the history of our beautiful and brutal species. Humankind hovers on a precipice. On one side is almost unimaginable climate disaster in which those least responsible for the climate crisis suffer most from its deadly consequences. That is, the world's impoverished people – who are disproportionately people of color – will continue to be killed and displaced by an ecological reality caused largely by the beneficiaries of industrial capitalism who are disproportionately white. This path would further the concentration of wealth, power, and privilege in the hands of a few. On the other side, however, is the potential before us: A world in which all people have the necessities for life with dignity and Earth's eco-systems flourish.

At this turning point, something new is asked of humankind – to forge ways of living that nurture rather than degrade Earth's life systems and that build equity among and between Earth's peoples. When something new is asked of humankind, something new is asked of religion. All of Earth's great faith traditions are called today to plumb their depths for wellsprings of moral-spiritual vision, hope, wisdom, and courage, and to offer these to the broader public.

One gift to be explored and offered by people who follow a subversive dark-skinned Jew from ancient Palestine is the strange and compelling story of divine love incarnate on this roving planetary speck called Earth. Love as it is revealed in the best of Christian – as well as Jewish and Muslim – traditions makes claims that shake the foundations of the world. The beginning point is God's love. The claim is breath-taking: The holy intimate Mystery whom Christians, Jews, and Muslims call God loves this world and each of us with a love that will never cease, a love more powerful than any other force in heaven or earth, a love that hungers fiercely for justice especially for "the least of these." Secondly, we human creatures are created and called to recognize this gracious love, receive it, relish it, revel in it, and trust it. And finally, after receiving and trusting that love, we are to embody it in the world by loving as God loves. We are beckoned to join with God's Spirit of justice-making Earth-relishing Love in its steadfast commitment to gain fullness of life for all, to heal and liberate. Jewish tradition refers to this as Tikkun Elan (to heal the world).

Never before have the stakes in heeding our calling to justice-making love been so high. Will the Christian movement step up to the plate?

I believe that two things are key. One is re-understanding neighbor-love ("You will love your neighbor....") as not only an interpersonal virtue but as a calling that shapes the political and economic structures of life. Here is where this volume comes in and becomes an utterly profound gift to the church and the world. This volume holds invaluable instruction in love as a political-economic-ecological vocation.

A second key is learning what I refer to as "critical mystical vision." It begins by asking: What in any given circumstance is assumed to be natural, normal, inevitable, or divinely ordained that, in fact, may be just a social construct and not inevitable nature, normal, or divinely ordained at all? Where does systemic evil parade as good? Where does systemic injustice hide behind the blinders of privilege?

These are dangerous question. They are liberating questions. I pose them to students in every class that I teach.

These questions challenge us to "see what is going on." That is, to see through the myths that structure our lives together. Myths? Yes, like the myth that advanced global capitalism is necessarily the way of the future. Or the myth that our cheap food, clothing, transportation, and electronics are actually low cost, rather than bearing deadly costs for vast numbers of people and for Earth's life-systems. Or the myth that poverty, racism, and ecological degradation can be overcome by private goodness and generosity in private life. (These virtues are necessary and of infinite worth. Yet addressing structural evil calls also for structural solutions. Flight into privatized morality breeds moral oblivion in the face of unjust systems.)

Ah, but daring to see "what is going on," where the vision is systemic brutality invites despair. Therefore, if we are to love well in the face of systemic injustice, we will cultivate critical mystical vision, the capacity to practice three forms of vision at one time:

- Seeing "what is going on" in whatever situation is at hand, and especially unmasking systemic evil that masquerades as good.

- Seeing "what could be," that is, life-giving, socially just and eco-logically regenerative ways of living and structuring our life in common. These alternatives are signs of hope breaking through the volcanic wasteland of economic and ecological violence.

- Seeing ever more fully the sacred Spirit of life coursing throughout creation and luring us – despite all evidence to the contrary – into abundant life for all. "When our days become dreary with low-hovering clouds of despair...let us remember that there is a creative force in this universe, working to pull down the gigantic moun-tains of evil, a power that is able to make a way out of no way and transform dark yesterdays into bright tomorrows" (Dr. Martin Luther King, Jr.).

Christian life has at its heart the crucial task of holding these three in one lens. Vision of this sort is subversive because it nurtures "courage to think differently." It reveals a future in the making and breeds hope for moving into it. Enter again the power of this volume. It is a splendid guidebook in subversive, hope-enlivening moral vision.

FOREWORD

"I have set before you life and death, blessings and curses. Choose life so that you and your descendants may live" (Deut. 30:19). A great choice, a great calling, is before humankind and its religions today. With this book, George Johnson and his collaborators plant seeds for growing love as a political-economic-ecological calling and for growing critical mystical vision. May we the readers cultivate and harvest those precious seeds so that we may have the courage to think differently and to choose life.

Cynthia D. Moe-Lobeda

Professor of Theology and Social Ethics

Pacific Lutheran Seminary, July 2016

INTRODUCTION

The writer of the fourth gospel in the New Testament included an encounter in the life of Jesus that deserves more attention than it receives in many churches today. It is the meeting between Nicodemus and Jesus. There have been various attempts to interpret this story. Many are used to support a particular theological bias such as baptismal regeneration or evangelical evangelism efforts. But everyone, I think, agrees that Jesus is telling Nicodemus that a change is needed in his thinking and values.

> **Unless one is born again (anew) one cannot enter or understand the Kingdom of God.**
>
> *John 3:3*

Jesus is telling Nicodemus (and us) that one needs to think differently if one is to become part of the movement that will change the world. To be born again involves a new perspective, a new world view, a new center, a paradigm shift, a new orientation. Jesus introduced an alternative wisdom that involved a different mind-set.

Following Jesus involves a change in one's thinking. This may begin to happen at a specific memorable encounter or experience, but it most certainly will evolve and grow over time. Everyone's story about being born again is different. Paul says in II Corinthians 3:18, "We are all being changed from one degree of glory to another." Often this change in thinking involves struggle and resistance. We are not always comfortable with change.

To think differently is especially difficult when we have been schooled to think a certain way for a long time and have based our values and beliefs on what we consider to be solid authority. Acts 10 tells about Peter, who was convinced that his theology about Jew/Gentile relationships was faithful to scripture and correct. We read how Peter had an experience that caused him to think differently. He resisted. He had scripture and tradition to support his beliefs. His leadership and reputation were at stake. He had experienced great success after his Pentecost sermon where 3,000 were converted. His resume included a three-year stint with Jesus and witnessing first hand the crucifixion and empty tomb. But Peter needed to change his thinking. It took a powerful experience and great courage to bring about a change. It is interesting to note the different times in Peter's life that he was led to think differently. Remember the washing of feet in John 13? Check it out.

We are living in a world and a time where some difficult decisions are required of us. Our choices will result in life or death for millions of people. Every day the news of our world tells of one crisis after another. There seems to be no escape from being impacted by conflicts that threaten our lives of privilege and security as well as the lives of those living on the margins, and creation itself. Articles in this book will illustrate this. Simplistic or easy answers don't work any longer. If we want the Kingdom to come and God's will to be done, we need courage to think differently.

There is so much new information to read about and learn. How does one connect the dots? How does one put things into perspective or know who to believe, whom to trust? How does what is happening and what is being said fit into our faith values? Some of what we hear and read is deeply colored by a specific political agenda or economic bias. Are we being programmed into a way of thinking that supports primarily my security, my agenda, my tribe with little regard to how it impacts the world? Have we been co-opted by the system?

Lately I have re-read some of the material that has been written by authors I deeply respect, but had been set aside or returned to the bottom of the pile so I could read new stuff. Both old and new books have caused me to rethink and revisit some long-held beliefs and values. This has motivated me to put some of these writings together in this volume where one can glean from many sources what people are saying about the need to think differently. I am grateful to the authors and publishers who have given permission to share the writings in this book. Space limitations have forced me to leave out many excellent articles.

The material is divided into seven sections with an appendix of various teaching resources. This book does not need to be read from beginning to end; one can easily pick and choose where to begin. Discussion questions are added to many articles for use in reflection, classes or small groups. Some articles are taken from small group study guides or Bible studies on the topic of social justice.

The kind of thinking needed today is not always easy or comfortable. I remember the struggle I went through 50+ years ago on the issue of divorce. My parents were devout conservative Christians. I attended a Christian high school, a church-related college (Augustana) and a Bible school before entering seminary to become a pastor. I felt fairly secure in my beliefs and feelings about divorce. While the Bible is not always consistent in its teaching about divorce, for me it was clear that divorce was wrong for those who took the Bible seriously.

Then my senior year at the seminary, while still single, I met Vivian, a devout Christian, who had been divorced. Falling in love with her forced me to think differently about divorce. It was a struggle emotionally as well as spiritually. I searched the scriptures. I counseled with seminary professors and parish pastors. And yes, I prayed. Vivian did all these things too.

One of the complications that surfaced for me was a rule that forbade any seminary student from being ordained if divorced or married to a divorced person. This meant that if I married Vivian, I would not be able to serve as pastor in my denomination. Divorce was allowed among church members, but not pastors. I petitioned to have the rule set aside in my case, but the national church board for my denomination turned my request down.

The congregation in California that had already extended me a call to serve as their assistant pastor invited me to come and serve them as a lay person if I decided to marry this divorced woman. I finally resolved my conflict on divorce with the help of some wonderful friends and counselors. The president of the seminary, Dr. Rogness, was the most helpful. So after much struggle and tears we married and moved to California in 1960. I served the church that called me as the lay Parish Associate. In 1962 the national church changed its mind regarding divorce among clergy allowing me to be ordained.

I share this story to demonstrate that it can be a painful process to think differently when one is programmed to think in ways that seem right until critically examined. But it also can be liberating. It also demonstrates that a church body can change its thinking. History records some dramatic shifts on the part of churches and institutions around such issues as slavery, the role of women, interracial marriage, and sexuality.

Not everyone who reads this book will change his or her thinking. Not everyone needs to change or should change. Some values should never be changed. The authors included in this volume invite us to think more deeply about issues that really matter. They encourage us to be open and to engage in conversation and Biblical reflection as we make decisions and choices that really matter.

Think differently. Different than what? What change in thinking are we talking about? Brian McLaren, an evangelical author and pastor, has written a book called *Everything Must Change*. Certainly we don't want to change everything. What McLaren writes about is the call for a radical and provocative way of understanding Jesus' core message, a message that gives us purpose and passion as we address the economic, environmental, political, and social dysfunctions that have dominated our world today.

To think differently means to engage in conversation and look at the deeper questions that don't have easy answers. To think differently means to challenge what we hear and read in the media; to think critically about how the Bible has been interpreted; to refuse to be programmed by economic and political systems that benefit the powerful and divide the world into haves and have-nots; to use our minds as well as our hearts in creative analysis and decision making. It means to be open to evaluating traditions and beliefs that no longer work in our changing world.

Another thing that has helped me think differently is to see things from other peoples' perspectives. When I visited and engaged in conversation with the poor in the United States and in other countries, I listened to how they read and interpreted the Bible. For many Latinos and others who have been exploited and oppressed, the Magnificat in Luke 1:46-55 is their favorite Bible passage; not John 3:16 that I was taught to memorize and believe was the best summary of the Bible. I changed my perspective when I realized how people of privilege and power see the Bible differently than those who live on the margins. I learned to ask questions like: Who benefits from interpretations I have been taught? Why is the study of economic oppression and liberation so important in interpreting the Bible? (Read the Tamez article.) What is good news to someone living in poverty? What is essential in the Biblical message?

Other questions worthy of discussion might include: When we are influenced to think differently are we betraying important loyalties, our heritage, our family values, our faith? When confronted with conflicting ideas, who do you believe? How can I think differently in a way that will give significance to my life. Will it make any difference if I think differently? If compassion is the bottom line, how does this impact how we relate to other religions?

These are important questions to ask when we encounter issues and ideas that challenge us to think differently. One of the things that has helped me in the struggle is to ask the question: Does my way of thinking help me to love God and love my neighbor? That seems to be the bottom line for the authors in this book. It is not a bad question for all of our decisions. I'm sure there are other cultures than these listed in this book that you are connected and passionate about. One cannot cover the waterfront in one volume. I will appreciate your feedback.

One of my favorite hymns is Harry Emerson Fosdick's "God of Grace and God of Glory." The refrain reads . . .

Grant us wisdom, grant us courage for the living of these days.

George S. Johnson
georgesjohnson@gmail.com

In a Culture of Irrelevant Religion and Idolatry

My wife and I have a tradition. Each evening at 5 we have a wine and cheese hour when we discuss, share, plan and enjoy each other. Often our conversation includes the state of the world and the state of religion. We both agree that so much of today's religion seems irrelevant and boring.

The United States does not lack for religion, nor the opportunity to practice any religion. Surveys indicate that a high percentage of citizens believe in God. Yet the quote from the Call To Action newsletter (see page 280) suggests it is irrelevant religion that makes possible the giants threatening to destroy us. They are: poverty and hunger, violence and war, environmental degradation, and domination and greed.

The Gospels say that "Jesus opened their minds" as he went about his teaching and healing ministry. John Cobb, Jr., a professor of mine when I attended School of Theology in Claremont. CA, encourages us to think more honestly about what we believe and why we believe. Thinking is not an easy task. Cobb says that if we want genuine renewal in the church we will have to become a thinking church. He reminds us that thinking is not an enemy of faith.

The sermon, *"The Peril of Worshipping Jesus"*, that Harry Emerson Fosdick preached at First Presbyterian Church in New York City in the 1920s suggests that *worshipping* Jesus can become a substitute for *following* Jesus. By dressing Jesus in metaphorical creeds and sacramental adoration we have escaped his moral insights and ethical demands. When I read this sermon I ask myself, why were we discouraged from reading Fosdick's sermons when I was at the seminary? Was he too liberal, too provocative…or just not Lutheran. Re-reading them now has helped me to think differently about current issues that really matter.

George S. Johnson

CHAPTER ONE

EXCERPTED FROM

Becoming a Thinking Christian

by John B. Cobb, Jr.

This book is for you if you are a committed lay Christian in one of the oldline Protestant churches. It invites you to become aware of the beliefs by which you live and to think about them. That means that it invites you to become aware that you are already a theologian and to become a good one.

To be a good theologian is to be a Christian who thinks. Thinking is hard. You cannot profit from this book without thinking.

Some suppose that there is a contradiction involved in this. Books for lay-people should be easy. That is wrong. Laypeople are just as capable of hard intellectual work as are professional theologians. Many laypeople have proven their intellectual prowess again and again in their chosen vocations (doctors, lawyers, managers, engineers, etc.). But most laity are not accustomed to *this* particular kind of thinking about *this* particular subject. Many very intelligent people are still operating out of a simplistic view of faith. Too many have been led to assume that faith is incompatible with intellectual challenge and integrity. They have stopped expecting the church to ask this of them. But that is the problem to which this book is addressed. It calls for thinking about that problem and thinking to overcome it. That is why it is a demanding book.

Still it is written for you as a layperson. That means that the thinking it calls for and talks about, and the way it talks about it, does not require the kinds of knowledge that only specialists are likely to have. It does refer to a few features of the Christian tradition that may not be familiar to you, but it explains them sufficiently for the purpose in ways that are not obscure.

The hard thinking it calls for is about yourself and your own beliefs. The subject is one you know well! The topics are familiar. What is hard is to *think* about them. The book cannot make that easy. Nothing can, except practice.

If you read the book just for information about what I am saying, it may not be so hard. But then the book will fail. *The purpose of this book is to encourage you to think – as a Christian.*

The best way to encourage someone to think is to ask questions and interact with the answers. That is the method of dialogue, and dialogue in its finest form involves just two people. Your answer to one question determines what the next question should be. Unfortunately, a book cannot offer that kind of personal interaction. That means that a book is not the best way to help you. Long, sustained conversations would be far better. Thus this book encourages you to find conversation partners.

What most books do is to give you the ideas of the author. These are often excellent, and sometimes they stimulate you to think in new ways. But no amount of learning about the ideas of others takes the place of thinking *for yourself*, and the general stimulus of encountering new ideas usually does not go far toward making you think carefully and critically.

A book can do more to encourage you to think for yourself than just stimulate you with new ideas, and this one tries to do so. It can give examples of the sort of careful and critical thinking that can bring your Christian faith to bear on important issues. Some of these examples may connect with the way you think about the same matters. That may make it easier to get started on your own thinking. But these examples can only be suggestive.

In general, the arguments presented in this book are convincing to me, and in that sense you will learn, as in most books, what the author thinks. But that is not the main point here. The effort is to lay out arguments in ways that will enable you to agree or disagree at each step, and then to develop different arguments where you make different judgments. If the book succeeds, your thinking will take its own course; otherwise it will not be your thinking. Sometimes it will lead to conclusions that are quite different from those presented.

But if the book succeeds, you will not simply assert your disagreement with conclusions. You will make explicit the bases of your views and examine these bases with some care to see whether you find them Christian. That is hard, partly because the relation among ideas is not easy to clarify, but also because we do not like to question beliefs that we have held, sometimes for a long time.

The book also contains some abstract talk about why it is important that you, as a lay Christian, think, how you can get started, some steps your thinking may take, what sources you may need to draw on, and where all this may take you. To understand what you have not previously thought about is also a kind of thinking that is demanding.

You can become a better theologian than many of the professionals! That is because becoming a professional theologian is more a matter of thinking about other people's beliefs than about one's own. This book will try to clarify the difference. If you become serious about being a theologian, at times you will need help from the professionals – maybe a lot of help. But you will not expect them to do your thinking for you! Real Christian theology is not a matter for professionals. It is for Christians who think. Professionals may do that, too. But that is because they are Christians who think, not because they have the specialized knowledge that makes them professionals.

I will be pleased if pastors realize that their needs are much the same. They, too, are part of the *laos*, the people of God, and they are not professional scholars. There is not guarantee that their theological education turned them into good theologians. It may have introduced them to the various disciplines of their teachers. It may have encouraged thinking about how to respond to some of the problems of leading a congregation and serving its people. It may have informed them about the theologies of important thinkers in past and present. But it may not have encouraged them to think very much about their own beliefs. If they have not acquired the habit of thinking on that topic, then this book is for them, too.

It won't hurt professional theologians to listen in. Sometimes professionals suppose that lay Christians become theologians by being introduced to the academic disciplines of the professionals. Indeed, too many Christians have bought into that idea of what a theologian is. They know they don't have time or inclination to go far down that road; so they leave theology to the experts. The consequences for individual Christians and for the church are disastrous. If we want church renewal, we will have to renew thinking in the church.

In fact, if there is a renewal of thinking in the church, there will be church renewal. Without it, there won't. Trying to renew the church with gimmicks, or merely by arousing emotion, will not do the job. The church is strong only when it lives by the mature convictions of its members. Mature convictions are shaped in thought.

I have been thinking for some time about the separation of what is called theology – what I as a professional theologian have been doing – and the life of the church and its members. The separation has seemed to me, increasingly, to be disastrous for both. I have been complaining about it, writing about it, and lecturing about it. In one sense this book comes out of that thinking.

Becoming better theologians does not ensure that we will agree with one another. We have already noted that the results may be to make our differences sharper. At one level, that is regrettable. But a church engaged in serious debate over matters of great importance will be far healthier than the present one. And the world will benefit from a critical examination of its secular assumptions even if all Christians do not agree on the analysis and prescription.

Christians cannot afford a continued shrinking of the sphere within which we think *as Christians*. The world cannot afford to lose the benefit of Christian vision and wisdom. For the sake of both church and world, we all need to become better theologians.

EXCERPTED FROM

Holy Discontent

by Diana Butler Bass

◆◆◆

From *Chistianity After Religion*, Copyright © 2012, reproduced with permission of
HarperCollins Publishers

On the final day of 2010, a friend sent me a New Year's greeting wishing me the gift of "discontent" and enclosed this prayer:

> *O God, make me discontented with things the way they are in the world
> and in my own life. Make me notice the stains when people get spilled on.
> Make me care about the slum child downtown, the misfit at work, the people
> crammed into the mental hospital, the men, women and youth behind
> bars. Jar my complacence, expose my excuses, get me involved in the life of
> my city and world. Give me integrity once more, O God, as we seek to be
> changed and transformed, with a new understanding and awareness of our
> common humanity.*

Not many people think of discontent as a gift. As the prayer points out, however, discontent is the beginning of change. Only by noticing what is wrong, seeing the systems and structures that do not foster health and happiness, can we ever make things different. If people were satisfied, there would be no reason to reach for more, no motivation for creativity and innovation. Discontent is one short step from the longing for a better life, a better society, and a better world; and longing is another short step from doing something about what is wrong. Indeed, restlessness possesses a spiritual quality: "Blessed are the poor in spirit," said Jesus, "for theirs is the kingdom of heaven" (Matt. 5:3).

In the last decade, Americans have witnessed the power of discontent – especially in politics. In 1990, approximately one in ten voters considered themselves "independents"; in 2010, that had risen to nearly four in ten. "Unaffiliated" became the largest political party in the United States, with both Democrats and Republicans lagging behind. One *Politics Daily* article proclaimed "Independent Voters Fed Up with Entire Political System,"citing over discontent with the structure of two-party politics. Such discontent contributed to the rise of the Tea Party, but the Tea Party did not corner the market on political restlessness. In 2006, discontent led to the election of a Democratic House; in 2008, to the nomination and election of Barack Obama. And in 2010, political progressives, environmentalists, Christian conservatives, and other groups articulated equal – but not nearly as well organized as the Tea Party's – anxiety, discontent, and anger with the way things are.

Of course, discontent can easily become rage. Rage is frightening, especially when it is combined with fear, lies, or violence. But it is also a sign that on a vast scale people want change. From politics to business to education, people are longing for new structures that resonate with and respond to their day-to-day experience, giving them a sense of participation and voice and a real stake in the future. "Everybody has an agenda for themselves and not for the people," said Tim Tennis, a forty-five-year-old factory worker from Ohio, to writer Linda Killian. "The people are not being heard. The politicians are doing what they want and getting away with it." But rage only results from discontent when restlessness is unfocused or its longings remain unfulfilled. When channeled wisely and fueled by a hopeful vision for the future, discontent can be the beginning of genuine social transformation by inspiring courageous action.

The rise of political unaffiliateds parallels the rise of religious unaffiliateds, as discontent has led to defections from most major religious groups. The two movements are not identical, but they share in the same spirit of frustration about institutions, authority, and leadership. As the old two-party system of American politics has become bogged down in issues, styles, and practices of the past, so too is American religion has been much more diverse than American politics, of course, giving people a wider range of choices than politics. But even denominations can roughly be grouped into liberal and conservative "parties," a reality that has led some scholars to suggest that American religion is essentially a two-party system.

Even more nuanced renderings, however, made American faith into a tripartite world – liberals, conservatives, and the "middle." Or Protestants, Catholics, and Jews. Or liberal Protestants, evangelical Protestants, and Catholics. The addition of "other" for Buddhists, Hindus, and Muslims stretched the world of religious parties. But even that seems less than adequate. In the same way that political independents feel that labels and parties have failed them, so religious people feel the same – opting out of the system because of anger, boredom, sadness, a sense of disconnection, lack of control, or whatever. In a very real sense, those who describe themselves as "spiritual" are a protest vote against churches of all sorts – mainline Protestant, Catholic, and evangelical. Or perhaps the "spiritual" are swing voters of the faith world, unsure as to where they might land.

If you are the one being voted against, it does not feel very good – especially if you or your congregation is doing the hard work of listening to the needs of the world and trying to respond in hopeful and imaginative ways. But even satisfied believers and congregations can learn from discontent. When people leave, or even when they drift, they are saying "This idea, group, or path no longer makes sense. The organizations that once enabled me to live well in the world no longer help. There must be a different way."

The religious unaffiliateds are primarily young adults. In the United States, somewhere in the range of 25 to 30 percent of the population under thirty neither attend religious services nor have any religious preference, although about half of the unaffiliated group still say that they believe in God or understand themselves to be spiritual. Whatever else may be said of them, they are profoundly disappointed in religion, religious ideologies, and organizations as those things currently exist. In a 2004 survey, the Barna organization found that young adults who are outside of church hold intensely negative views of Christianity: 91 percent think that Christianity is "antihomosexual," 87 percent say Christians are "judgmental," 85 percent accuse churchgoers of being "hypocritical," and 72 percent say Christianity is "out of touch with reality." Only 41 percent think that Christianity seems "genuine or real" or "makes sense" while only 30 percent think that it is "relevant to your life."

Those numbers are sobering, especially to Christians who find meaning in their congregations, have worked for social justice for LGBT (lesbian, gay, bisexual, or transgender) persons in their churches, or who practice their faith in loving ways. Because such statistics are hard to hear, they are easy to dismiss as the ignorance of youth or a lack of maturity: "Ah! The discontent of youth! I once felt the same. But when they grow up and have children, they will see things differently!" However, in a roundabout way, their criticism actually demonstrates authentic spiritual longing. Somewhere these young adults have evidently heard that Christianity is supposed to be a religion about love, forgiveness, and practicing what Jesus preached and that faith should give meaning to real life. They are judging Christianity on its own teachings and believe that American churches come up short. Thus, their discontent about what is may reflect a deeper longing for a better sort of Christianity, one that embodies Jesus's teaching and life in a way that makes a real difference in the world.

Paul, the pastor who e-mailed to tell me he quit church, left because he was longing for something better. Tired of trying to maintain an institution and quelling quarrels, Paul still loved much of what faith was about; he cared about the "spiritual disciplines of study, worship, confession and forgiveness, discernment, fellowship, and mission." Despite the fact that he thought the church had become "irrelevant," he clearly dreamed of being part of a community that embodied these spiritual practices. He desired a different sort of church, a robust community that connected people to God and to one another. For two decades, he had worked to create such a church and failed. He said he was watching his denomination "self-destruct." But the undertow of longing still pulses through his note. His frustration and sadness are matched by the wish for a fuller life of faith and a better church. Paul's story is one of leaving and longing, just like Ellen's. They both left, but still long to find a community where a more just and loving form of Christian faith is enacted.

During a lecture to a group in California, I stated that about 30 percent of Americans consider themselves "spiritual but not religious," A man in the audience shouted out, "That's the state slogan of California!" The phrase "spiritual but not religious" is the contemporary way of trying to explain some sort of connection to God, separate from, in tension with, or in opposition to religious institutions. The same polls that find religion on the wane also find this thing called "spirituality" on the upswing; Americans are showing intense fascination for everything from new sorts of communal gatherings for worship to individual mystical experiences, to classical prayer and meditation practices. At first, many religious leaders hoped such experimentation was a passing fad – a spiritual search on the part of a restless baby-boomers' grandchildren are even more discontent than their elders, it is increasingly difficult to dismiss spirituality as a sort of cultural phase. To speak of "spirituality" simultaneously signals discontent with religious institutions and longing for a new, different, and deeper connection with God, one's neighbor, and oneself and creation.

Religious discontent is indistinguishable from the history of spiritual renewal and awakening. Religion is often characterized as contentment, the idea that faith and faithfulness offer peace, security, and certainty. In this mode, God is depicted in kindly ways, the church as an escape from the cares and stresses of the world, and religious leaders as pastors, the spiritual caretakers of the flock. Although most faith traditions do offer such surety to believers, religion has another guise as well – the prophetic tradition. In the prophetic mode, faith discomforts the members of a community, opens their eyes and hearts to the shortcomings of their own lives and injustice in the world, and presses for human society to more fully embody God's dream of healing and love for all peoples.

Religious faiths struggle between the pastoral and the prophetic, comfort and agitation. In a very real way, institutions are inherently pastoral – they seek to maintain those things that give comfort by baptizing shared values and virtues of a community. They reinforce the way things are (or were) through appeals to divine or supernatural order. They are always slow to change. Institutions resist prophets. Prophets question. They push for things to be different. They push people to behave better toward one another. They want change.

The history of Christianity can be told as a story of the tension between order and prophecy. Jesus came as a prophet, one who challenged and transformed Judaism. A charismatic community grew up around his teachings and eventually formed into the church. The church organized, and then became an institution. The institution provided guidance and meaning for many millions. And then it became guarded, protective of the power and wealth it garnered, the influence it wielded, and salvation it alone provided.

Many of the people in the church did not seem to notice, but some did. What the church taught seemed at odds with their experience of life or God. They became increasingly disenchanted with what the church offered. Discontent grew. They questioned the way things were done. They experimented with new ideas and spiritual practices. They met on the sly, singing subversive songs and praying to their favorite (and often unapproved) saints, and served people the institution overlooked or oppressed. They bent the rules and often broke them. The established church typically ignored them, sometimes tolerated them, often branded them heretics, tried to control them, and occasionally killed them. When enough people joined the ranks of the discontented, the institutional church had to pay attention. In the process, and sometimes unintentionally, the church opened itself up for genuine change and renewal.

Today, the movements of the discontent are remembered by names many people revere: the Benedictine renewal, the Franciscan movement, the Brethren of the Common Life, the Protestant Reformation, the Anabaptist community, the Methodist and evangelical revival, the Great Awakening, the Oxford movement, the Pentecostal revival. Others, I suspect, are remembered by no grand title.

In my own search for family history, I discovered one such small movement. During the 1920s, some of my ancestors – who were most likely Lutherans – left their traditional church for the passion of Pentecostal experience. They rejected the faith of the Old World in favor of embracing the fervor of the Spirit and leaving behind a contented existence of roasting coffee, delivering ice, and being carpenters, praised by those who knew them for their "fine Christian character." They became spirit-filled preachers and church planters, and one relative was a singing evangelist who helped spark a revival on Maryland's eastern shore. They refused to attend more respectable churches, and women stood up to authoritarian husbands in a quest to pray in tongues. Their memory is not recorded in any scholarly book, Instead, from the seeds of spiritual discontent, they changed themselves, their households, their neighborhoods, and their families' future. That single spiritual outburst, my ancestors' wild, abandoned leap into Pentecostal fervor, still reverberates in my life almost a century later. They changed history, not as grand leaders who started a new church, but in little bits at a time.

No historian can even guess how many small movements of individuals or congregations have existed in the past, movements made up of those who experienced God in new ways that remade their lives and communities without much notice or credit. Some movements lasted only a short time and were local events; others lasted decades or centuries and spread throughout Christendom. Such things are part of the long historical process of renewing faith. How would any religious tradition stay alive over hundreds or thousands of years if not for the questions of discontent and the creativity brought forth by longing?

Robert Jones, director of Public Religion Research, remarks of this history: "There's a sense in which the spiritual, experiential elements are always overflowing the bounds of the official religious channels . . . Much of religious history is about the institutions trying to catch up with and channel those outbursts." Organized religion fears such outbursts; but spiritual outbursts almost always precede real reform. Might spiritual discontent be today's prophetic edge, needling institutions to listen, to change, to be more responsive and relevant? Are the outbursts signs of some new form of faith?

———————— EXCERPTED FROM ————————

The Peril of Worshiping Jesus

by Harry Emerson Fosdick

❖❖❖

The world has tried in two ways to get rid of Jesus; first, by crucifying him, and second, by worshiping him. The first did not succeed. It required more than a cross to stop the influence of that transcendent character. Like an airman taking off against the wind and using the very force of the opposing air to rise by, so Jesus took off on his amazing flight. The cross did not crush – it lifted him.

The world, therefore, foiled in its first attempt to be rid of Jesus by crucifying him, turned to the second, far more subtle and fatal way of disposing of great spiritual leadership – it worshiped him. Throughout history it has been true that when a spiritual leader has been too powerful to be crushed by opposition there has been still another way to escape his moral insights and his ethical demands, and that is to worship him. To dress him up in elaborate, metaphysical creeds, hide his too-piercing eyes in the smoke of sacramental adoration, build beautiful sanctuaries where his challenging social ideals may fade out in vague mysticism, get him off somewhere on a high altar, pray to him, sing to him, do anything for him rather than let him get back again where he started, walking the common ways of men and talking about how to live – that always has been the most successful way of getting rid of Jesus.

If at first this seems a dangerous thing to say, remember that Jesus himself said it. He did not fear being opposed. He knew that the blood of the martyrs is the seed of the church, and concerning his own cross John reports his saying: "I, if I be lifted up from the earth, will draw all men unto myself." He did not fear being opposed; he feared being worshiped.

For one thing, he saw his own contemporaries by this method getting rid of their prophets. First, their fathers had hated the prophets, opposed them, stoned them, sawn them asunder. Then, when the prophets proved too powerful in personality and influential in message to be disposed of in that way, the ever-available, second method had been tried. Listen to Jesus, himself, as he describes it - "Woe unto you, scribes and Pharisees, hypocrites! For ye build the sepulchres of the prophets, and garnish the tombs of the righteous, and say, If we had been in the days of our fathers, we should not have been partakers with them in the blood of the prophets. Wherefore ye witness to yourselves, that ye are sons of them that slew the prophets."

Jesus saw that stoning the prophets on one side and garnishing their sepulchers on the other, different as the two things appear, come practically to the same end: they are two ways of getting rid of the prophets, escaping what the prophets really stood for, dodging their moral message. The fathers who killed the prophets and the children who garnish their sepulchers belong to the same race, says Jesus, and are up to the same thing – they are evading the spirit of the prophets.

Even in his lifetime, Jesus feared this way of being evaded. How else will you explain his stern rebuke to the sentimental woman who cried, "Blessed is the womb that bare thee, and the breasts which thou didst suck"? Jesus came back at her like thunder, saying, "Yea rather, blessed are they that hear the word of God, and keep it." It is as though you could hear him saying to himself, See, they are beginning to worship me; they are evading what I am driving at by adoring emotions about me; they will get rid of me yet, as they have gotten rid of the prophets, by idolizing me. Or how else will you explain his swift retort to the man who came bowing to him, saying, "Good Teacher"? Said Jesus, "Why callest thou me good? None is good save one, even God." One can fairly read his thoughts as though he said to the man, Beware of worshipful deference to me – I fear it; come, stop this bowing and this "Good Master"; what about your attitude to the kind of living I am standing for, whose springs are in God? And once, as though to leave no doubt that this fear of being worshiped was ever before him, he cried, "Not every one that saith unto me, Lord, Lord, shall enter into the kingdom of heaven; but he that doeth the will of my Father who is in heaven." O, wise Master, with what prophetic eye you saw the way men would successfully evade you! For all these centuries since, cherishing evils that your spirit would have spurned, all Christendom has been saying from countless temples, "Lord, Lord!"

It is an amazing thing that the historic church has so unanimously worshiped Jesus and has so seldom stopped to ask what Jesus himself would think of it. Is it not true that most Christians have taken it for granted that Jesus would enjoy it – enjoy being prayed to, sung to, talked about in exalted, theological terms, and enshrined on the high altars of the church? Do not many Christians still suspect that he would feel grieved, hurt, rejected, and jealous if he were not thus adored? All this, however, obviously is the reflection of our own littleness. Little people like extravagant praise, adoration, flattery. Little people push their egos to the front, claiming attention and wanting to be idolized; but great personalities are never like that. When a capacious soul comes, standing for something that he cares so much about he will die for it on Calvary, you cannot flatter him. He has identified himself with something greater than himself, of which he regards himself as the incarnation and instrument. He thinks of himself as the vehicle and agent of an eternal matter. He does not want his ego idolized; he wants his cause supported.

Take the truth into a realm quite different from religion and consider Abraham Lincoln, who, if you use the word "worship" as we are using it this morning, in its general and human sense, comes as near being worshiped as any American. That began when he died, While he lived men tried to crush him by opposition, but he was too strong to be overcome. When he died, however, they began using the other method to dispose of him. They adored him. They garnished his sepulcher. Nothing too marvelous could be said of him. But in the ten years after he died Congress put into effect a policy towards the South that denied everything Lincoln had stood for and wanted. They praised his name and they scuttled his policies. They flattered his memory and denied his magnanimity. They alike adored Lincoln and refused to follow him, so that they made the reconstruction era in the South one of the horrors of our history.

What would Lincoln have said? We know. Stop this evading of my spirit by praising me! What do I care about the idolizing of my ego? I want my cause supported. Of course Lincoln would have said that because he was a large soul, and not a little one.

Can one doubt, then, what Jesus' attitude would be? We all sing, for example, that great hymn,

> ## In the cross of Christ I glory,
> ## Towering o'er the wrecks of time.

Who wrote that? Sir John Bowring. Who was he? He was the British Governor at Hong Kong at a time when the British Empire was forcing the opium traffic on China, and he was the agent of the imperial policies. Everybody acknowledges, our British brethren first of all, that the forcing of opium on China was one of the most outrageous things in Western history. Well, the man who was Governor of Hong Kong while that policy was in force had written, year before, "In the Cross of Christ I Glory."

You will recall the man who said that he could take care of his enemies himself, but prayed to be delivered from his friends. Jesus Christ might have said that. The most disastrous events in the history of his movement have not come from his opposers, but from his worshipers who said, "Lord, Lord!"

When today I plead against the peril of worshiping Jesus, you see it is not because I, myself, do not exalt him. You know I do exalt him. He is supremely great. That constitutes the seriousness of the situation. He is really great – not to be flattered, not to be pleased by creedal praise or sacramental worship, wanting just one thing so much that he died for it – the Divine Will done in personal lives and social relationships. And the tragedy is that it has proved too deceptively easy to join in forcing opium on China while at the same time singing "In the cross of Christ I glory." I am not specially blaming Sir John

Bowring; we cannot do that. He was like the rest of us. He was not consciously hypocritical, but a sincere, honest, and in many ways eminently admirable man. He simply fell victim, as many of us have fallen, to this most popular of all ways of getting rid of Christ. We would not crucify him, not one of us, but, alas, we worship him – we dispose of him that way. We say, "Lord, Lord!"

Consider, for one thing, how easy it is to get rid of Christ by worshiping him, because thereby we can substitute emotions for morals. There are two sets of faculties in us, the esthetic and the ethical – the sense of beauty and the sense of duty – and Christ appeals to both. Especially as the tradition of history has woven its alluring spell about him, setting him in stories that begin with singing angels over Bethlehem and end with worshiping women in a garden, he is beautiful. He has been set to music, glorified in poetry, enshrined in architecture, until the approach to Christ is clothed in beauty. But when we approach Christ esthetically, through beauty, it may end in emotional adoration only, saying, "Lord, Lord!"

So you, a youth here in New York City, may adore your mother. How do you adore her, emotionally or morally? That is, do you simply love her with tender sentiment, or are you living the kind of life which does honor to her and developing the sort of character which, if she knew about it, would make her glad? The difference is deep. Mothers at their finest are beautiful and most men adore them; but it is one thing to have the emotional sentiments of the heart go out to a mother and it is another thing to be morally true to her. It would be strange, indeed, if some youth here did not at this moment acutely feel the difference. Well, Christ must acutely feel the difference in his disciples. Indeed, he never said, "Worship me!" He said, "Follow me!"

To put the matter in a figure that combines both beauty and morals, Christ played his life like music meant to be played over again. When Beethoven wrote a symphony, he did not write it merely to be admired but to be reproduced. When once a Beethoven has created harmony, one does not have to be Beethoven to reproduce it. It can be played again and again. So Christ, in his unselfishness, his faith in God, his reverence for personality, his practice of brotherhood, his devotion to a nobler social order, was not creating a piece of music for the world to stand before and cry, "How lovely!" He wanted it reproduced – played again and again by boys and girls, men and women, on all the human instruments that God had given them, until the whole earth should be full of his music.

He wanted that, but he has not seen that – only here and there has that come to pass. What he has seen is something different – countless millions of people worshiping him emotionally but not morally. Emperors like Constantine, drenched in blood, who murdered his own wife, his son, and other more remote and less significant relatives, worshiped Christ. Ecclesiastics who sold their influence for private gain and stained the garments of the church with fornication and simony have worshiped Christ. Men who believed that little babies were damned to eternal hell have worshiped Christ. Men who persecuted their fellows for conscience sake and made the torture chambers of Christendom the horror of the world have worshiped Christ. Churches that have shut off their fellow Christians from the kingdom of God because of diversities in theology that Jesus never heard of and would have scorned as mint, anise, and cumin, have worshiped Christ.

John Newton ran a slave ship between Africa and the slave markets of his time in the days when the horrors between decks were enough to make even the reading of them turn one white. He wrote in his diary that he had never known sweeter or more frequent hours of divine communion than on his slave journeys, and every Sunday he read the church liturgy twice with his crew. How incredible, in retrospect, such a combination of worshiping Christ with ruthless inhumanity appears? Yet how many have been and are guilty of it and how few, like John Newton, see new light, repent of their blindness, and change, as he did, both opinion and life!

You see what we have done with Christ – we have kept his name on the label, but we have changed the contents of the bottle. That is a summary of much of Christendom's history – the name kept on the label, "Christ," but the contents not of his moral quality.

We cannot suppose – can we? – that that suddenly has stopped in our time? Upon the contrary, the churches of this country are full of people who worship Christ, who have no more idea what Christ means about war, race relationships, the color line, about the money standards of the day, the profit motive in industry, than Constantine had about Christ's attitude toward his bloody imperialism, or the Duke of Avla about Christ's care for the victims of his persecution. This seems to me the very nub of the Christian problem today. The crucial matter is not theological controversy. Real problems are involved there, but they are not the crux. The crux is moral. A Christianity that worships Christ emotionally but does not follow him morally is a conventional sham, and too much of our ecclesiastical Christianity today is precisely that. Let us say it to ourselves in our beautiful churches, amid the loveliness of our architecture, lest we should ever be tempted to substitute esthetics for ethics or formal worship for downright righteousness. Jesus would care more about our attitude towards the color line or war than he would care about all our processionals, however stately, and all our architecture, however fine. For obviously, Jesus above all else, intended to be taken in earnest morally.

We cannot, then, leave our text in history. It comes down the centuries, accumulating significance with every year, and walks up to our own doors and knocks. "Not every one that saith unto me, Lord, Lord."

Consider how easy it is to dispose of Christ by worshiping him, because we can thereby substitute theological opinion for spiritual experience. In this regard, much of Christianity has gotten rid of Christ just as Buddhism has gotten rid of Buddha. Think what you will about the basic presuppositions of Buddha's philosophy – and I heartily disagree with them – he nevertheless, was a tremendous character, and his noble eightfold path of moral living is noble. At first men fought against him, but that did not succeed; he was too great to be overthrown by opposition. Now, however, conventional Buddhism has gotten rid of him by worshiping him. It is one of the strangest ironies in the history of religion. For Buddha himself did not believe in a personal God at all, and now Buddhism has made a personal God out of him. That disposes of him! Now they can build up rituals, construct theologies, worship him in sacramental regularities, and his noble eightfold path of moral living can be obscured in the smoke of incense. The Christians, however, are no better than the Buddhists in that regard. That is what we have done with Jesus.

I can imagine some one saying, But, then, do you not believe in the divinity of Jesus? To which I answer that I believe in the divinity of Jesus with all my faculties if we can come to an understanding about what we mean be divinity. Are you willing to start with John's idea of divinity in the New Testament: "God is love"? That is divinity – love. Divinity is not something supernatural that ever and again invades the natural order in a crashing miracle. Divinity is not in some remote heaven, seated on a throne. Divinity is love. Here and now it shines through the highest spiritual experiences we know. Wherever goodness, beauty, truth, love are – there is the Divine. And the divinity of Jesus is the divinity of his spiritual life.

If some one says, Well, we all have some of that divine spark in us; we all have some goodness, truth, love, and therefore on that basis the divinity of Jesus differs from ours in degree, indeed, but not in kind, I answer, Are you afraid of that conclusion? Of course the divinity of Jesus differs from ours in degree but not in kind. You cannot imagine there being one God and two kinds of godlikeness. Paul prayed that his disciples might be filled unto all the fullness of God. John said, "He that abideth in love abideth in God, and God abideth in him." Was the God that Paul and John prayed might be in them a different kind of God than was in Jesus? To be sure not. There is only one God. To say therefore that God was in Christ seems to me no theological puzzle at all. I think God was in my mother, the source of all the loveliness that blessed us there! And I rise up from that with a profound sense of the reality of what I am doing when I profess my faith that God was in Christ.

If, now, some one says, Very well, but that reduces Jesus to our level, I answer, How do you make that out? I feel in relationship to Christ like a landlocked pool beside the sea. The water in the landlocked pool is the same kind of water that is in the sea. You cannot have one sea and two kinds of seawater. But look at the landlocked pool, little, imprisoned, soiled it may be in quality, and then look at the sea, with deeps and distances and tides and relationships with the world's life the pool can never know. So is my life beside his. So is my soul beside his soul. The same God, to be sure, but what a contrast the difference in capacity can make!

If, then, we mean by Jesus' divinity the quality of his spiritual life, of course I believe in it and glory in it. But the historic church too often has meant something else, has pushed him far off to a supra-mundane world, throned him in a distant heaven, garbed him beyond all recognition in heavily brocaded garments of theology, until the real Jesus has been gotten rid of altogether. Listen to this about Jesus of Nazareth: "The second person in the Trinity, being very and eternal God, of one substance, and equal with the Father, did… take upon him man's nature," so that "two whole, perfect, and distinct natures, the Godhead and the manhood, were inseparably joined together in one person, without conversion, composition, or confusion." They have done that to the divine teacher of Galilee, and they have gloried in it when all the time they were getting rid of him, - at last successfully crucifying him, - laying him in a theological tomb and rolling a great stone before the door.

I read recently a passage from a sermon that seemed to me to cry out for an answer – the preacher was glorying in the fact that Jesus had conquered Europe. Very conceivable, said the preacher, that Jesus might appeal to Asia, but what a marvel that he should appeal to Europe, to hard-headed, practical, militant Europe! What does the preacher mean – Jesus conquering Europe? What Jesus conquered Europe? A conventionalized Jesus was unlike the real one as the floral patterns on wallpaper are unlike the flowers of the field. A Jesus who was called by the most resplendent, metaphysical titles in history, but who supported bloody imperialism, blessed bloody persecutions, gave his benediction to economic exploitation, put his cross on the banners of the most sanguinary crusades in history, insisted on the damnation of infants to hell, and said that slavery was ordained of God. That caricature of Jesus has, as a matter of plain history, too largely conquered the Western world. But the Jesus of the Good Samaritan, the Prodigal Son, the Beatitudes, the Jesus who used a little child as his symbol of the kingdom's spirit, the Jesus who said, "Ye cannot serve God and mammon," and "A man's life consisteth not in the abundance of the things which he possesseth," the Jesus who reverenced every human personality and died that there might come a kingdom of God and human brotherhood on earth – that Jesus has not yet conquered either Europe or America.

To be sure, I know that this is not all there is to religion. Christianity is more than ethical effort. If you take the word "worship" in its original meaning, "worthship" – the recognition of worth – then there are few things more important that we ever do. And especially we moderns need ever to grow quiet, like pools at evening, in the presence of the highest that we know in Christ, that his beauty may be reflected in us. If that is what one means by "worship" then we should worship him with all our hearts. We need, however, to imagine what would happen if somehow he could be released from all the brocaded velvets and golden crowns of our too-conventional and formal adoration and could speak to us in his own voice. How little he would care for anything that did not involve personal character and social righteousness! How little he would care whether a man idolized his ego, if only he possessed his spirit! What a company he would claim as his own – men and women of all races, colors, creeds, religions, some who had worshiped him and some who had not, in whom he found his spirit! For he supremely would care that what he stood for should permeate the world. Not every one, not *any one*, who merely says, "Lord, Lord!" but he that doeth the Father's will!

EXCERPTED FROM

Theological Education

by Walter Brueggemann

From Theological Education: Healing the Blind Beggar from the February 5-12, 1986 issue of
The Christian Century magazine, reproduced with permission of *Christian Century*

Mark 10:46-52 records a standard healing miracle. There is a person in need who comes to Jesus. Jesus acts and the person is healed. We may be jaded enough not to believe in the story, or else so familiar with it that we don't notice what is going on. It is, however, a story that has much to tell us about what it is that theological education should be helping the churches to do.

We should first notice that the man is described as "a blind beggar." That is an interesting juxtaposition. He has a physical ailment – he wants his sight back – but he is also a beggar. I wonder about the relation between his blindness and his status as a beggar. Perhaps he was blind and therefore could not get an education and could not work, and so he ended up as a beggar. Perhaps. But there are blind people who do not end up as beggars. Perhaps, because he was a beggar, he never had access to nutritious food or to health care, and so became blind. The cause-and-effect relationship between the man's poverty and his blindness is difficult to determine. It may be enough simply to note that physical ailments often accompany poverty and powerlessness. When one quits caring and hoping for things, one often gives up on physical well-being as well.

The social location of the man looms larger in the narrative than we may at first recognize. For the story does not simply concern the blind beggar and Jesus. There is a third actor: "many of the people." They are a nameless, faceless mass. We might say that they represent public opinion or peer pressure. I do not know what they have to do with the man's blindness, but surely they have something to do with his status as a beggar. It is in relation to them that he is a beggar. They establish the norm which categorizes him as such.

The odd action of "many of the people" draws attention to them. The text says, "They told him to hold his tongue." They wanted the beggar silenced.

The people's effort to silence the blind beggar reflects their wish to keep him a beggar – dependent and blind. If the man were healed, if he were to shake off his powerlessness he would begin to demand food and care. Eventually he would enter the job market and perhaps even reclaim his patrimony that he had lost. If he were to do that, it may mean that someone else would lose status. The blind beggar's silence, on the other hand, would ensure that the status quo would be maintained. In a similar way every society, powerful institutions – churches, schools, courts, hospitals – serve to keep people in their designated slots.

The action in the story is begun by the blind beggar: "He cried out." He turns out to know more and trust more and ask more than the people expected from a blind beggar. First, he addresses Jesus with a Christolog title: "Son of David." He knows it is "Messiah time, the time when the blind see and the poor have their debts canceled and beggars become citizens again (cf. Luke 7:22-23). Who would have thought that a blind beggar would know it was this time? Second, he dares to issue an imperative. He asks that the power of the powerful one (Jesus) be given to one who has no claim except courage to cry out. The blind beggar names and entreats Jesus. The people rebuke him, but he asks again. He will not be dismissed. He gains his voice from his hope and belief that Jesus is the Messiah. He had waited enough for the promises which God had made even to blind beggars. God now needs to be enjoined to those promises.

The people do not want to concede that it is the time for fulfillment. They have an interest in postponing that time, because it would mean sharing power with beggars and being surrounded by more people who speak out and make claims.

The beggar does not speak in vain. Jesus says, "What do you want me to do?" The beggar has been heard. The beggar's response to Jesus is terse and unambiguous: "I want my sight back." I want to be whole. I want access to public life. If I get my eyes, I will quit this begging. I want my dependency to end. I am entitled to more. And I will have it.

Jesus' response is quick and simple. "Go, your faith has cured you." His faith has done it. His faith is an act of hope which refuses to settle for the status quo: "Faith is the assurance of things hoped for, the conviction of things not seen" (Heb. 11:1). This blind man's only resource was things hoped for, things not seen, and such faith gave him sight. Faith is an overt act of self-assertion by which the man knows he is entitled to healing. In asserting his faith, the beggar performs an act of subversion; he violates all the conventions and steps out of his assigned role. Faith is the courage to speak, to announce for oneself a new possibility.

This emphasis on the beggar's act may sound like auto-therapy, as if it is the beggar who heals himself. But, of course, this healing happens only with Jesus as the partner in dialogue. The narrative makes this point in a quite understated way. It is the key presence of Jesus, the name of Jesus, that evokes the hope and that gives the beggar the nerve and the occasion to speak (v. 47). The outcome, in spite of the resistant crowd, is that the beggar receives his sight. Then, we are told, "He followed him." The beggar becomes a disciple, committed to a new life of obedience. This healing does not just allow the man to do his own thing. His new health binds him to his healer.

The meaning of this healing narrative can be summarized this way:

- The man's illness reflects a powerlessness in society that leads to economic disadvantage and physical liability (the two tending to go together).

- The community wishes to perpetuate the man's powerlessness by forcing him to be silent.

- Hope leads the man to speak out, which is an act of social subversion.

- It is the availability of Jesus as a committed partner in dialogue that permits healing to take place. In that dialogue, there is power to transform life. And the unreported result of that transformation is that the community's life is transformed as well.

What does all this have to do with theological education? I suggest that these four points correspond directly to four crucial areas of need in theological education.

- Theological education that promises healing and liberation must have the *sociological imagination* (in C. Wright Mills's term) to see that healing is mediated through social processes and social structures. Religion is never simply about "me and Jesus." It is also never simply a matter of psychology, as if problems are just in one's psyche or have to do only with one's self-understanding. Blindness is related to being a beggar, and one is always a beggar in a social context. Theological education in America must overcome its sociological indifference and naïveté. A massive investment in social criticism is needed in the American church, for it is the structures of our society and institutions, wittingly or not, that define people as beggars and that render them blind. In short, theological education must teach students to read Marx as discerningly as they now read Freud.

- Theological education that promises healing and liberation must face the fact that a key issue in healing, salvation and liberation is power. The key transaction in the healing narrative is the *seizure of power* by the blind beggar. The question of power has been kept off the table in recent times by a religiousness that emphasizes a personal, psychological quest for happiness, comfort or meaning. But this gospel narrative does not lie. It insists that raising the power issue and jeopardizing the power monopoly of the many are essential to the process of healing. In ministry, the issues of who has power and how it is held, shaped or monopolized are crucial. Those who are kept powerless will not be healed; they will remain beggars.

- Theological education that promises healing and liberation must recognize that the first step in gaining power is *bringing things to speech*. The key turn in the narrative is when the blind beggar is able to speak of his pain. The first marvel of the story is that the beggar, rather than be silenced, cries out in pain and hope for the messianic reality.

We face a crisis of speech in our time. (I do not say "language," with which scholarship is now fascinated, for I refer here to the act of speaking, not the structure of language – *parole, not langue*.) The crisis of contemporary speech is caused by the silence of those who are on the margins of society. It is also caused by speech that, warped by the modes of technology, involves an exchange of information but does not personally address another person ("Son of David") or announce something about oneself ("have mercy on me"). Where there is neither address nor announcement, there will never be healing, salvation or liberation. History moves and life is transformed when the powerless get speech. We need, therefore, in all our institutions, to be asking: Who has speech? Who does the talking? Who does the decisive speaking?

Theological education has been peculiarly entrusted with the treasure of serious speech, of address and announcement. In the scriptural tradition which authorizes us, it is the speech of the poor that begins history (ef. Exod. 2:23-25). In preaching and liturgy it is the speech of the "little ones" that releases transforming energy.

• Theological education that promises healing and liberation must be *unashamedly Christological*. The healing narrative in Mark is clearly about Jesus. Without Jesus there would be no story to interest us, even as there would be no chance for healing. It is only in the presence of Jesus that the blind beggar is able to seize power.

In recent years we have been fascinated by the models of health defined by Freud, by Eastern religion, by technology, by philosophy. Our situation now is like that of the beggar; the other cures have failed. The cry to the Son of David is the last and only hope.

A Christological focus in theological education does not mean using slogans or invoking a magical name. Rather, it refers to the disclosure of truth, given in the crucifixion and resurrection, about where the power of life comes from. The power of life does not come from the usual sources administered by society, nor from any special "gnosis" among us, but only from the news of God's sovereignty and graciousness and in acts of self-abandonment and obedience. Our culture nurtures us in different truths and tempts us with other disclosures, but the blind beggar shows us that there is only one way to life.

Theological education, then, requires attention to all the factors that we find in the story of the blind beggar. It requires realism about social conditions; awareness of the issues of power and powerlessness; concern to attend to those who have been silent to speak; and an emphasis on the centrality of Jesus. Out of all of that comes wholeness. We are not told exactly how wholeness comes, but the concluding message is: "Your faith has cured you."

We are invited by this narrative to relearn the healing process as it is given to us in evangelical faith. (I use the word "evangelical" in its proper sense as the adjectival form of "gospel," and not with all the unfortunate contemporary distortions of the term.) We need to relearn that process, for it is different from a magical conversion, and does not rely on technical solutions alone, as if it were no different from fixing a lawn mower.

Excessive fascination with technical healing is dangerous because it only increases the monopoly of power and drives beggars into deeper blindness. The issues in healing and in education are not technical but political.

Alternatives to technical healing which are preoccupied with the self are also to be handled gingerly, because we do not contain within us the power for life. Pastoral healing, messianic healing, has to do with the formation of a community of joy and obedience.

We are – all of us – blind beggars, with genuine hurts and handicaps. We are – all of us – part of the crowd and we try to silence the groans of others because they are a threat to our position. All of us stammer for speech and all of us wonder if we have the nerve to voice our hope in the Messiah. All of us imagine that we know what time it is, but we are not sure.

It is time for theological education to notice the categories of healing that are offered in Mark 10:46-52.

The issue before theological education is whether we will overcome its own vested interests and learn the healing process revealed by Jesus. Without that process, beggars will remain blind and the blind are sure to remain beggars. But new power and fresh possibility are offered wherever Jesus is Lord.

Idols in the Church
Possible Blindspots in our Theology and Practice
by George S. Johnson

————— ✦✦✦ —————

I was a senior at the seminary when the late Warren Quanbeck preached a series of chapel talks on "Idols in the Church." Somehow those homilies have remained in my memory bank over the years. I think his thoughts are worthy of some conversation today as well.

Professor Quanbeck talked about the Bible, the church and the sacraments getting more attention than the Gospel. We had been studying idolatry as a problem in the life of Israel and the early church, but I wondered . . . certainly modern Christians don't bow to idols. Our struggles were against racism, consumerism, greed, war and exclusivity, not those things like the Bible, sacraments and the church that are so central to our faith. We don't bow to any golden calf . . . do we?

Maybe idol is not the best term to use in calling for a critical look at our theology and practices in the church today. Idols in this article refer to those things we believe or practice that become substitutes or an escape from what is essential, what is primary, what is ultimate. Idols are not necessarily bad or unimportant. The problem comes when they get more attention than they deserve, or take our attention away from what should have first priority in our theology and practice.

I have been part of the Lutheran family for 75 years, educated in Lutheran schools and trained in orthodox Lutheran theology. I think I understand the importance of grace and justification by grace through faith. They were central in my preaching for most of my years in the parish. My church is important to me. That is why I feel free to raise questions about its theology and engage in critical thinking.

As Director of the Hunger Program of the former American Lutheran Church I was exposed to the pain and exploitation of the so-called third world. When

I talked about it, wrote about it and encouraged people to become advocates for the poor and hungry, I wondered why Christians were not more interested in addressing the root causes of the pain that people all over the world were suffering. I asked myself, "Why hasn't the religious community taken more leadership in changing the values and structures that have messed up our world? Why hasn't the Biblical teaching of justice been proclaimed and followed?"

> **"Why hasn't the religious community taken more leadership in changing the values and structures that have messed up our world?"**

It is not that we are not concerned about social problems of our day. We collect money, we bring food, we build houses for homeless, we take mission trips to New Orleans or Mexico, and a few of us will even write letters to our representatives in government. Charity is important to us. And it should be.

But when the hard facts hit the road we discover that nothing has changed that much. The rich keep getting richer and the poor keep getting poorer. In spite of all our charity and grace preaching we continue to dominate others, put profit before people, destroy the environment and support the status quo. Working to end poverty is not part of our theological discussion. We stand in long lines to receive the bread and wine but few stand in line to help those whose rights have been ignored or denied. We say the systems that deal with immigration, energy and healthcare in our country are broken. I wonder if our theology is broken.

The Ark of the Covenant (a wooden chest) became very important to the people of Israel during the early part of their history. It contained the 10 commandments. They bowed down to it. It was where they experienced the presence of God. However, when it became an idol with almost superstitious elements attached to it, Jeremiah called for an examination of its usefulness. He told them to get rid of it. (Jeremiah 3:16) We all have our own arks that have become traditions and practices needing examination. Maybe we need a Moses to come down from the mountain and expose our modern golden calves.

1. For example: the *Bible* we treasure has become an idol for many. It can so easily be used to distract us from what is central. How many years have we debated the gay/lesbian issue in our churches? At the center of the debate is the interpretation of the Bible. It matters what the Bible says, but as Gerd Theissen reminds us, we need to discover what is essential in the Bible.

The Bible is not God. We may say that but live as though it is. When it comes to what the Bible says about sexuality we become literalists, but when it comes to what the Bible says about money and greed we refer to the metaphorical use of literature by the authors? Are we not all selective literalists? When my interpretation of the Bible is the only correct one, then we can make the Bible an idol that distracts us from what is central to our faith.

Worship of the Bible might stem from our neglect of adult education in our congregations. How many active members have learned what the Bible is and what it is not? A twenty minute sermon each Sunday will not do it. Perhaps a greater emphasis on adult learning will help us learn how to read the Bible, how to interpret the Bible and how to recognize that the Bible is not God, but one of the ways God is revealed to us. Worship of the Bible can sap our energy needed to love God and our neighbor. As Dorothee Soelle says, we have locked God up in the Bible and liturgy instead of using the Bible and liturgy as eyeglasses to understand our everyday lives.

At one of our family reunions my niece told me that she and her husband were looking for a church where the pastor believed the Bible. "Oh", I said, "Have you found some pastors who don't believe the Bible?" She finally admitted that what she meant was that she wanted a pastor who interpreted the Bible the way she did.

It can be a sign of arrogance that ends discussion when we simply say "But the Bible says" or "Doesn't the scriptures say?" Luther suggested that both the

Bible and plain reason should be used in discerning what the Bible teaches. He also warned against the Bible becoming a paper Pope.

2. The *Church* is another example of how something that we treasure becomes an idol, something that can become a substitute for what is most important. After Emperor Constantine declared Christianity to be the state religion in the 4th century, the church began to adapt itself to the ways that were patterned after the Empire. Since then we have constantly struggled with how to be faithful to the teachings of Jesus and remain in good standing with governing powers and economic systems.

George Barna and Frank Viola in their book, *Pagan Christianity*, remind us how much of what we do in Christian gatherings each Sunday is not rooted in the scriptures but in the pagan culture and rituals of society. The hierarchical structures of church leadership today match the structures of leadership in the Roman Empire. Visit the consecration of a Bishop to observe what the authors mean. Or note how members sit passively in the pews while one person with authority announces the evangelical truth. This has led to a lack of encouragement for critical thinking among the laity.

We tend to put more emphasis on the Sunday worship in a building than we do on loving our neighbor. I was made aware of this recently when one young couple in my *Practicing the Faith* class told me that they had decided to practice being the church on Sundays rather than going to church. So each Sunday now they pack up some food and survival necessities and walk into the canyons of San Diego County near where they live. They learn to know the migrants who sleep there in shacks and have a meal with them. Word and sacrament are present in their effort to be church. They experience the presence of God.

Our worship of the church is also manifested in ecclesiastical certitudes. I (an ordained pastor) was asked to come up to the altar one Sunday during communion to read the words of institution in the communion liturgy. The intern who was leading worship and preaching that day had not yet received ordination. He could do everything except say the words of institution, according to the rules as explained by the Bishop. He could preach and pray but not say certain words in the Eucharistic liturgy. Some idols are hard to let go of.

3. Another practice in the church that can become an idol is the *Sacraments*. Keep in mind that an idol can be a good thing, important, but something that diverts our attention away from what is primary and essential. A study of the history of the sacraments in the church can be helpful in learning about the evolution of their development and reasons for their elevation. The sacraments can be either helpful or a distracting in our calling to "do justice, love mercy and walk humbly with God."

The *Hunger Times*, a tabloid used by the Hunger Programs of the three predecessor bodies of the Evangelical Lutheran Church in America quoted an Episcopalian bishop who said, "I want the congregations in my diocese to be as energized and active in feeding the poor as they are in participating in the Eucharist."

 A few Sundays ago we had a Bread for the World letter writing Sunday in our parish. Almost everyone lined up to come forward that Sunday to receive the elements at the Eucharist and experience the presence of Jesus. I wished there had been that same line of people willing to write a letter on behalf of the poor and hungry in the world. And I wished that the subversive words and action of Jesus that caused his death would be lifted up in the Eucharist. What are we called to remember in the words, "do this in memory of me."

What would be wrong with a church that reminded its members that they would experience the presence of Jesus in the lives of the excluded in their community as much as they did in the sacraments? Is not this good biblical theology? (Matthew 25) What happened to the sacrament that Jesus instituted for us just before he was executed. I mean the practice of washing one another's feet (servanthood) . . . or hands if it is easier? Jesus' command to *"do this"* is just as important as the *do this* in the communion liturgy. Has not our strong emphasis on the Eucharist promoted a kind of individualism in our theology?

Larry Rasmussen in *Earth Community, Earth Ethics*, says that "sacramentalism recognizes and celebrates the divine in, with and under all nature, ourselves included. In the sacrament of creation we celebrate our relationship, care and respect due the sacred." An idol can be a substitution or a distraction from pure religion, "to visit the orphan and widow in their affliction, loose the bonds of injustice and let the oppressed go free."

4. I wonder if our emphasis on *Reformation Theology* has become an idol in the Protestant church. It is almost as though we need to get permission from Martin Luther or John Calvin before we can take a stand or talk about changing our theological perspectives.

An idol can be something that has served a good purpose but has become a practice or dogma that has overshadowed a more important truth or current reality. Grace yes, but there is more that needs to be declared. Has "grace alone" become an idol?

No one would suggest that we are not saved by grace or that our own efforts or beliefs can earn us any merits toward our salvation. What has challenged me to think about grace alone as an idol was a chapter in Walter Brueggemann's book, *The Covenanted Self*. He questions the use of the word "alone" that Luther places together with the word grace. Brueggemann suggests that Lutheran theology of grace is Paul or Augustine's interpretation of Jesus, and may be a misreading of Paul. Krister Stendahl, a Lutheran, agrees.

Has "grace alone" become a distraction or escape mechanism from ethical living . . . from obedience to Christ's commandment to love our neighbor? Is this why the Sermon on the Mount has remained on the sidelines in our preaching and teaching? Why was it so central for Bonhoeffer and King?

Could it be that our emphasis on grace has led us to be less active in the Kingdom work of making a difference in the world? I know what our theology says. If we preach grace enough people will respond by loving their neighbor and loving our enemies. Has it worked that way? Really?

Was it the lack of grace preaching that led to the rise of the Third Reich in the 30s? . . . to apartheid in South Africa? . . . to slavery in our country both before and after the civil war? . . . to the opposition to equal rights for women and minorities only a few decades ago? . . . to the treatment of Native Americans by Christians in our early history? . . . to our continued support for war and exploitation of less developed countries? . . . to our destruction of the environment in modern times? Was it "grace alone" that was missing? I don't think so.

It was a good Lutheran pastor in Germany who, during the second World War, said . . . "We have gathered like eagles around the carcass of cheap grace and there we have drunk the poison that has killed the life of following Jesus. We have given away the Word and Sacraments wholesale without asking awkward questions . . . We have poured forth unending streams of grace. But the call to follow Jesus is hardly ever heard." *From "Cost of Discipleship" by Dietrich Bonhoeffer*

5. Do I dare suggest this next possible idol in the church? Have we made an idol of *Jesus* in our theology and practice? In Mark 10:18 Jesus passed off a compliment by saying, "Why do you call me good? No one is good but God alone." On other occasions Jesus shifted the attention away from himself as God so that the focus could be on something more important; his teaching about the Kingdom of God.

This need not take away the divinity of Jesus or the important teaching of the incarnation. Where we get tripped up is in our devotion to Jesus that has distracted us from Jesus' teachings. Has our attention to the son of Mary and Joseph become an escape from the responsibility to carry out his mission?

In the Apostles' creed we confess what is central to our faith. But nothing is said in this ancient creed about what Jesus taught . . . his message . . . his invitation to follow him. Does this mean that beliefs about who Jesus is; his birth, death and resurrection are more important than our relationships to each other and to creation? Much of idolatry can be on an unconscious level. It can be a tradition never really examined.

In a book of sermons by Harry Emerson Fosdick, *Answers to Real Problems*, there is a sermon entitled, "The Peril of Worshiping Jesus." (See chapter three of this volume.) He says the world has tried two ways to get rid of Jesus. One was to crucify him. When that didn't work they used a more subtle technique. They worshiped him. To escape his moral insights and ethical demands, Fosdick says, the world has dressed him up in elaborate metaphysical creeds and sacramental adoration. Jesus never said, "Worship me!" He said, "Follow me!"

I have suggested that there are theological blind spots that have kept us from dealing with our global crisis, the inequalities that are a matter of life and death to millions of people in today's world. We need some critical reflection on what these blind spots are. You may have a different list.

Following the holocaust it was said that, "no theological statement should be made that is not credible in the presence of burning children." How might we state that differently to fit our situation today? Joerg Rieger in his book, *God and the Excluded* says that we need to become aware of how our theology has led to our complicity in the current structures that have contributed to the exclusion of so many from the abundant life Jesus talked about.

One thing that can help us in this critical self-reflection is a willingness to listen to those who have been and are excluded. When I took a few members of the church I served in Long Beach, California, to Latin America to learn about hunger and exploitation, my theology was challenged. I discovered why Mary's song in Luke 1:46-55 is more precious to them than John 3:16. Since then the person, mission and teachings of Jesus have new meaning for me. I have had to rethink some of my theology.

Solidarity with the poor means more than taking up offerings for them, or building wells and preaching good sermons about poverty and justice, important though that is. Jesus told his followers to invite the poor to their banquets and parties. This means being at table with them. It means listening and being present with them in their struggles. It means face-to-face encounters and seeing through the windows they see through every day. It means going to their tables, not just inviting them to ours.

Maybe Brian McLaren is right when he says, *Everything Must Change*. (Title of his recent book.) He isn't suggesting we throw everything out, but be open to examining our current theology and practices.

I do not claim any certainty in my conclusions. I do have some questions. What I wish for is more conversation.

In a Culture of Exclusion and Thin Democracy

People have become upset and fed up with the way the rich keep getting richer and the poor keep getting poorer. They have taken to the streets and become part of the occupy movement. Inequality has become a hot topic and has become part of the conversation in the media as well as education centers. Some pastors and religious leaders are mentioning it, though carefully, in their sermons and newsletters. Is it just a phase we are going through or is it something that calls for action, for courage to think differently.

I recently taught a six-week class on poverty at the Irvine United Congregational Church where my wife and I worship quite regularly. We explored the Biblical passage where Jesus announces his mission as he begins his ministry in Galilee,

> ## "The Spirit of the Lord is upon me to preach good news to the poor."
> *Luke 4:18*

We started the class by sharing what we thought being poor was like and if we were poor what would good news be to us. It was not difficult to realize that, as Robert McAfee Brown says, we who are the non-poor have managed to take the sting out of those Biblical passages that lift up the cry of those living in poverty. Who can deny that the non-poor end up running the church today and set the agenda and budgets of most congregations?

Frances Moore Lappé has an interesting history of concern for the hungry of the world. She grew up in a United Church in Texas and while in graduate school realized that she needed to think differently about why so many people are hungry in our world. Lappé helps us move past the barriers of greed and powerlessness. Her insights help us to probe the root causes of the biggest threats to our planet and to think differently about a richer form of democracy and happiness.

You will be surprised at the keen insights regarding oppression and exclusion from Brita Gill-Austern, a professor of pastoral care at Andover Newton Theological School. She uses important findings from Miroslav Volf's book *Exclusion and Embrace* to awaken us to the powerful, contagious and destructive end of exclusion.

According to poet Carl Sandberg, exclusion is the ugliest word in the English language.

Few parables in the New Testament get at the dangers of inequality as well as the story of the rich man and Lazarus. What Jesus condemns in this text is not wealth per se but wealth in the midst of poverty. Luke16:19-31

George S. Johnson

O For a World

O for a world where everyone respects each other's ways
Where love is lived and all is done with justice and with praise

O for a world where goods are shared and misery relieved
Where truth is spoken, children spared, equality achieved

We welcome one world family and struggle with each choice
That opens us to unity and gives our vision voice

The poor are rich, the weak are strong, the foolish ones are wise
Tell all who mourn: outcasts belong, who perishes will rise

O for a world preparing for God's glorious reign of peace
Where time and tears will be no more, and all but love will cease

Miriam Therese Winter, 1987
Can be sung to "O For a Thousand Tongues" tune AZMON

EXCERPTED FROM

Something Worth Getting Mad About

by Bill Moyers

✦✦✦

From *Inequality Matters,* compilation Copyright © 2005 by Demos: A Network for Change. *The Fight for Our Lives,* © 2005, reproduced with permission by The New Press, www.thenewpress.com

Some things are worth getting mad about. These two stories from the same page of the same day's *New York Times,* for example. Under a six-column headline across the top, the Times of March 10, 2004, tells us that the annual tuition at Manhattan's most elite private schools has reached $26,000 – for kindergarten as well as high school. Lower down the page, in a story with a two-column headline, we learn about a school in Mount Vernon, New York, just across the city line from the Bronx. Its student body is 97 percent black. Nine out of ten kids qualify for free lunches. One out of ten lives in a homeless shelter.

During Black History Month, a sixth-grader sets out to write a report on Langston Hughes but cannot find a single book about the man in the library. It's not fluke: this is a library with only one book on Frederick Douglass, and none on Rosa Parks, Josephine Baker, or Leontyne Price. In fact, apart from a few Newbery Medal books bought by the librarian with her own money, the shelves are filled with books from the 1950s and 1960s. A child's primer on work begins with a youngster learning how to be a telegraph delivery boy. In another book, the dry cleaner, the deliveryman, and the cleaning lady – in fact, all the characters – are white, as all the students in the school were at the time the book was written. A 1967 book about telephones points out that while most phones have dials, a few of the newer models have buttons. The library has no computer. It doesn't even have a card catalog.

And here's something else to get mad about: Caroline Payne has continually been turned down for jobs because of her appearance. Her Medicaid-financed dentures don't fit, and her face and gums are distorted. Caroline Payne is one of the protagonists of David Shipler's The Working Poor: Invisible in America.

She was born poor, and though she once owned her own home and earned a two-year college degree, she has bounced from one poverty-wage job to another all her life. She has the will to move up, but not the resources to overcome a succession of unexpected and overlapping problems – a mentally handicapped daughter, a broken marriage, a sudden layoff that forces her to sell her few assets and give up her home. "In the house of the poor," Shipler writes, "the walls are thin and fragile and troubles seep into one another."

Here's something else: the House of Representatives, now a wholly owned subsidiary of the corporate, political, and religious right, has approved new tax credits for children. Not for poor children, but for families earning as much as $309,000 a year – the very families that have already been showered with tax cuts. The editorial page of the *Washington Post* calls this "bad social policy, bad tax policy, and bad fiscal policy. You'd think they'd be embarrassed" the *Post* says. "But they're not."

Nothing seems to embarrass the political class in Washington these days. Not the fact that more children are growing up in poverty in America than in any other industrial nation; that millions of workers are making less money in real dollars than they did twenty years ago; that working people are falling behind even as they put in longer and longer hours; or that while we have the most advanced medical care in the world, forty-five million Americans – eight out of ten of them in working families – are uninsured and cannot get basic care.

Astonishing as it seems, scarcely anyone in official Washington seems to be troubled by a gap between rich and poor that is greater than it has been in half a century – and greater than that of any other Western nation today. *Equality* and *inequality* are words that have been all but expunged from the political vocabulary. Poverty still gets mentioned every now and then, but in an airy, offhand way. Next to nothing is said, for example, about the profound shift in poverty that is under way in America today. For years we were told that those people down there at the bottom were single, jobless mothers. The poor themselves were counseled that if they wanted to move up the economic ladder, they had only to go to school, work hard, and get married. But now we see poverty where it was not supposed to be: among people who have followed the program to the letter – families with two parents, a full-time worker, and a head of household with more than a high school education. These are the newly poor, whom our political elites expect to climb out of poverty on a downward-moving escalator.

The Stanleys and the Neumanns come to mind. These two Milwaukee families – one black, one white – lost their breadwinners in the first wave of downsizing in 1991 as corporations began moving jobs out of the city and out of the country. In a series of documentaries over the next decade, my public TV colleagues and I chronicled their efforts to cope with wrenching changes and find a place for themselves in the new global economy. The Stanleys and the Neumanns are the kind of people my mother would have called "the salt of the earth." They love their children, care about their communities, go to church every Sunday, and work hard all week.

To make ends meet after the layoffs, both mothers had to take full-time jobs. Both fathers became seriously ill; when one father had to spend two months in the hospital, the family went $30,000 in debt because they didn't have adequate health coverage. We were present with our camera when the bank began foreclosure on the modest home of the other family because they couldn't meet the mortgage payments. Like millions of Americans, the Stanleys and the Neumanns were playing by the rules and getting stiffed. By the end of the decade they were running harder and slipping further behind, and the gap between them and prosperous Americans was widening.

They love America, and their patriotism turns a personal tragedy into a political travesty. When our film opens, both families are watching the inauguration of Bill Clinton on television. By the end of the decade, they have tuned out. They no longer believe they matter to those who run the country; they don't think their concerns will ever by addressed by the governing class. They are not cynical – they are too religious to be cynical – but they know the system is rigged against them.

And so do we. For years now a small fraction of American households have been garnering an extreme concentration of wealth and income while large corporations and financial institutions have obtained unprecedented power over who wins and who loses. In 1960, the gap in terms of wealth between the top 20 percent and the bottom 20 percent was thirtyfold. Four decades later it is more than seventy-five-fold. Such concentrations of wealth would be far less of an issue if the rest of society were benefiting proportionately. But that's not the case. The pressures of inequality on middle- and working-class Americans have grown more severe despite the general prosperity (which is why we called our documentaries about the Stanleys and Neumanns *Surviving the Good Times*). In the words of the economist Jeffrey Madrick, "The strain on working people and on family life, as spouses have gone to work in dramatic numbers, has become significant. VCRs and television sets are cheap, but higher education, health care, public transportation, drugs, housing, and cars have risen faster in price than typical family incomes. Life has grown neither calm nor secure for most Americans, by any means."

This is a stunning turn of events for a nation saturated with paeans to "the American Dream." Ours was not supposed to be a country where the winner takes all. Through a system of checks and balances, America sought to maintain a healthy equilibrium. Because equitable access to public resources is the lifeblood of any democracy, Americans made primary schooling free and universal. Because everyone deserves a second change, state laws were changed to protect debtors, especially poor ones, against rich creditors. Charters to establish corporations were open to most if not all (white) comers, rather than held for the elite. Government encouraged Americans to own their own piece of land, and even supported squatters' rights. Equal access, long a promise implicit in our founding documents, gradually became a reality for millions of us in the twentieth century. My parents were knocked down and almost out by the Depression and stayed poor all their lives. Nevertheless, I went to good public schools, and my brother made it to college on the GI Bill. When I bought my first car with a borrowed loan of $450, I drove to a subsidized university on free public highways and rested in state-maintained public parks. I was one more heir to a growing public legacy that shaped America as a shared project and became the central engine of our national experience.

Until now.

America is undergoing a profound transformation. The radical political elite that has gained ascendancy over politics has made inequality the objective of a sustained campaign, described by the (now defunct) Center for the Renewal of American Democracy as "a fanatical drive to dismantle the political institutions, the legal and statutory canons, and the intellectual and cultural frameworks that have shaped public responsibility from social harms arising from the excesses of private power." From land, water, and other natural resources, to media and the broadcast and digital spectrums, to scientific discovery and medical break-throughs, a broad range of America's public resources is moving toward elite control, contributing substantially to those economic pressures on ordinary Americans that, says Jeffrey Madrick, "deeply affect household stability, family dynamics, social mobility, political participation, and civic life."

You could have seen it coming by following the Great Divider – money. After a long career covering Washington, the veteran reporter Elizabeth Drew concludes that "the greatest change in Washington over the past twenty-five years – in its culture, in the way it does business and the ever-burgeoning amount of business transactions that go on here – has been in the preoccupation with money." Campaign money has "flooded over the gunwales of the ship of state and threatens to sink the entire vessel," writes Jeffrey Birnbaum, who spent nearly twenty years as a political reporter for the *Wall Street Journal*. "Political donations determine the course and speed of many government actions that – though we often forget – will deeply affect our daily lives."

Senator John McCain describes elections in the United States today as nothing less than an "influence-peddling scheme in which both parties compete to stay in office by selling the country to the highest bidder." During his brief campaign for president in 2000, McCain was ambushed by dirty tricks from the religious right in South Carolina and drowned in a flood of cash from the wealthy cronies of George W. Bush, who was sworn in for a second term under a canopy of cash - $40 million to $50 million – supplied for his inauguration by the very corporations waiting offstage for the payback.

And what a payback! Here's how it works:

> When powerful interests shower Washington with millions in campaign contributions, they often get what they want. But it's ordinary citizens and firms that pay the price and most of them never see it coming. This is what happens if you don't contribute to their campaigns or spend generously on lobbying. You pick up a disproportionate share of America's tax bill. You pay higher prices for a broad range of products from peanuts to prescriptions. You pay taxes that others in a similar situation have been excused from paying. You're compelled to abide by laws while others are granted immunity from them. You must pay debts that you incur while others do not. You're barred from writing off on your tax returns some of the money spent on necessities while others deduct the cost of their entertainment. You must run your business by one set of rules, while the government creates another set for your competitors. In contrast the fortunate few who contribute to the right politicians and hire the right lobbyists enjoy all the benefits of their special status. Make a bad business deal; the government bails them out. If they want to hire workers at below market wages, the government provides the means to do so. If they want more time to pay their debts, the government gives them an extension. If they want immunity from certain laws, the government gives it. If they want to ignore rules their competition must comply with, the government gives its approval. If they want to kill legislation that is intended for the public, it gets killed.

I'm not making this up. And I'm not quoting from Karl Marx's *Das Kapital* or Mao's *Little Red Book*. That was *Time* magazine. From the heart of America's media establishment comes the matter-of-fact judgment that America now has "government for the few at the expense of the many."

It is easy to understand why Franklin Delano Roosevelt feared a government by money as much as a government by mob. It is easy to understand why the Stanleys and the Neumanns were turned off by politics. They and millions like them have been the losers in a class war that disarmed them of political influence before defeating them.

Looking backward, it all seems so clear that we wonder how we could have ignored the warning signs. What has been happening to working people is not the result of Adam Smith's invisible hand but the direct consequence of corporate money, intellectual activism, the rise of a literalistic religious orthodoxy opposed to any civil and human rights that threaten its paternalism, and a string of political decisions favoring the interests of wealthy elites who have bought the political system right out from under us.

To create the intellectual framework for this revolution in public policy, these elites funded conservative think tanks that churned out study after study advocating their agenda. To put muscle behind these ideas, they created a formidable political machine. Thomas Edsall of the *Washington Post* is one of the few mainstream journalists who has covered the class story. "During the 1970s," he writes, "business refined its ability to act as a class, submerging competitive instincts in favor of joint, cooperative action in the legislative area." Big-business political action committees flooded the political arena with a deluge of dollars. And the wealthy elites built alliances with the religious right – Jerry Falwell's Moral Majority and Pat Robertson's Christian Coalition – who gleefully contrived a cultural holy war as a smoke screen behind which the economic assault on the middle and working classes would be waged.

The unmitigated plunder of the public trust has spread a spectacle of corruption across America. For its equivalent one has to go back to the first Gilded Age, when the powerful and the privileged controlled politics, votes were bought and sold, legislatures corrupted, and laws flagrantly disregarded, threatening the very foundations of democracy. It was a time – now is another – when the great captains of industry and finance could say, with Frederick Townsend Martin, "We are rich. We own America. We got it, God knows how, but we intend to keep it."

And they will, unless, reading this book, you get mad – mad enough to get organized.

EXCERPTED FROM

Getting A Grip

by Frances Moore Lappé

◆◆◆

This is the question that's propelled my life for decades now. It *is* really bewildering. We know that no human being actually gets up in the morning vowing, "Yeah, today I'm going to make sure another child dies needlessly of hunger," or muttering, "Sure, I'll do my part to heat the planet and obliterate entire species."

Yet each day over twenty-five thousand young children die of hunger and poverty, and roughly one hundred more species are forever gone. And the crises are not abating; they just keep whacking us: global climate chaos, terrorism, racial and religious divides, life-stunting poverty, pandemic disease . . . and now our own government's betrayal of constitutional principle.

Again . . . *why?*

I think for a lot of us, there is no real answer. Things just keep happening. We know *we're* not in control, and it seems like nobody is.

Sure, some people believe the problem is just us – human beings are just screwed up. Whether you call it original sin or simple selfishness, it's just who we are. Others are more targeted in assigning blame. For them, the root cause of our planet's crises is those *particular* people . . . the evil ones. Osama bin Laden, George W. Bush, Saddam Hussein, Dick Cheney. Still others believe we have no choice. We must conform to the now-proven economic laws of the global marketplace or suffer an even worse fate.

For all their many differences, the consequences of these views are similar. They leave us powerless. With no grip on how things got so bad, we have no clue as to where to start to correct them. So we're tempted to seize on any gesture of charity or any burst of protest – any random act of sanity. For a moment, at least, we can feel less useless in the face of the magnitude of the crises. Ultimately, though, acts of desperation contribute to our despair if we're unable to link our specific acts to real solutions.

Feeling powerless, we're robbed of energy and creativity, with hearts left open to fear and depression. No wonder the World Health Organization tells us depression is now the fourth leading cause of lost productive life world-wide – expected to jump to second place in fifteen years. Or that suicide worldwide now exceed homicides by 50 percent.

But what if…what if…together with our friends, family, and acquaintances, we could probe the root causes of the biggest threats to our planet? What if we were able to grasp something of the common origins of these threats and then identify powerful entry points to interrupt them? And more than that, what if we could then feel we are shifting the destructive underlying patterns toward health?

Now, that's power. Our power.

Peeling Away the Layers

Over the years, I've come to sense that blaming the evil other stumbles on what logicians call an attribution error, the misplaced identification of cause. And it's a pretty serious error, for it releases us from asking really helpful questions: What is it about the current order we ourselves are creating that elicits so much pain and destruction? And peeling to the next layer: What are our own unexamined assumptions and beliefs that leave us feeling so powerless?

In the late nineteenth century, for example, Indians outnumbered the British civil servants ruling them by three hundred thousand to one. Yet Indians' widespread belief in their powerlessness continued until Gandhi and others re-framed reality, revealing the power that was theirs all along. In 1930, Indians declared independence and, sparked by Gandhi's example, thousands walked over two hundred miles to the sea to protest the British salt tax. Within seventeen years, the Indian people had ousted their colonial rulers.

It's pretty easy to see how mental concepts – ideas about reality – disempower others, whether it's a belief in a ruler's "divine right" or a conviction about the inferiority of a lower caste. It's much harder to perceive the mental straight-jackets we ourselves don every day.

Our future, though, may well depend on giving it a try.

In *The Anatomy of Human Destructiveness*, social philosopher Eric Fromm observes that all human beings carry within us "frames of orientation" through which we make sense of the world. They determine – often literally – what we can see, what we believe humans are made of, and therefore what we believe is possible. In other words, just about everything.

Now this trait might be just fine . . . *if* our frames are life-serving, but, Fromm warns, they aren't always. To stir us to realize the danger within this unique aspect of our humanness – our filtering through socially determined frames – Fromm came up with this mid-bending declaration: "It is man's humanity that makes him so inhuman."

Cultures live or die, Fromm is telling us, not by violence, or by chance, but ultimately by ideas. And unfortunately for our precious planet, much of the world appears locked within sets of ideas, including our ideas about democracy, that actually contribute to our "inhumanity" – whether that means inflicting or ignoring the suffering and loss mounting worldwide.

Inside the front cover, please see what I call a *Spiral of Powerlessness*. It is the scary current of limiting beliefs and consequences in which I sense we're trapped.

Its premise is "lack."

There isn't enough of anything, neither enough "goods" – whether jobs or jungles – nor enough "goodness" because human beings are, well, pretty bad. These ideas have been drilled into us for centuries, as world religions have dwelt on human frailty, and Western political ideologies have picked up similar themes.

"*Homo homini lupus* [we are to one another as wolves]," wrote the influential seventeenth-century philosopher Thomas Hobbes. Repeating a Roman aphorism – long before we'd learned how social wolves really are – Hobbes reduced us to cutthroat animals.

> **Private interest . . . is the only immutable point in the human heart.**
>
> *Alexis de Tocqueville,*
> *Democracy in America, 1835*

From that narrow premise, it follows that it's best to mistrust deliberative problem-solving, distrust even democratic government, and grasp for an infallible law – the market! – driven by the only thing we can really count on, human selfishness. From there, wealth concentrates and suffering increases, confirming the dreary premises that set the spiral in motion in the first place.

What this downward spiral tells me is that we humans now suffer from what linguists call "hypocognition," the lack of a critical concept we need to thrive. And it's no trivial gap! Swept into the vortex of this destructive spiral, we're missing an understanding of democracy vital and compelling enough to create the world we want.

Democracy? Why start there?

Democracy is *the* problem-solving device much of the world now embraces as the way to meet common needs and solve common problems. So if our definition of democracy is flawed, we are in big trouble.

Elections Plus a Market . . . That's Democracy?

To see what's missing, let's explore a bit more the dominant conception of reality in which our nation's culture, especially our view of democracy, is grounded. As just noted, its foundational premise is scarcity – there just isn't enough of *anything* – from love to jobs to parking spots. In such a world, only one type of person thrives. So if you peel away all the fluff, humans must have evolved as competitive materialists, elbowing one another out in a giant scramble over scarce stuff.

Absorbing this shabby caricature of humanity, we understandably see ourselves as incapable of making a success of democratic deliberation – assuming a selfish nature, we're sure somebody will always muck it up. Not to fret, though. We've been assured with ever-greater intensity since the 1980s that if real democracy – deliberating together to shape a common purpose and strategies – is suspect, there's a perfect solution: Just turn over our fate to an impersonal law that will settle things for us. Privatize and commoditize all that we can – from health care to prison management to schools – in order to take full advantage of what Ronald Reagan called "the magic of the market."

And government? It's something done *to* us or for us by taking "our money," so the less of it the better.

From these assumptions, it is easy to see why most Americans grow up absorbing the notion that democracy boils down to just two things – elected government and a market economy. Since in the United States we have both, there isn't much for us to do except show up at the polls and shop.

I like to call this stripped-down duo Thin Democracy because it is feeble.

We breathe in this definition like invisible ether, so it's easy to jump over an unpleasant fact: Real democracy and our peculiar variant of a market economy are based on opposing principles. Democracy derives from the Greek: *demos* (people) plus *kratos* (rule). Thus democracy depends on the wide dispersion of power so that each citizen has both a vote and a voice. But our particular market economy, driven by one rule – that is, highest return to shareholder and corporate chiefs – moves inexorably in the opposite direction. By continually returning wealth to wealth, a one-rule economy leads to an ever-increasing concentration of power.

Lizzie's Lessons

In the early 1900s, Lizzie Maggie tried to warn us. Lizzie was a concerned Quaker, worried that one-rule capitalism would do us in. So she came up with a board game she hoped would entertain us but also serve as an object lesson: It may take all night, but the rules of the game eventually drive property into the hands of one player, ending the fun for everybody.

Well, Lizzie's idea got into the hands of Parker Brothers. They called it Monopoly, and the rest, as they say, is history – history that, in this case, reveals just what Maggie was trying to tell us about one-rule economics. Just five companies sell well over half of all toys in America. More generally, in 1955, sales of the top five hundred corporations equaled one-third of the U.S. gross domestic product. They now account for two-thirds.

As corporate wealth concentrates, so does private: Here in the United States, between 1979 and 2001, family income among the wealthiest 5 percent leapt by 81 percent, but families in the bottom 20 percent saw virtually no gain. The gap separating America's average CEO's compensation and average worker's pay has widened tenfold in a generation, so today the CEO earns as much by lunchtime on the first day of the year as a minimum wage worker earns the entire year.

In the United States over the last four years, the share of economic growth going to corporate profits increased by over two-thirds, while the share rewarding workers fell, even as their productivity continued to rise. Today America's biggest employer, Wal-Mart, pays its workers in inflation-adjusted dollars only 40 percent as much as the biggest employer in 1969, GM, paid its employees – not to mention the workers' benefits now stripped away.

For the first time, the four hundred richest Americans are all billionaires, with combined wealth of $1.25 trillion, roughly comparable to the total annual income of half the world's people. Worldwide, the number of billionaires is exploding. Growing eight times faster than the global economy, it is now at 946 people with a total wealth almost 40 percent greater than the entire GDP of China.

So we didn't learn from Lizzie. We didn't get it – that to keep the game going, we citizens have to devise rules to ensure that wealth continually circulates. Otherwise, it all ends up in one player's pile. (In my household, it was usually my brother's!)

Yet under the spell of one-rule economics, most economists ignore this truth, as well as new jaw-dropping evidence that markets, by themselves, don't create livable societies:

Worldwide, during the 1990s, every one hundred dollars in economic growth reduced the poverty of the world's billion poorest people by just *sixty pennies*.

Denial runs so deep, though, that the pro-corporate British journal, *The Economist*, apparently with a straight face, can describe inequality deepening worldwide as a "snag" in the system. And well-meaning academics, with Columbia University's Jeffrey Sachs in the lead, can rally us to end global poverty by exporting our assumed-to-be successful economic model to them.

So we remain blind to Thin Democracy's pitfalls.

Thin Democracy's Pitfalls

Death to open markets. Despite the myth of competitive capitalism, writes economist James Galbraith, "[C]orporations exist to control markets and often to replace them. Two companies have succeeded in controlling roughly three-fourths of the global grain trade; one, Monsanto, accounts for 88 percent of the area planted worldwide with genetically modified seed and/or seed with biotech traits. Six corporations control most global media, from publishing to movies, and five control almost two-thirds of U.S. gasoline sales.

In our one-rule economy, concentrated economic power is inevitable, destroying the very open, competitive market that was the rationale for the whole set-up to begin with. Wasn't it? Competitive, fair markets cannot be sustained, it turns out, outside of a genuinely democratic polity.

Just as with the protection of civil liberties, open markets depend on us, on our creating and continually monitoring rules that keep them open.

Corporations want the opposite; they seek control over markets to ensure highest returns – not because they're run by bad people, but because the rules we've set up encourage them to.

History bears out this truth: it was only when Americans did step up to the plate, especially in the period from 1933 to 1945, and created fairness rules – including the right of workers to organize, Social Security, and a legal minimum wage – that our country experienced a dramatic narrowing of the gap between most of us and a tiny minority at the top. The approach fostered broad-based economic prosperity for decades: Our median family income grew four times faster between 1947 and 1973 than it has since – as America has forsaken Lizzie's commonsense insight.

Unfortunately, Thin Democracy's pitfalls don't stop here.

Warping of politics. Concentrated economic power, flowing inevitably from a one-rule economy, ends up infecting and warping our political system, as well. Sixty-one lobbyists now walk the corridors of power in Washington, D.C., for every one person we citizens have elected to represent our interests there.

The liberty of a democracy is not safe if the people tolerate the growth of private power to the point where it becomes stronger than their democratic state itself. That, in its essence, is fascism . . .

Franklin Delano Roosevelt, 1938

When citizens are outnumbered sixty-one to one, private power supersedes public power – as FDR warned us seven decades ago. Little wonder! To pick just a few frightening examples:

- for almost six years after 9/11, the chemical industry lobby was able to resist measures needed to secure fifteen thousand chemical plants against attack.

- while five thousand Americans die annually from food-borne illnesses, the food industry is able to block mandatory recalls.

- ex-oil lobbyist Philip Cooney was so tight with the Bush White House that he edited official reports to downplay climate change.

- pharmaceutical lobbyists helped craft a healthcare law that forbids Medicare to negotiate drug prices – while we pay double what Europeans do for identical drugs.

So more and more Americans feel their democracy has been stolen, and they know by whom. Ninety percent of us agree that corporations have too much influence in Washington.

Deeper Dangers

More than unworkable, Thin Democracy is dangerous. The power it gives corporations to put their own short-term gain ahead of our survival is only one danger.

The fragility of centralized power. Contrary to lessons drummed into us, concentrated power is often not resilient, efficient, or smart. The Inca and the Aztecs, huge civilizations, fell to conquistadors in no time, while the leaderless, decentralized Apaches fended off harsh attacks for two centuries. Concentrated power often isolates itself and thus fails to learn. Think only of the, "I'm in the decider" bunker stance of the Bush White House that led the U.S. into Iraq, one of our country's most horrific foreign policy blunders.

Missing problem solvers. The flipside is that the centralized power of Thin Democracy leaves most of us feeling powerless, robbing the planet of just the problem solvers we most need. It encourages us to look to the "market" or to CEOs or to government higher-ups for answers, but our planet's problems are too complex, pervasive, and interconnected to be addressed from the top down. Solutions depend on the insights, experience, and ingenuity of people most affected – all thwarted when citizens are cut out and manipulated, and when decisions get made secretly by the few.

Put slightly differently, solutions require in-the-moment inventiveness and widespread behavior changes, and both depend on the engagement and "buy-in" of citizens. So Thin Democracy undermines precisely the broad-based commitment our world so desperately needs.

Misaligned with our nature. Thin Democracy can't create healthy societies because it is misaligned with human nature in two ways. Denying our rich complexity, *it fails to tap the best in us and fails to protect us from the worst.*

By "best" I mean several innate needs and capacities I explore in Chapter 2. They include our needs to connect with others, for basic fairness, and for efficacy, as well as the need to feel that our lives matter, which for many people means contributing to something grander than our own survival.

Forcing us to bury these needs, Thin Democracy fuels paralyzing despair and alienation.

Ironically, Thin Democracy doesn't register our really negative potential either. Let me be clear. I don't mean the capacity of a tiny minority of us; I mean the vast majority. The Holocaust doesn't prove what a crazed dictator and some sadistic guards will do. Actually, it proves the depravity most normal people will express, given the "right" conditions.

To bring home this unhappy truth, British historian Christopher Browning reports that as late as March, 1942, the vast majority – 75 to 80 percent – of all victims of the Holocaust were still alive, but "a mere eleven months later" most were dead.

These murders happened, Browning says, because "ordinary" people became killers. He tells, for example, of Reserve Battalion 101 – about five hundred men from Hamburg, Germany, many of whom were middle-aged reservists drafted in the fall of 1939. From working and lower middle-classes, these men with no military police experience were sent to Poland on a bloody mission – the total extermination of Jews in Poland's many remote hamlets.

Within four months, they had shot to death, at point-blank range, at least thirty-eight thousand Jews and had another forty-five thousand deported to the concentration camp at Treblinka.

"Though almost all of them – at least initially – were horrified and disgusted," over time, social modeling processes took their toll, as did guilt-induced persuasion by buddies who did the killing, until up to 90 percent of the men in Battalion 101 were involved in the shootings.

I first learned about Battalion 101 from Philip Zimbardo. You might recognize the name. Zimbardo is the professor who organized the infamous "prison experiment" at Stanford in 1971. He put young people who'd "tested normal" into a mock prison setting where they were divided into prisoners and guards, dressed for their roles, and told the experiment would last two weeks.

But on the sixth day, Zimbardo abruptly halted the experiment. He had to. Using some techniques eerily similar to those in Abu Ghraib prison over three decades later, the "guards" had begun brutalizing their "prisoners" causing severe emotional breakdown. Professor Zimbardo has since acknowledged that one reason he stopped the experiment is that his girlfriend told him he himself had begun behaving like a warden – "more concerned," as he put it later, "about the security of 'my prison' than the needs of the young men entrusted to my care . . . "

In the last one hundred years, humans have killed roughly forty million other humans not in war, as we normally define it, but in massive assaults on civilians, from the fifteen million lost in the Russian Gulag to almost one million in Rwanda. Whether we're talking about a psychologist's carefully designed experiment or the current genocide in Darfur, the inescapable proof is in: Decent people do evil things under the "right conditions."

And what is one condition certain to bring forth brutality? Extreme power imbalances that arise inevitably in a range of social orders. One of these is Thin Democracy.

Failure to bring meaning. Finally, Thin Democracy is dangerously vulnerable because its materialistic premise can't satisfy our higher selves' yearning for transcendent meaning.

Thin Democracy's narrow, insulting assumptions about human nature cannot sustain dedication and sacrifice. Many U.S. soldiers now risk their lives in war, believing they're serving a high calling. But the built-in logic of one-rule economics mocks their idealism. Since 9/11, thousands of American soldiers have made the ultimate sacrifice in Iraq, while executives of U.S. armament corporations have made a killing, doubling their own compensation.

At the same time, Thin Democracy's demeaning materialism and its concentrated wealth help to swell the numbers of excluded people who feel humiliated and angry. Understandably, these feelings open some hearts to extremist, violent ideologies – both religious and secular – that claim high moral ground and offer adherents everlasting glory.

"My grandmother's gone to heaven because she shot the Israelis," explained six-year-old Israa, as she played beneath a photo of seventy-year-old Fatima Najar, who blew herself up in Gaza in 2006. Young men have long seemed most susceptible to violent ideologies, but a sixty-five-year-old in Gaza told the British *Observer*, "I know at least twenty of us [elder women] who want to put on the [suicide bomber's] belt." They've "found a use for themselves," she said.

How deep runs our need to feel useful, a need unmet for so many people in today's world. Ultimately, Thin Democracy can't hold a candle to the fanatics' uplifting, absolutist visions – right or left.

In all, Thin Democracy gives democracy itself a bad name. Its profound shortcomings help to explain why in many countries' initial enthusiasm for it is now waning. In 2000, two-thirds of Latin Americans polled said they were dissatisfied with democracy. Between 2000 and 2005, in ten African countries, polls show citizens' preference for democracy falling – in Tanzania by almost half.

Humility and Hope

In "getting a grip" myself, I've tried to shape a way of seeing the world that has explanatory power for me: Our primary obstacle, I lay out here, is that we're stuck in an unworkable mental map that cannot come to grips with local-to-global crises – Thin Democracy.

My diagnosis is hard-nosed about human frailty without writing off our species as incorrigible, for I am reminded almost daily that, as creatures of the mind, we have the unique power to bring to consciousness a failing mental frame – those core assumptions shaping our view of reality – and to remake it with new information and experience.

Each person has the biological power to interrupt detrimental, derogatory beliefs and generate new ideas. These new ideas, in turn, can alter the neural circuitry that governs how we behave and what we believe.

Andrew Newberg, M.D., Author, *Why We Believe What We Believe*

We can intentionally evolve more life-serving mental maps. Imagine that!

But to walk this journey presumes a certain kind of humility. With all our fancy forecasting – from ten-day weather reports to the "Fed's" inflation predictions – we can be lulled into believing we can see into the future pretty well. But actually, we can't. History doesn't unfold in neat, even increments. It moves in messy, surprising jolts, and in this unprecedented era, the surprises could even intensity.

And here's the big upside: Recognizing that in this unique moment it is not possible to know what's possible…we discover we are free. We're free to throw ourselves into the most thrilling, planetary struggle our species has ever known. We can probe deeply, asking together, What might be a richer understanding of democracy – one strong and vital enough to meet today's challenges, and compelling enough to stand up to extremists' claims?

In nine parts, this little book explores this path.

EXCERPTED FROM

Taking Oppression Seriously

by Brita L. Gill-Austern

One of the most stunning facts of being human is that each individual shares 99.9 percent of the same DNA with all other humans. Yet it is that less than one-tenth of 1 percent of difference that creates a good deal of the havoc, conflict, war, and oppression in our world. The differences between us lead to many acts of dehumanization and practices of exclusion toward the one or ones we consider "other." The human race is still struggling with learning how to deal with its differences in ways that can contribute to the beauty, richness, and meaning of life, rather than be the source of such unrelenting oppression and suffering.

In this essay, I argue that the vitality of life and creation rests upon the interplay of difference and unity. Drawing upon the work of Miroslav Volf, I will show how human beings unable to maintain the creative tension between difference and unity consistently turn to various practices of exclusion to deal with difference. These practices of exclusion further the disconnections between us that dehumanize us all and contribute to oppression and the suffering that follows in its wake. I will argue that one form of exclusion, poverty, is maintained through the practice of abandonment and indifference. Finally, I will develop a definition of practices of practical solidarity and show how in the face of oppression they can move us away from practices of exclusion to practices of practical solidarity.

Diversity, Difference, and Unity are the Dance of Creation

The Mexican writer Octavio Paz wrote: "What sets the worlds in motion is the interplay of differences, their attractions and repulsions. Life is plurality, death is uniformity" (1985, 17). This truth is also built into our common creation story. As theologian Sallie McFague reminds us:

> The common creation story radicalizes both oneness and difference. From one infinitely hot, infinitely condensed bit of matter (a millionth of a gram) some fifteen billion years ago, have evolved one hundred billion galaxies, each its billions of stars and planets... Biologists have found in a single square foot of topsoil an inch deep an average of 1,356 living creatures, including 865 mites, 265 springtails, 22 millipedes, 19 adult beetles and various numbers of other forms. From one millionth of a gram of matter, unimaginable unity, has evolved unimaginable diversity. (1993, 38)

If anything can be said about the creative source of the world, it is that the Source of All loves diversity and unity. The common creation story tells us that the basic dynamic of the universe is a constant dance between distinctiveness and communion, with every distinctive part of the universe being attracted to another part. The basic dynamic of the universe is also at the heart of genuine care and justice making. Care, pastoral theologian Peggy Way reminds us, "seeks embrace, the embrace of difference and hence the embrace of the possibility of community" (2005, 59).

The problem of difference, of seeing "the other" as object rather than subject, permeates our individual and communal lives. As a species we still need to work on the dance that makes distinctiveness and difference belong to the experience of communion rather than disconnection. All too often we interrupt the dance of creation that binds difference and communion, diversity and unity together, by treating difference as a threat to both identity and community. Too often we deal with differences by and through practices of exclusion, which also foster systemic oppression. To bring creative change, we must address directly the practices of exclusion that oppress others based on perceived and real differences and find ways to model and incarnate for others practices of practical solidarity.

Practices of Exclusion

Carl Sandburg called "exclusion the ugliest word in the English language." No doubt because of all that ugliness it spawns in human life. Exclusion results from a failure to hold in creative tension what we know of reality from the beginning of creation: we are both distinct and differentiated from everything else and also a part of and drawn into an inescapable web of interdependence, reciprocity, and mutuality that yearns for communion.

We deal with difference, according to Volf in his book *Exclusion and Embrace*, through the violence of exclusion. To heal the disconnections that divide us we must look at what Volf calls "the powerful, contagious and destructive evil of exclusion" (1996, 30). Practices of exclusion are rooted in our interpersonal and familial histories. They thrive, as do weeds in a garden, when identity is seen exclusively through the lens of our own tribe or culture, when we are blinded by our captivity to that culture, and when the narcissism of self-absorption prevents us from recognizing the historical realities of others.

Volf identifies four forms of the violence of exclusion in the ways in which we deal with difference, each of which can make life hell on earth.

First, he names the *violence of expulsion*, when we intentionally and often violently exile others from community or proclaim that "they" do not belong. In such objectification of the other, we create a rationale for violence. Some of the most horrific practices of expulsion depend upon hatred and evoking it in others (1996, 74). Expulsion takes its most extreme form through the elimination of "the other" in such historical events as the ethnic cleansing in the Balkans, the Holocaust, the genocide of Rwanda. The exclusion of expulsion says fundamentally: You do not belong to the family of humanity; you are "other," you are vermin, rats, scum, and therefore I have the right to kill you. The exclusion of expulsion can also be found in discrimination, in the workplace, in ghettos and white suburbs, in schools of privilege, and in prisons filled with those made poor by structures that perpetuate economic inequality.

Second, we deal with difference, according to Volf, by the *violence of assimilation*. This is a milder form of eliminating the identity of the other, which occurs when we incorporate the other into our reality by obliterating his or her reality. The other only exists through the lens that the assimilator creates in order to make him or her become like oneself. Distinctiveness is swallowed up, repressed, or denied. Volf, drawing on Claude Levi-Strauss, says that exclusion by assimilation rests on a deal: "we will refrain from vomiting you out, if you let us swallow you up" (ibid.). We see this in the United States when acceptance of immigrants is based on their becoming just like "us," giving up their language, customs, and culture.

Another common pattern for dealing with difference is through subjugating the other. We designate others as inferior in some way, then use them or exploit them to increase our wealth, or inflate our egos (1996, 75). When we do this we are often operating out of an ideology of scarcity, whereby we exclude others from scarce goods be they economic, social, or psychological. This is exclusion made concrete in practices of domination, revealing our desire to be alone at the center. We see these patterns of exclusion in the history of colonization, in much of our global market economy, and in gender relations in many part of the world.

Finally, Volf says, we practice *exclusion by the indifference of abandonment*. Here we deal with difference by pretending we just do not see. We see, but pass over to the other side. We see, but we keep our distance so that the other has no claim on us. We see, but we divert our attention to other things. We see, but we feel powerless, so we push this seeing from consciousness. The exclusion of indifference, when the "other" becomes anonymous or invisible to us, grows like mold in a basement. Volf reminds us that when the other lives at a distance, indifference can be more destructive than hate (ibid., 77).

Underlying most forms of oppression and practices of exclusion are persistent and pervasive patterns of disconnection. These patterns of disconnection not only lay a foundation for oppression, fundamentally they also create an attitude that we are not responsible. Patterns of disconnection are at the root of some of our most intractable social problems: violence, war, racism, ecological devastation, homophobia, and the increasing economic inequality in our world. These problems and others are maintained and exacerbated by patterns of exclusion that reify such feelings of disconnection.

The Exclusion of the Practice of Abandonment of Those Made Poor

An attitude of indifference lies beneath the practice of abandonment and we see its expression most vividly in the abandonment of those who have been made poor. I focus on the practice of indifference and abandonment and the patterns of disconnection that give rise to it for three reasons: first, I believe it is the practice of exclusion to which the majority of U.S. citizens are most susceptible; second, in our historical moment it has the most power to spawn suffering and evil; and finally, I believe this is the practice of exclusion where faith communities and our practices of care can make the greatest impact. The Gospels are permeated with Jesus' concern for exclusion. The good news of Christ's welcoming embrace comes again and again to those who are abandoned to live on the margins of exclusion.

The problem of abandonment stems from a lack of connection. We exclude and abandon others when we feel no connection with them or we fail to recognize our connection. When there is no sense of connection, the expected common reaction is indifference, which leads to abandonment. Without relationship, we lose a sense of responsibility to the other.

Where is the place in our world where the exclusion of indifference and abandonment is most evident? Many would argue that it is in the growing gap of economic inequality that allows an increasing abandonment of the poor. Only indifference and abandonment of the poor would allow the richest 10 percent of the world's population to receive 49.6 percent of the world's total income, while the bottom 60 percent receives 13.9 percent. Economic inequality eventually leads to more social breakdown and disconnection (Collins and Yeskel 2005, 30).

Salvadoran theologian Jon Sobrino points to the fact that, quantitatively, poverty constitutes the most painful suffering on this planet. He calls its day-to-day, death-dealing reality "the world's most serious wound" (1992, 22). The greatest weapon of mass destruction in our world today is poverty; nothing else comes close. All the casualties of all the wars in the world do not equal those who die because of causes related to poverty. The oppression of those whom minister Delle McComick, executive director of the experiential educational organization Borderlinks, calls "the made poor," the largest percentage of whom are persons of color, by the vast economic inequalities of our nation and our world, is one of the most urgent moral issues of our time and the greatest challenge to the witness of faith communities.

Way reminds us in her book *Created by God: Pastoral Care for All God's People* (2005) that pastoral care is faithful living by finite creatures in their particular historical context. Our particular historical context demands that we give increased attention to the exclusion practiced through abandonment by the "haves" of the "have-nots" of our world. How can one billion people, almost one fifth of the world's population, live on less than a dollar a day unless much of the world simply accepts their fate with indifference and abandons them to their plight?

Behind the statistics of poverty from all corners of the world are millions of stories of individual women, children, and men whose exclusion from power and the world's resources has resulted in lives of unbelievable hardship and premature death. In the United States it is becoming harder to deny the death-dealing power of the exclusion of indifference and abandonment. In this country we have seen that the poorest were most at risk by Hurricane Katrina. One out of six persons in New Orleans did not own an automobile, and therefore were dependent upon public or government-provided transportation to evacuate. They lived in the lowest, most flood-prone parts of New Orleans. Some think Katrina has begun to shake us out of our slumber. But if you look at the slow rebuilding of New Orleans and what has happened to many of its former residents, we need to wonder. We give generously immediately following a crisis, we write checks, we gather food for food banks and open our doors for soup kitchens, but the underlying structures that continue to fuel inequality, and are the most resistant to change, remain in place.

The indifference of abandonment, and the form of politics it generates, comes at least in part because we have lost a sense of connection to those who suffer from the impact of poverty. The great divide between the "haves" and " have-nots" in our world can only be crossed by building connective bridges that foster relationship and a sense of community with those outside our immediate circle. Because we are knit together in an inescapable web of mutuality and interdependence, we need each other to be fully human. Without recognition of this interdependence, the self and other are dehumanized. A "re-humanization" of the self and other can happen through connection with those outside of our immediate circles or "lifestyle enclaves." This movement can be facilitated by practices of practical solidarity in congregations that deepen our sense of connection to those who live on the margins.

Simon Kneebone, cartoonist. Reproduced with permission of New Internationalist magazine.

———— EXCERPTED FROM ————

Charity Can Be a Dangerous Solution

by Shane Claiborne

✦✦✦

Layers of insulation separate the rich and the poor from truly encountering one another. There are the obvious layers like picket fences and SUV's, and there are the more subtle ones like charity. Tithes, tax-exempt donations, and short-term mission trips, while they accomplish some good, can also function as outlets that allow us to appease our consciences and still remain a safe distance from the poor. Take this poignant example you may have caught wind of: it was revealed that Kathie Lee garments, which have earned Wal-Mart over $300 million in sales annually, were being produced by teenage girls working in abysmal conditions in Honduran sweatshops. These girls, as young as thirteen, worked fifteen-hour shifts under the watch of armed guards and received thirty-one cents an hour. But the great irony is that the garments they were making for Kathie Lee were sold under a label that promised that "a portion of the proceeds from the sale of this garment will be donated to various children's charities." More recently, Kathie Lee has been an advocate for workers' rights. Charity can be a dangerous insulator.

It is much more comfortable to depersonalize the poor so we don't feel responsible for the catastrophic human failure that results in someone sleeping on the street while people have spare bedrooms in their homes. We can volunteer in a social program or distribute excess food and clothing through organizations and never have to open up our homes, our beds, our dinner tables. When we get to heaven, we will be separated into those sheep and goats Jesus talks about in Matthew 25 based on how we cared for the least among us. I'm just not convinced that Jesus is going to say, "When I was hungry, you gave a check to the United Way and they fed me," or, "When I

was naked, you donated clothes to the Salvation Army and they clothed me."
Jesus is not seeking distant acts of charity. He seeks concrete acts of love:
"you fed me... you visited me in prison... you welcomed me into your home
. . . you clothed me."

With new government funds and faith-based initiatives, the social-work
model can easily entangle the church in the efficiency of brokering services
and resources in a web of "clients" and "providers" and struggling to retain
God's vision of rebirth, in which we are all family. Faith-based nonprofits
can too easily be the mirror image of secular organizations, maintaining the
same hierarchies of power and separation between rich and poor. They can
too easily merely facilitate the exchange of goods and services, putting plenty
of professionals in the middle to guarantee that the rich do not have to face
the poor and that power does not shift. Rich and poor are kept in separate
worlds, and inequality is carefully managed but not dismantled.

When the church becomes a place of brokerage rather than an organic
community, she ceases to be alive. She ceases to be something we are,
the living bride of Christ. The church becomes a distribution center, a place
where the poor come to get stuff and the rich come to dump stuff. Both go
away satisfied (the rich feel good, the poor get clothed and fed), but no one
leaves transformed. No radical new community is formed. And Jesus did not
set up a program but modeled a way of living that incarnated the reign of
God, a community in which people are reconciled and our debts are forgiven
just as we forgive our debtors (all economic words). That reign did not spread
through organizational establishments or structural systems. It spread like
disease – through touch, through breath, through life. It spread through
people infected by love.

Often wealthy folks ask me what they can do for the Simple Way. I could ask
them for a few thousand dollars, but that would be too easy for both of us.
Instead, I ask them to come visit. Writing a check makes us feel good and
can fool us into thinking that we have loved the poor. But seeing the squat
houses and tent cities and hungry children will transform our lives. Then

we will be stirred to imagine the economics or rebirth and to hunger for the end of poverty.

Almost every time we talk with affluent folks about God's will to end poverty, someone says, "But didn't Jesus say, 'The poor will always be with you'?" Many of the people who whip out this verse have grown quite insulated and distant from the poor and feel defensive. I usually gently ask, "Where are the poor? Are the poor among us?" The answer is usually a clear nugatory. As we study the Scriptures, we see how many texts we have misread, contextualized, and exegeted to hear what we want to. Like this one about the poor being among us, which Jesus says in the home of a leper and after a poor marginalized woman anoints his feet with perfume. The poor were all around him. Far from saying in defeat that we should not worry about the poor, since they will always be among us, Jesus is pointing the church to her true identity – she is to live close to those who suffer. The poor will always be among us, because the empire will always produce poor people, and they will find a home in the church, a citizenship in the kingdom of God where the "hungry are filled with good things and the rich sent away empty."

I heard that Gandhi, when people asked him if he was a Christian, would often reply, "Ask the poor. They will tell you who the Christians are."

Joel Knoffman, artist, used by permission.

Rich Man and Lazarus

A Group Bible Study by George Johnson

Luke 16:19-31

—— ◆◆◆ ——

Adventure and Challenge

This study is an adventure into one of the most challenging parables told by Jesus. The subject of wealth in the midst of poverty is the major theme. No text is more crucial to our understanding of the Church's responsibility in a world where hunger is rampant and the economic crisis is causing great suffering.

The format used here is best adaptable for small groups or family devotions where participants are encouraged to reflect and enter into the discussion. You could divide it into two sessions. Copies may be reproduced so that everyone can participate. The text reads as follows:

"There was a rich man, who was clothed in purple and fine linen and who feasted sumptuously every day. And at his gate lay a poor man named Lazarus, full of sores, who desired to be fed with what fell from the rich man's table; moreover the dogs came and licked his sores.

"The poor man died and was carried by the angels to Abraham's bosom. The rich man also died and was buried; and in Hades, being in torment, he lifted up his eyes, and saw Abraham far off and Lazarus in his bosom. And he called out, 'Father Abraham, have mercy upon me, and send Lazarus to dip the end of his finger in water and cool my tongue; for I am in anguish in this flame.' But Abraham said, 'Son, remember that you in your lifetime received your good things, and Lazarus in like manner evil things; but now he is comforted here, and you are in anguish. And besides all this, between us and you a great chasm has been fixed, in order that those who would pass from here to you may not be able, and none may cross from there to us.'

"And he said, 'Then I beg you, father, to send him to my father's house, for I have five brothers, so that he may warn them, lest they also come into this place of torment.' But Abraham said, 'They have Moses and the prophets; let them hear them.' And he said, 'No, father Abraham; but if someone goes to them from the dead, they will

repent.' He said to him, 'If they do not hear Moses and the prophets, neither will they be convinced if someone should rise from the dead.'"

Luke 16:19-31 (RSV)

Background

The Gospel of Luke portrays Jesus as one who has a special concern for the poor, the outcast, the forgotten ones in society. This compassion for the poor in Luke is reinforced by Jesus' clear warnings about the dangers of wealth and the importance of the right use of possessions. If we are serious about listening to and following Jesus, we will need to look more carefully at his teachings regarding wealth and poverty. This parable is about discipleship, what it means to be a follower of Jesus in a hungry world.

Three verses that will help us get a feel of the context are:

- Jesus' statement in Luke 18:24, "How hard it is for those who are rich to enter the kingdom of God." Don't jump to verse 27 until you live a bit with verses 24 and 25.

- The description of his audience in Luke 16:14, "The Pharisees, who were lovers of money, heard all this and they scoffed at him."

- The statement regarding faithfulness in Luke 16:13, "No servant can serve two masters . . . You cannot serve God and mammon (money)." The idolatry of money is here pictured as the chief rival of devotion to God.

Getting Started

To break the ice and give everyone the feeling of involvement in this study, ask each person to share with two other people (or with the whole group) the answer to two of these

- When I was a child (ages 6-12) the thing I remember about learning to share is . . .

- One of my conceptions of what it means to be poor is . . .

• A person who has taught me valuable lessons about ministry with the poor is . . .

How Do You Feel

• The parable pictures two extremes, the rich and the poor. The life style of both is pictured for us with a description of diet, money, clothes, shelter, health care, pleasures and choices. The stark contrast is highlighted. Share examples of the contrast between the rich and poor today. Feelings are important as well as facts. What are your *feelings* (not rationalizations) about scenes of poverty or evidences of wealth? Share with one another what your first thought in the morning and last prayer at night might be if you were the rich man in this parable... if you were Lazarus. What would your feelings be?

No More Guilt Please

• Many of us are wealthy when you realize that many people in the world have an income of less than $500.00 a year per person. And the gap between the have's and have-not's is widening. The extreme contrast between rich and poor fits the description of our society and that of millions of poor people today. A common tendency among affluent Christians is to justify our accumulations and thereby avoid warnings given by Jesus regarding wealth and possessions in the midst of poverty. Do any of the following tendencies describe your way of dealing with Jesus' teachings on wealth and poverty? Pick one or two to share and discuss in small groups. Then pick one that you think best describes the Church today.

• I find comfort in knowing that there are a lot of people wealthier than I.

• I try to avoid pictures of bloated bellies and firsthand encounters which make vivid the misery and violence of poverty. It only makes me feel more guilty.

• I have tended to spiritualize passages in the Bible about poverty, hoping that it refers primarily to the spiritually poor.

- I remind myself that many godly people in the Bible were wealthy and that prosperity can be a sign of God's blessing.

- I ask questions, resort to clichés and/or argumentation, or quote other passages.

- I become more generous in sharing my possessions so that others benefit from my wealth.

- I stress justification by faith, the priority of evangelism and God's love for everyone including the rich.

- I live in forgiveness knowing that the poor will always be with us.

- I don't hear that much preaching or teaching about wealth and poverty or warnings about the use of possessions. At least I don't seem to be bothered much.

- I argue that if it were not for some of us having wealth, (capitalism) how would the poor be helped?

Sacred Idols Exposed . . . Ouch

- A dominant theme here is the great reversal of roles in the next life. The situation for both the rich man and Lazarus completely changed after their death. Remember, a common attitude among Jesus' listeners was that wealth was a sign of God's blessing and poverty a curse upon sinfulness … or at best a result of laziness or disobedience. With this in mind, what risks did Jesus take in telling this parable? What sacred idols of today get exposed in this parable?

Stay With The Text

- Why is the rich man tormented while poor Lazarus ends up in Abraham's bosom? Our answer to this is the key to our understanding Jesus' warning. We who are among the non-poor sometimes tend to read more into this parable than is said by Jesus. Some call this escapist interpretation. It is important to stay with what Jesus tells us here.

Nothing is said about "right belief" or how the rich man acquired his wealth. All we know about the two is their relative wealth and poverty. What it says is that the rich person was punished and poor Lazarus was granted a state of bliss. Remember the context, "How hard it is for a rich person to enter the kingdom of heaven." (18:24)

Discuss these options as you seek to complete this sentence according to what you think the text says. The rich man was punished ("being in torment" v. 23) because . . .

- He was rich.

- He was rich in the midst of poverty.

- He was rich and did not share with the poor sufficiently.

- He was rich and insensitive to the plight and presence of Lazarus.

- There is not enough information in the text to help us know why.

- He must have been an unbeliever or attained his wealth dishonestly.

- One must be careful lest this passage become a tool for revolutionaries or leftists.

- Other teachings of Jesus' help us here, such as...

No Secondary Issues Here

- How shall we interpret this parable? How can we apply it? Whatever we do we cannot escape its warning to affluent Christians and the Church living in an affluent society. We cannot ignore its concrete social and economic realism. Sharing wealth does not create a faith relationship with God but is a frequent test or evidence of whether such a relationship exists. The accumulation of wealth in the midst of poverty and how we handle our possessions (assets) are not peripheral to our understanding of, and participation in the kingdom of God. Is not Jesus saying that holding on to our wealth and feasting sumptu- ously every day while Lazarus suffers at our gate, can lead to wrath and separation? Is there not here a serious warning about accumulation of money and privileges as well as insensitivity to poverty?

What questions does this parable raise for you at this point in the study? What ethical decisions must we make in light of global hunger today? Discuss the meaning of the phrase "preferential option for the poor." Can one hold on to more than is needed and still claim to follow Jesus?

A Social Conscience

- Have someone read the following statement from Dom Helder Camara, a Brazilian archbishop, who has devoted his life to seeking justice for the poor.

I used to think, when I was a child, that Christ might have been exaggerating when he warned about the danger of wealth. Today I know better, I know how very hard it is to be rich and still keep the milk of human kindness. Money has a dangerous way of putting scales on one's eyes, a dangerous way of freezing people's hand, eyes, lips and hearts."

Offer examples of how money can put scales on our eyes . . . and freeze our lips and hearts. Bishop Camara has been criticized (even called a communist sympathizer) for his work to bring justice to the poor. Why does this happen? How can we prepare the Church for such opposition? How does greed hinder the development of a social conscience?

Please Tell My Brothers

- The second half of the parable deals with the call to repentance. The story is a warning to the rich. It says *'watch out lest the kingdom of God be forever closed to you.'* But it is told in order to help the rich person. The affluent are called to change, to redirect their lives and to heed the warning about holding on to wealth while those at the gate are suffering from poverty with all its sores and indignities. Reread vs. 27-31. The rich man thought that if Lazarus were to rise from the dead and warn his brothers, they would repent. Abraham

didn't seem to agree (v. 31). Many of us wait until something sensa-
tional or dramatic happens before we change. What leads or motivates
us to repent… to change our attitudes, priorities and life styles? Can
the Church repent? When is guilt redemptive? (Discuss).

Moses And The Prophets

• Twice the phrase "Moses and the prophets" is repeated. In other
  words, what Jesus taught about loving one's neighbor, charity and
  justice toward the poor, was an essential teaching of the Old
  Testament. The warnings about neglecting the poor and oppressing
  the needy are numerous in all Jewish literature. Mary, a Jew, sang
  about it in the Magnificat. (See Luke 1:52-53.) Read the following
  passages to help you catch a glimpse of what "Moses and the prophets" say about wealth and poverty: Isaiah 58:6-11, Amos 5:11-15,
  Lev. 19:9-10, Deut. 15:7-11, Exodus 22:25-27, Jer. 22:13-17. What
  common themes do you find? How does the Bible help us develop a
  social conscience as well as a personal conscience?

Who Is My Lazarus

• In addition to Moses and the prophets, there is another element which
  called the five brothers to repentance regarding their accumulation of
  wealth. That is the presence of the poor at their gate. Wealth itself is
  not condemned. It is wealth in the midst of poverty that is so unacceptable. The presence of Lazarus reveals our greed, our covetousness,
  our unjust systems, our escapist theology that keep us from heeding
  Jesus' warning.

Matthew 25:31ff suggests that we meet Jesus in the lives of the hungry,
naked, prisoners, etc. Which of the following might best describe the
Lazarus at your gate? That is, what is the human element that calls
you to repent and change regarding greed, covetousness, idolatry and
accumulation of possessions in the midst of poverty? Choose two and
discuss in a small group of three or four.

- Stories of hunger and starvation in the United States or in the world.

- Crowded closets, garages full of things seldom used. Having so much in comparison to the millions who live and die in poverty.

- Experiencing anxiety, emotional stress and other health warnings due to: overwork, desire to get ahead, keeping up one's sense of worth based on achievement, meeting expectations of others, wanting what others have.

- Having visited with and listened to poor people… a "firsthand" encounter with poverty…an immersion trip to a less developed country or area.

- A sermon, a book, an art form, a movie, a play that pictured some aspect of the violence of poverty.

- The daily newspaper, TV news cast or special TV hunger appeal.

- The role model and compassion of someone whose life is devoted to seeking relief and justice for the poor and oppressed.

- Some other source that is a Lazarus to me… (Describe).

Enough Is Enough

- Perhaps the rich man allowed the element of greed and covetousness to blind his eyes and harden his heart to the pressure and predicament of Lazarus. The poor man was at his gate yet he didn't really see him or know him. Bishop Camara says money has a dangerous way of putting scales on our eyes. When is enough enough? When is it time to identify covetousness in our lives and call a halt to our accumulation of more things, more money, more security, more conveniences?

Choose one or two of the following and share with the group why you chose it. Enough is enough when . . .

- We have enough to meet our basic needs of food, shelter, health care and education.

- We have two or more coats and our sisters and brothers or neighbors have none.'

- We discover that luxuries have become necessities.

- We are embarrassed to invite poor people into our homes or when we become secretive about how much we really have accumulated for the future.

- We are not embarrassed over the stark contrasts between the rich and the poor of the world, or when we fail to grieve over the presence and plight of Lazarus.

- We would refuse to change places with others who are victimized by poverty and begin to put the blame on them.

- We discover that others are starving to death and need our help, while in our churches we give an average of less than $4.00 per member to the hunger appeal each year.

- Military budgets soar and arms expenditures become large portions of foreign aid in order to keep revolutions from happening where the poor begin to organize and fight to protest and change the systems that keep them poor.

What Can We Do?

Where is the gospel in all this? Is there something encouraging, hopeful, positive that I can receive from this text? Yes, there is good news, but the good news begins with the truth. Luke's purpose is to tell the truth about the kingdom of God. Sometimes the good news comes in ways we don't expect or want. Here, the Word of God comes in the warning and call to repent. It is because of Jesus' compassion for both the rich and the poor that he tells this parable. Jesus here speaks to those who still have the opportunity to hear Moses and the prophets and to change.

The good news is that God has given us time to repent, grace and courage to be about it. Read the story of Zacchaeus in Luke 19:1-10. Note the new joy of repentance in his witness. He was a new person. The change is in his attitude and actions toward the poor.

There are only two ways to answer a call to repent: to repent or refuse to change for whatever reason. Agreeing that one should repent is not repentance. Nor is feeling sorry. Action is needed. Following are some positive ways to respond to this text. Do any of them fit your situation or thinking at this point? Share with the group what you would like to do in response to God's Word to you in this study.

- I will cease my denial mechanisms which have kept me from really seeing Lazarus at my gate. To do this, I will plan some way to visit an agency that has direct contact with the poor, hoping to get a closer look and greater sensitivity to what is really happening to them. Some day also, I hope to visit a third world country as a learner, not a tourist.

- I will read more about Jesus' teachings regarding poverty and wealth. To do this I will plan to read one book such as: *Diet for a Hot Planet* by Anna Lappé, *The Missing Class* by Katherine Newman and Victor Tan Chen, *The Spirit Level* by Richard Wilkinson and Kate Pickett, *Social Justice Handbook* by Mae Elise Cannon, *How Much Is Enough* by Arthur Simon or *Earth Democracy* by Vandana Shiva.

- I will begin altering some of the ways I celebrate Christmas when it comes around. As a start, I will plan to cut back my Christmas spending by 25% and give that 25% to the poor. This, of course, may mean some explanation to those significant others in my life which will become part of my response.

- I will become a member of Bread for the World so that I might be better informed about what my government is doing for the poor and hungry… and learn how I can use my citizenship to be an advocate for the Lazaruses of today.

- I will watch more carefully my accumulation of things, conveniences and luxury items. During the next 12 months I will match dollar for dollar everything I spend for clothes, appliances, sporting equipment, jewelry, books and entertainment for myself. For every dollar I spend, I will give a dollar to my church's hunger appeal. (If you want to move more gradually, you could choose one or two of the above categories.)

- I will become more active in sensitizing people to the plight and presence of Lazaruses in our society and world. To do this, I will find one thing I am presently doing that is not as important as helping Lazarus and I will gracefully pull out. In its place, I will join a group or mission project that enables me to use my time and talents to educate and mobilize people around the plight and presence of the Lazaruses who lie at our gates.

- I will become more vocal and assertive at my place of work and with my friends in standing up for poor and oppressed people.

- I will begin this next month to give a special offering of 1% or 2% of my income, over and above my present giving to my congregation. (Zacchaeus was more radical.) I will designate it specifically for the poor. I will become better informed and more actively involved in seeing that this money is used not just for relief but also for long-range development and justice for the hungry of the world.

- I will use one of the special gifts (talents) I have to advance the cause of justice and more equity. Examples: compose a song, write a poem or story, draw a picture, create a dance, build or repair something, begin a group study, join a hunger walk, volunteer for an agency, start a campaign, give a speech, write letters, become a tutor, serve meals. I will choose one and stay with it.

- I will begin next week to fast one major meal a week and give the amount saved from that meal to the poor. I will do this without calling attention to myself or upsetting the schedule of others. The time I would ordinarily be eating I will use for prayer, meditation, reflection or reading about the Lazarus in today's world.

- I will pray for a social conscience and a change in my attitude toward wealth, poverty and the poor. To do this, I will start taking sides in the rich/poor conflict. This means I will cease being neutral. In my desire to follow Jesus, I will by word and deed demonstrate my bias for the poor. I will defend their cause, speak and vote against those who oppress or neglect them and I will be willing to risk in order to help them attain greater justice.

- I will seek to become a friend of someone who is poor, get to know this person and where possible, invite her/him into my home. (Isaiah 58:7, Luke 14:12-14).

- I will learn to celebrate food with a deeper appreciation of those who produce it . . . knowing that to eat food and enjoy it glorifies God . . .

In a Culture of
Biblical Certitudes
and Ignorance

Many of us have found that while discussing a different approach to a controversial issue someone might say, "But the Bible says…" It can cut off conversation and make it sound like there is only one way to interpret what the Bible says. But that is not so. As was noted in the introduction to this book, even the apostle Peter has to change his mind to Biblical certitudes.

In this chapter the authors help us to read the Bible again with an openness to see issues differently and see things in the Bible we haven't seen before. Many people are hungry for a new way of reading the Bible. Some have left their churches because of the very narrow, dogmatic, and simplistic approach to Biblical literature. It takes courage to question and challenge what one has been taught or what those in authority have taught over the years.

One of the first discoveries one makes in reading the Bible again is that everyone tends to read the Bible out of their own economic lenses. Why is it that many Christians from the developing world see things from the Bible that we who are among the privileged do not see. Why hasn't oppression been a major topic of study in Western seminaries? It is central to the Biblical story of God's salvation acts.

As you read Elisabeth Schüssler Fiorenze's exerpts from *Feminist Biblical Interpretation* you will be challenged in your patriarchal ways of reading the Bible. She reminds us that the Bible is not just a religious book, but also a political book. It has political significance, not only for women, but for everyone in the struggle for liberation and self identity. Fiorenze points out that women's experiences can add much to our reading and understanding of the Bible. The gender issue is still with us.

Some time ago I developed a series of small group Bible studies around the theme: Jesus and Conflict. The study included in this chapter demonstrates that Jesus questioned and challenged traditional ways the Torah was being interpreted in the religious community. We need to be reminded that Jesus faced conflict and opposition when he dared to interpret the scriptures and traditions differently. How do we handle it when we face that conflict today? How has your church handled it?

George S. Johnson

EXCERPTED FROM

Reading the Bible Again

by Marcus J. Borg

◆◆◆

The key word in the title of this book – *Reading the Bible Again for the First Time* – is "again." It points to my central claim. Over the past century an older way of reading the Bible has ceased to be persuasive for millions of people, and this one of the most imperative needs in our time is a way of reading the Bible anew.

Reading and seeing go together. On the one hand, what we read can affect how we see. On the other hand, and more important for my immediate purpose, how we see affects how we read. What we bring to our reading of a text or document affects how we read it. All of us, whether we use reading glasses or not, read through lenses.

As we enter the twenty-first century, we need a new set of lenses through which to read the Bible. The older set, ground and polished by modernity, no longer works for millions of people. These lenses need to be replaced. The older way of seeing and reading the Bible, which I will soon describe, has made the Bible incredible and irrelevant for vast numbers of people. This is so not only for the millions who have left the church in Europe and North America, but also for many Christians who continue to be active in the life of the church.

The need for new lenses thus exists within the church itself. The older lenses enabled Christians of earlier generations to experience the Bible as a lamp unto their feet, a source of illuminations for following the Christian path. But for many Christians in our time, the older lenses have become opaque, turning the Bible into a stumbling block in the way. 1 Yet not all Christians agree about the need for new lenses. Many vigorously defend the older way of seeing the Bible. For them, what seems to be at stake is nothing less than the truth of the Bible and Christianity itself.

Conflicting Lenses

Conflict about how to see and read the Bible is the single greatest issue dividing Christians in North America today. On one side of the divide are fundamentalist and many conservative-evangelical Christians. On the other side are moderate-to-liberal Christians, mostly in mainline denominations. 2 Separating the two groups are two very different ways of seeing three foundational questions about the Bible: questions about its origin, its authority, and its interpretation.

The first group, who sometimes call themselves "Bible-believing Christians: typically see the Bible as the inerrant and infallible Word of God. 3 This conviction flows out of the way they see the Bible's origin: it comes from God, as no other book does. As a divine product, it is God's truth, and its divine origin is the basis of its authority As a contemporary bumper sticker boldly puts it, "God said it, I believe it, that settles it." The sticker may be unfair to many who hold this position, but it was created by an advocate, not a critic.

For these Christians, the Bible is to be interpreted literally, unless the language of a particular passage is clearly metaphorical. From their point of view, allowing nonliteral interpretation opens the door to evading the Bible's authority and making it say what we want it to say. They typically see themselves as taking the Bible with utmost seriousness and often criticize moderate-to-liberal Christians for watering it down and avoiding its authority. They also commonly see themselves as affirming "the old-time religion" – that is, Christianity as it was before the modern period. In fact, however, as we shall see, their approach is itself modern, largely the product of a particular form of nineteenth- and twentieth-century Protestant theology. Moreover, rather than allowing the Bible its full voice, their approach actually confines the Bible within a tight theological structure.

The second group of Christians, most of whom are found in mainline churches, are less clear about how they *do* see the Bible than about how they do *not*. They are strongly convinced that many parts of the Bible cannot be taken literally, either as historically factual or as expressing the will of God. Some people who reach this conclusion leave the church and are seeking a way of seeing the Bible that moves beyond biblical literalism and makes persuasive and compelling sense.

Their numbers are growing; 5 never before has there been so great an appetite for modern biblical scholarship among mainline Christians. They are responding strongly and positively to a more historical and metaphorical reading of the Bible. At the grass-roots level of mainline churches, a major de-literalization of the Bible is underway.

Though these Christians know with certainty that they cannot be biblical literalists, they are less clear about how they *do* see the origin and authority of the Bible. They are often uncertain what it means to say that the Bible is "the Word of God" or "inspired by God." Though they reject grounding the Bible's authority in its infallibility, they are unsure what "biblical authority" might mean.

Thus it is not surprising that even within mainline denominations, there is conflict about how to see and read the Bible. At the national level, most of these denominations have vocal minority movements protesting what they perceive to be the loss of biblical authority. At the local level, some congregations are sharply divided about how to see the Bible. The conflict also divides families. In many conservative Christian families, one or more members have either dropped out of church or become part of a liberal church. The reverse is also true: many liberal Christian families have seen one or more of their members become conservative Christians. Some families have been able to negotiate this conflict with grace. But in many, it has been a source of division, grief and hand-wringing.

The conflict about the Bible is most publicly visible in discussions of three issues. First, in some Christian circles, "creation versus evolution" is the primary litmus test of loyalty to the Bible. The second issue is homosexuality: May practicing gays and lesbians be full members of the church? May the unions of gay and lesbian couples be blessed? May gays and lesbians be ordained? This debate is often cast in the form of accepting or rejecting biblical authority.

A third lightning rod for the conflict is contemporary historical Jesus scholarship. For the last decade, the quest for the historical Jesus has attracted widespread media attention and public interest, especially among mainline Christians. But it has generated a strongly negative reaction among fundamentalist and conservative-evangelical Christians. From their point of view, questioning the historical factuality of the gospels strikes at the very foundations of Christianity.

The Roots of the Conflict

The border between fundamentalist and conservative-evangelical Christians is hard to draw. A fundamentalist has been defined as "an evangelical who is angry about something." 6 But some conservative-evangelicals are not fundamentalists and have no interest in defending, for example, the literal factuality of the Bible's story of creation or the complete historical accuracy of all the words attributed to Jesus. But what they do share in common is an understanding of the authority of the Bible grounded in its origin: it is true because it comes from God.

Fundamentalism itself – whether Christian, Jewish, or Muslim – is modern. It is a reaction to modern culture. 7 Christian fundamentalism as an identifiable religious movement originated early in the twentieth century in the United States, with its immediate roots in the second half of the nineteenth century. 8 It stressed the infallibility and inerrancy of the Bible in everyday respect, especially against Darwinism and what it called "the higher criticism" (by which it meant the scholarly study of the Bible as it had developed primarily in Germany in the nineteenth century).

The roots of the evangelical understanding of the Bible are older, going back to the Protestant Reformation of the sixteen century. The Reformation replaced the authority of the church and church tradition with the sole authority of scripture. John Calvin and Martin Luther, the two most important leaders of the Reformation, both had a strong sense of biblical authority. But it was in the second and third generation of the Reformation that claims for the infallible truth of the Bible were made. "Plenary inspiration" – the notion that the words of the Bible were dictated by God and are therefore free from error – was emphasized by those later Reformers.

The realization that these developments are relatively recent is important. The explicit description of the Bible as inerrant and infallible by fundamentalists and some conservative-evangelicals cannot claim to be the ancient and traditional voice of the church. Yet both fundamentalism and the notion of the Bible as "God's truth" (and thus without error) have their roots in an older, conventional way of seeing the Bible widely shared by most Christians for a long time.

Top. 18

Given who we have become, one of the imperative needs of our time is a re-visioning of the Bible and Christianity. I deliberately hyphenate the word "re-vision" in order to distinguish what I mean from a common meaning of "revision" (without a hyphen). We often use the latter word to describe the improvement of something that had been poorly done – for example, a manuscript or a term paper. But that is not what I mean.

Rather, to re-vision means "to see again." The emphasis upon "seeing again" also reminds us that the older form of Christianity is not "traditional Christianity" but was an earlier way of seeing the Bible and the Christian tradition. What is needed in our time is a way of seeing the Bible that takes seriously the important and legitimate ways in which we differ from our ancestors.

The way of seeing and reading the Bible that I describe in the rest of this book leads to a way of being Christian that had very little to do with believing. Instead, what will emerge is a relational and sacramental understanding of the Christian life. Being Christian, I will argue, is not about believing in the Bible or about believing in Christianity. Rather it is about a deepening relationship with the God to whom the Bible points, lived within the Christian tradition as a sacrament of the sacred.

EXCERPTED FROM

Bible of the Oppressed
by Elsa Tamez

Oppression and liberation are the very substance of the entire historical context within the scriptures. God's self revelation occurs in the midst of the experiences of oppression and the yearning for liberation. Today the poor and the hungry as well as the rich are experiencing God in the same kind of struggle.

For the Bible oppression is the basic cause of poverty, not the only cause, but the basic cause. To understand what is behind the poverty and hunger in the world one must understand oppression.

"There is an almost complete absence of the theme of oppression in European and North American biblical theology."

Biblical words for oppression

- *"Nagash"* means to oppress, exploit, force, overwhelm with work. See Exodus 1:14, Isaiah 58:3, Deut. 15:2, Zech. 9:8.

  Nagash means someone is trying to profit through exploitation of others. Those afflicted live in a state of anxiety as they carry out the orders of the oppressor.

- *"Anah"* means to oppress, exploit, humiliate, degrade, dominate. See Gen. 15:13, Deut. 26:6, Exodus 3:7, Psalm 119:107, II Samuel 13:12, 14.

  Anah also includes making someone feel dependent. It is accompanied by human degradation and humiliation.

- *"Lahats"* means to oppress, press or squeeze, harass. See Exodus 3:9, Jer. 30:19-21, Isaiah 19:20, Amos 6:14.

The basic idea of this word is crushing which elicits a reaction, a cry of pain and a call for quick liberation.

- **"Ashaq"** means rob, obtain by violence, extort, do injustice. See Ezek. 22:12, Mic. 2:1-2, Hos. 12:7, Jer. 22:13, Lev. 19:13.

The primary purpose of this oppression is to accumulate wealth by robbing one's neighbor and committing acts of violence.

- **"Daka"** means to grind, pulverize, crush. See Ps. 94:5, Ps. 89:11, Jer. 44:10, Isaiah 3:15, Isaiah 19:10.

It follows that when oppression is ruthless it reaches the innermost being of a person.

Good News of Liberation

The narrations of the Old Testament attribute every act of liberation to Yahweh. In the Bible the historical agent of liberation is Yahweh acting through the oppressed. At the same time it is the oppressed who determine that they will no longer yield to the oppressor and who are fully convinced that God, Yahweh, gives them strength enough to win the victory.

In the Israelites' view Yahweh is the manifestation of justice. The terms **tsedeq** (justice, righteousness), **mishpat** (right judgment), **hesed** (mercy, steadfast love) and **emet** (truth, fidelity) define God's presence. See Psalm 89:14. The justice of God is not an attribute which human beings have attributed to God, but rather refers to the historical action of God in experiences of liberation. It is God's faithfulness to the community.

In the magnificat (Luke 1:46-53), Mary is speaking not merely of individuals undergoing moral change but of the restructuring of the order in which there are rich and poor, mighty and lowly. She had a clear understanding of the Old Testament concept of justice.

"Where is the life (John 10:10), the love (I John 4:20), the freedom (John 8:32), that the gospel proclaims? Clearly something has gone awry in the

reading of God's word. Struggle, life and liberation have been replaced by passivity, resignation and submission. In other words, the gospel has been reduced to a set of individualistic terms relating only to the spiritual order."

Tamez draws two conclusions about the poor as seen by the Bible. First, poverty is regarded as something decidedly negative; it is a scandalous condition and the manifestation of a degrading human condition. Secondly, this situation of poverty is not the result of some historical inevitability nor is it just the way things are. It is the result of the unjust actions of oppression.

In her concluding chapter Tamez talks about conversion as the affirmation of life. Conversion, she writes, means radical transformation of the person and a change of outlook which shows itself in concrete acts of justice. (Jer. 34:15, Jer. 22:15-16, Matt. 3:7-9, Matt 7:21)

Tamez concludes by reminding us that liberation is a process, a task that must continually be accomplished anew. Yet the supreme self revelation of God in human form (Jesus) reminds us that God's reign here on earth has begun. So we continue to pray "Your kingdom come, your will be done on earth as in heaven."

Discussion Questions

• Look up the verses that describe the various biblical words for oppression. Think of examples of each type of oppression in today's society. Who speaks for the victims of the oppressed in your community?

• Is justice a 'gospel' term for you? Or law? What do you think it is for oppressed people? For Mary in Luke 1? How is it preached in your church?

Feminist Biblical Interpretation

by Elisabeth Schüssler Fiorenza

———— ❖❖❖ ————

Feminist theology begins with the experiences of women, of women-church. In our struggle for self-identity, survival, and liberation in a patriarchal society and church, Christian women have found that the Bible has been used as a weapon against us but at the same time it has been a resource for courage, hope, and commitment in this struggle. Therefore, it cannot be the task of feminist interpretation to defend the Bible against its feminist critics but to understand and interpret it in such a way that its oppressive and liberating power is clearly recognized.

A feminist hermeneutics cannot trust or accept Bible and tradition simply as divine revelation. Rather it must critically evaluate them as patriarchal articulations, since even in the last century Sarah Grimke, Matilda Joslyn Gage, and Elizabeth Cady Stanton had recognized that biblical texts are not the words of God but the words of men. This insight particularizes the results of historical-critical scholarship that the Bible is written by human authors or male authors. This critical insight of a feminist hermeneutics has ramifications not only for historical scholarship but also for our contemporary-political situation because the Bible still functions today as a religious justification and ideological legitimization of patriarchy.

To speak of power is to speak of political realities and struggles although we might not be conscious of this when we speak of the power of the Word. The Bible is not simply a religious but also a profoundly political book as it continues to inform the self-understandings of American and European "secularized" societies and cultures. Feminist biblical interpretations therefore have a critical political significance not only to women in biblical religion but for all women in Western societies.

The Bible is not only written in the words of men but also serves to legitimate patriarchal power and oppression insofar as it "renders God" male and determines ultimate reality in male terms, which make women invisible or marginal. The interconnection between androcentric language and patriarchal power becomes apparent when we remember that in 1850 an act of Parliament was required to prohibit the common use of *they* for sex-indeterminable references and to legally insist that *he* stood for *she*. At a time when patriarchal oppression is on the rise again in American society and religion, the development of a feminist biblical hermeneutics is not only a theological but also a profoundly political task.

The controversies that have surrounded a feminist interpretation ever since Elizabeth Cady Stanton planned and edited *The Woman's Bible* indicate that such a feminist challenge goes to the roots of religious patriarchal legitimization. The recent, often violent, and seemingly irrational reactions to the *Inclusive Language Lectionary* amply prove this critical political impact of feminist biblical interpretation. Writing in the *Washington Post* James J. Kilpatrick makes his point succinctly:

> It is probably a waste of time, energy, and indignation to denounce the latest efforts to castrate the Holy Bible, but vandalism of this magnitude ought not to go unremarked.

If language determines the limits of our world, then sacred androcentric, that is, grammatically masculine, language symbolizes and determines our perception of ultimate human and divine reality. Those who protest an inclusive language translation as the "castration" of Scripture consciously or not maintain that such ultimate reality and authority are in the words of Mary Daly "phallocentric."

From its inception feminist interpretation of Scripture has been generated by the fact that the Bible was used to halt the emancipation of slaves and women.

Not only in the last century but also today patriarchal right-wing forces in society lace their attacks against women's rights and freedoms in the political, economic, reproductive, intellectual, and religious arenas with biblical quotations and appeals to scriptural authority. In countless pulpits and fundamentalist TV programs, such patriarchal attacks are proclaimed as the Word of God while the feminist struggle for women's liberation is denounced as "godless humanism" that undermines the "American family." Yet the political right does not simply misquote or misuse the Bible as a Christian feminist apologetics seeks to argue. It can utilize certain Scriptural texts because they *are* patriarchal in their original function and intention.

Feminist interpretation therefore begins with a hermeneutics of suspicion that applies to both contemporary androcentric interpretations of the Bible and the biblical texts themselves. Certain texts of the Bible can be used in the argument against women's struggle for liberation not only because they are patriarchally misinterpreted but because they are patriarchal texts and therefore can serve to legitimate women's subordinate role and secondary status in patriarchal society and church. While some of us have maintained that feminists must abandon the Bible and biblical religion, in these essays I seek to argue why feminists cannot afford to do so. We have to reclaim biblical religion as our own heritage because "our heritage is our power." At the same time I insist that such a reclaiming of our heritage can only take place through a critical process of feminist assessment and evaluation.

Reclaiming the Bible as a feminist heritage and resource is only possible because it has not functioned only to legitimate the oppression of *all* women: freeborn, slave, black and white, native American, European and Asian, immigrant, poor, working-class and middle-class, Third World and First World women. It has also provided authorization and legitimization for women who have rejected slavery, racism, anti-Semitism, colonial exploitation, and misogynism as unbiblical and against God's will. The Bible has inspired and continues to inspire countless women to speak out and to struggle against injustice, exploitation, and stereotyping. The biblical vision of freedom and wholeness still energizes women in all walks of life to struggle against poverty, unfreedom, and denigration. It empowers us to survive with dignity and to continue the struggle when there seems to be no hope for success.

A critical feminist hermeneutics of liberation therefore seeks to develop a critical dialectical mode of biblical interpretation that can do justice to women's experiences of the Bible as a thoroughly patriarchal book written in androcentric language as well as to women's experience of the Bible as a source of empowerment and vision in our struggles for liberation. Such a hermeneutics has to subject biblical texts to a dialectical process of critical readings and feminist evaluations. In order to do so it insists that *the* litmus test for invoking Scripture as the Word of God must be whether or not biblical texts and traditions seek to end relations of domination and exploitation.

In short, if we claim that oppressive patriarchal texts are the Word of God then we proclaim God as a God of oppression and dehumanization. The question is indeed "theological" in the strictest sense of the word, requiring not only a new naming of God but also a new naming of church and its use of Scripture. Such a process of naming transforms our metaphor of Scripture as "tablets of stone" on which the unchanging word of God is engraved for all times into the image of bread that nurtures, sustains, and energizes women as people of God in our struggles against injustice and oppression.

The hermeneutical center of such a feminist biblical interpretation – I therefore argue here – is the *ekklesia gynaikon* or women-church, the movement of self-identified women and women-identified men in biblical religion. When as a Christian I use the expression *women-church*, I do not use it as an exclusionary but as a political-oppositional term to patriarchy. It this becomes necessary to clarify here in what way I use the term *patriarchy* as a heuristic category. I do not use the concept in the loose sense of "all men dominating all women equally," but in the classical Aristotelian sense. *Patriarchy* as a male pyramid of graded subordinations and exploitations specifies women's oppression in terms of the class, race, country, or religion of the men to whom we "belong." This definition of patriarchy enables us to use it as a basic heuristic concept for feminist analysis, one that allows us to conceptualize not only sexism but also racism, property-class relationships, and all other forms of exploitation or dehumanization as basic structures of women's oppression.

Although public life and political self-determination were restricted in Athenian democracy to the freeborn propertied male heads of patriarchal households and reserved in the patriarchal church for ordained males, I understand women-church as the dialogical community of equals in which critical judgment takes place and public freedom becomes tangible. Women-church seeks to realize the fullest meaning of the Greek New Testament notion of *ekklesia* as the public assembly of free citizens who gather in order to determine their own and their children's communal, political, and spiritual well-being. The synagogue or church of women is the gathering of all those women and men who empowered by the Holy Spirit and inspired by the biblical vision of justice, freedom, and salvation continue against all odds the struggle for liberation from patriarchal oppression in society and religion. As such the feminist movement in biblical religion is not just a civil rights but also a liberation movement. Its goal is not simply the "full humanity" of women, since humanity as we know it is male-defined. The goal is women's (religious) self-affirmation, power, and liberation from all patriarchal alienation, marginalization, and exploitation.

> **"In this new emphasis on mission we have been led by the Spirit through the lives of people who are oppressed and powerless to a re-reading of the Holy Scriptures – to Moses confronting the authorities of Egypt, to Mary who sees the hand of God putting "down the mighty from their thrones."**
>
> *Margaret Wold*

EXCERPTED FROM

God Takes Sides

by Robert McAfee Brown

We have been brought up to believe in a God who is the God of all people – rich, poor, white, black, Asian, African, North American, South American. We are perturbed when we read that the belt buckles of German soldiers in World War I had the words Gott mit uns (God with us) inscribed on them, as though God were supporting the Germans rather than the French, Belgians, English and Americans . . .

The notion of God exercising indistriminate love toward all is a healthy protection against racists, who do not believe God really loves dark-skinned peoples, or against North Americans who instinctively feel that God is more concerned about them than about the unemployed workers who flock to Mexico City every day.

And yet there is something false and unbiblical about this view of God's relationship to the world's peoples, as we can see if we pit other groups against each other and ask whether God is equally their God. Is God as much the God of the torturers as the God of the tortured? Is God equally the God of the military dictator and the God of those who are murdered by the dictator? Does God have the same disposition toward the victim of a plant closedown in Akron, Ohio, as toward members of the board of directors who shut down the plant with no concern for what will happen to the workers?

Our conventional God is aloof from such things; any other God would be a partisan God – worse yet, a "political" God – taking sides with some of God's children and against others. And that is hard for us to swallow.

But it is not hard for the biblical writers to swallow. Indeed, they affirm such a God strongly. We will look at one passage, **the story of the exodus, that describes a very partisan God who takes sides with a vengeance. If it were only an isolated passage, we could dispose of it, but it has set its stamp on the whole Bible** and has become a paradigm passage for third world Christians living in situations of oppression and injustice similar to the Egyptian situation. To fail to take it seriously is to fail to take the Bible seriously . . .

Read Exodus 1:8-14; 2:23-25; 3:7-10.

. . . In the story of Exodus, and throughout the whole Bible, the main outlines of the story are clear:

1. *A class struggle is going on*

2. *God is aware of the struggle*

3. *God takes sides in the struggle*

4. *God calls people to join in the struggle*

We start with the people. And what is happening to the people? Clearly, *a class struggle is going on.* It would be easy for us to digest that claim if only the word "class" were omitted; who could disagree that a "struggle" is going on? But the term "class struggle" has been used deliberately.

In the modern world, Christians need to do more than bristle when they hear the words "class struggle." For although Karl Marx may have invented the term, he didn't invent the reality; he merely noticed it and called it to the attention of others… There are two classes of people involved in the Book of Exodus and they are locked in *struggle.* To reject the term is to reject the story.

It's a pretty uneven struggle. The Israelites are slaves, the king and his crowd are slaveowners… Here, there is a classic oppressor/oppressed situation, complete with intimidation, humiliation, forced labor, powerlessness, and genocide… What happens in such situations is that the oppressed "internalize their oppression"; they accept their lowly status as appropriate or inevitable

and, believing themselves powerless to produce change, they lose hope . . .
Their spirit is broken . . . *God is aware of the struggle* . . .

Things have gotten so bad that the Israelites cry out to God. They need help
. . . And the good news is that God is not exclusively wrapped up in contemplation of divine attributes but is aware of the Israelites' plight. God realizes
that certain covenantal agreements already referred to make it necessary for
something to happen... God does not side with the powerful... God promises
political liberation from the economic and social bondage Israel had endured
. . . God believes that religion and politics mix. For the God who just said "I
have come down to deliver them out of the hand of the Egyptians" follows
up by saying to Moses, "Come, I will send you to Pharaoh that you may bring
forth my people . . . " God calls people to join in the struggle . . .

God, while intervening on behalf of the weak, is quite prepared to use the weak.
Moses, for example, is as weak as they come; he ducks and weaves in every
possible way to avoid the body blow of an assignment. Piling up excuses
ranging from the fact that he doesn't know God's name to the fact that he stutters
and would therefore be a singularly ineffective negotiator with Pharaoh . . .

> We are discovering that the Bible says a great deal about the poor. It all seems askew, for while the poor do get a lot of attention in the Bible, the nonpoor get a lot of attention in the church, and usually end up running things. One reason for this is that the nonpoor have become the official interpreters of the scriptures and have managed to take most of the sting out of the passages dealing with the poor.

Discussion Questions

• In your opinion does God take sides? Does this mean God loves the oppressor less? Did Jesus take sides in his life and teachings? If so, in what ways? If we are called to take sides what risks are involved?

• Put yourself in this story. Using the Egyptian context, where would you fit into the Exodus situation? Use your imagination and become a person living in Egypt under Pharaoh. What's your occupation? How do you relate to the Israelite situation? To Moses? To Pharaoh's new laws? Talk about this in small groups.

TOLES © 1984 The Washington Post. Reprinted with permission of UNIVERSAL UCLICK.

Jesus and Biblical Interpretation

by George Johnson

◆◆◆

From a series of small group studies on Jesus and Conflict

Focus: To better understand Jesus' interpretation of scripture and how interpretation of the Bible can be the source of conflicts and opportunities in the church.

Gathering

1. Check in time. Share what's been going on in your life since you last met. Any decisions made? Any new people encountered? Any prayers answered or needed? Any surprises or blessings?

2. Go around the circle and share your thoughts on one of the following:

    a. A difference (different opinion or conviction) you have had with a friend, family member or relative on a social justice issue or social practice . . .

    b. A practice or value in the church or society that has changed over the last 30-40 years which you feel good about . . .

Learning

Mark 2:23-27

One Sabbath Jesus was going through the grain-fields, and as his disciples walked along, they began to pick some heads of grain. The Pharisees said to him, "Look, why are they doing what is unlawful on the Sabbath?" He answered, "Have you never read what David did when he and his companions were hungry and in need? In the days of Abiathar the high priest, he entered the house of God and ate the consecrated bread, which is lawful only for priests to eat. And he also gave some to his companions." Then he said to them, "The Sabbath was made for man, not man for the Sabbath."

Mark 3:1-7

Another time he went into the synagogue, and a man with a shriveled hand was there. Some of them were looking for a reason to accuse Jesus, so they watched him closely to see if he would heal him on the Sabbath. Jesus said to the man with the shriveled hand, "Stand up in front of everyone." Then Jesus asked them, "Which is lawful on the Sabbath: to do good or to do evil, to save life or to kill?" But they remained silent. He looked around at them in anger and deeply distressed at their stubborn hearts, said to the man, "Stretch out your hand." He stretched it out, and his hand was completely restored. Then the Pharisees went out and began to plot with the Herodians how they might kill Jesus. Jesus withdrew with his disciples to the lake, and a large crowd from Galilee followed.

Keeping the Sabbath was an important sign and symbol of Jewish devotion and commitment of their faith in God. They were very careful not to violate this commandment "Remember the Sabbath day to keep it holy." Several laws and traditions were adopted to protect this commandment. For example, plucking grain on the Sabbath was considered a violation of this law. So was practicing healing unless it was a matter of life and death.

1. Look at the text again in Mark 2:23-27. How would you describe the method or tactic Jesus used to answer their criticism? To what did he appeal? How did Jesus lift up the problem of biblical amnesia and certitudes?

2. Jesus could have said to his disciples – "Men, I know you are hungry, but let's not pluck grain from the field. It might be offensive to some who are very conservative in their interpretation of the scripture and tradition. We don't want to be a stumbling block to those who are needing to hear our message." But he didn't. Why do you think he allowed men to pluck grain on the Sabbath? Choose one to comment on. (Use your imagination).

    a. He didn't expect anyone to make an issue of such an insignificant matter.

    b. He purposely wanted to teach the Pharisees a lesson about when not to be too literal in one's interpretation. It was a teaching moment, an opportunity. Name a teaching moment that you have experienced.

c. He wanted to show that some laws need to be changed. The law may have served a good purpose at one time, but times change and some laws need changing. Can you think of one that needs to change today? Was Jesus approving civil disobedience.

d. Jesus didn't buy the argument that one should avoid controversy in order not to offend or build a wall for those who need to hear your message. How does this argument play out today?

e. Jesus probably didn't even notice what his disciples were doing and when it was brought to his attention he looked for a way to defend them. It was a good thing he knew his scriptures well.

f. Other.

3. How would you describe the principle of biblical interpretation that is expressed in Mark 2:27? What should be the bottom line in our interpretation of the Bible?

4. Read again Mark 3:1-7. A similar issue is at stake in this passage. What makes this situation a bit different than the situation in 2:23-27?

5. Verse 3:2 reads, "they" watched Jesus . . . so "they" could accuse him. What does this say to you about the "they"? Choose one and comment.

a. Some previous experience with Jesus had made them suspicious or at odds with his teachings. They brought their bias with them to the event. The bias was . . .

b. "Damned if you do...damned if you don't." When someone is out to get you, it doesn't matter what you do, it's going to be criticized. Is it as true in the church as well as elsewhere? Give an example when this was true for you.

c. The "they" were very strict in their observance of the laws and tradiltion. They were literalists with no room for flexibility or exceptions. Their chief concern was . . .

d. Jesus had a very "liberating" way to interpret the scripture. People were more important to him than laws. This often brought conflict. This says to me . . .

e. Knowing their critical attitude did not altar Jesus' agenda or action, He healed the man on the Sabbath. What was the risk here?

f. Other.

6. Mark 3:5 says that Jesus looked at the "they" (the people watching) with anger. He was grieved at their hardness of heart. What does this say to you?

a. Jesus got angry . . . therefore . . .

b. I am surprised the gospel writer points out Jesus' emotion of anger. I hadn't thought about anger from this story before. How does one reconcile this with our picture of Jesus as forgiving, loving and patient?

c. Conflict over interpretation of what is right and what is wrong often brings out strong emotions. An example of this in our day is . . .

d. Other.

7. The end of the passage (3:6) says the Pharisees immediately conspired how to destroy him. Luke's version (Luke 6:11) says they were filled with fury . . . How might this conflict early in Jesus ministry, have affected the remainder of his earthly ministry? What did he learn from it? What do we learn from it? Did he tone down his message?

8. For further discussion read the article "Appearing Before the Authorities" by Walter Brueggemann on page 202 of this book. What can we learn from this? Also see, "Was Jesus Subversive?" on page 262. How does this change or add to your thinking about Jesus death on the cross?

Caring/Sharing

1. Who or what experience has helped you to learn how to interpret the Bible?

2. Can you give an example of a time when you found it necessary to ask the broader question of how it affects peoples' lives rather than stick to a literal interpretation? What was the broader issue for you?

3. Choose one of the following areas where you may have changed your thinking. Was it related to an interpretation that no longer fits for you.

   a. Non-Christian religions

   b. Divorce

   c. Female clergy, gender issues

   d. Capitalism and socialism

   e. Gay/lesbian rights

   f. Interracial marriage

   g. Heaven and hell

   h. Capital punishment

   i. War and redemptive violence

   j. Suicide

   k. Global warming

   l. Jesus, the only way to God

   m. Healing ministry

   n. Sexual issues

4. What help would you like from your church in the area of interpretation of scripture and tradition? What could your group do to enable this help to happen?

5. When someone says, "It's in the Bible" or "Doesn't the scripture say?" or "Don't you believe the Bible?" you may want to respond "The issue is not what does the Bible say, but how does one interpret the Bible." Discuss this approach.

Closing

Sing a song together that might be appropriate to the season, or one that most everyone knows. One example might be: "Ubi caritas et amor" . . . Your leader will teach it to you. Or . . .

Now thank we all our God with heart and hands and voices,
Who wondrous things has done, In whom this earth rejoices;
Who from our mother's arms has blessed us on our way
With countless gifts of love, And still is our today.

Ubi Caritas, from Taize

(based on 1 John 4:7)

In a Culture of Individualism and Cheap Grace

There are different kinds of Christians and different kinds of Christianity just like there are different kinds of ice cream and different kinds of cars. Most of us can tell when we are being sold a cheap version of this or that. It usually never lasts very long...nor does it satisfy us in the long run. No one really wants the cheap version of anything.

When Dietrich Bonhoeffer, the German theologian who wrote *Cost of Discipleship*, talks about cheap grace he is referring to a kind of Christianity that doesn't call for disciplines and responsibilities, a Christianity that can't stand the test of adversity. In this chapter the authors help us to examine our Christianity and the foundations upon which it is being built. A gospel without demands has its appeal but does not square with the biblical message. Brueggeman's article in this chapter calls us back to a respect for the commandments and the sermon on the mount.

Rugged individualism, says religious sociologist Robert Wuthnow, has become a cancer in our society. It is slowly eating away our commitment to the common good and care for one another. During political campaigns speeches too often put the emphasis on what will bring economic prosperity and security to me and my tribe without much talk about the cost of proposed policies to the environment and to future generations and the rest of the world. Too much religion is also individual based. We need to think differently and question our self-centered culture.

Maybe we have focused too much on the poor and middle class without talking much about wealth and how it is attained. The myth that growth in income will eventually help the poor and middle class is exposed by Joerg Rieger, professor at Perkins School of Theology in Dallas, in his book, *No Rising Tide, Theology, Economics and the Futrure*. To advocate for the common good sounds like a form of socialism. Call it what you want, it is the foundation upon which this country was built and is central to the teachings of Jesus as well as most religions.

George S. Johnson

EXCERPTED FROM

Obedience That Is Not Legalism

By Walter Brueggemann

We may as well concede at the outset that we live, all of us, in a promiscuous, self-indulgent society that prizes autonomy. As a consequence, "obedience" is a tough notion, which we settle mostly either by the vaguest of generalizations, or by confining subject matter to those areas already agreed upon.

The fearfulness and avoidance of obedience, as conventionally understood among us, has in my judgment two root causes, both of which are alive and powerful, even though not often frontally articulated.

The first dimension of the problem is the Augustinian-Lutheran dichotomy of "grace and law," which runs very deep in Western theology. In his treatment of Paul, Augustine considerably upped the stakes of the issue in his crushing opposition to Pelagius, and Luther solidified that theological claim by boldly inserting the word "alone" in his reading of Paul, thus "grace alone." It is clear that by "law" Luther meant many different things, seemingly focused especially on life apart from the gospel. The result, however, has been a remarkable aversion to "works," as though obedience to the commands of God, that is, performances of "works," is in and of itself a denial of the gospel. Luther is of course much more subtle and knowing than this, but so he has been conventionally interpreted. The outcome has been a notion of gospel without demand, a notion that plays well in a "therapeutic" society.

An aspect of this strong dichotomy has been a latent but pervasive anti-Jewish stereotype. Thus "law" is easily assigned to the "Jews," and the Old Testament becomes a book of commandments that has been "superseded" by the free gospel of Christ. Such a common maneuver of course fails to understand the core dynamic of covenantal faith shared by Jews and Christians and inevitably feeds anti-Semitism.

It is sufficient here simply to observe that such a reading of the gospel of Paul, powerfully reinforced by a sustained German-Lutheran reading of Romans, is at least open to question. Krister Stendahl has proposed that Augustine and Luther have massively misread Paul, who is concerned not with "guilt," but with Jewish-Christian relations in the early church. And E. P. Sanders has contributed greatly to the exposition of Stendahl's proposal, so that this governing dichotomy needs to be seriously challenged and reconsidered. The task of such reconsideration is a difficult one, given the force of these old categories.

The second dimension of our problem is the Enlightenment notion of unfettered freedom of "Man Come of Age." Indeed, the central program of the Enlightenment has been to slough off any larger authority to which obedience is owed, and that with special reference to the traditional authority of the church. This notion of freedom is already rooted in Descartes' establishment of the *human* doubter as the norm of truth. Locke contributed to the cause with his notion of the human person as a rational, free decider, and Kant completed the "Turn Toward the Subject," in making the human autonomous actor the one who will shape functional reality. This Enlightenment ideology has received its popular form in a Freudian theory of repression in which human maturation is the process of emancipation from communal authority that is extrinsic to the individual person and therefore fundamentally alien to mature humanness. Thus the human goal is movement beyond any restraints that come under the category of repression.

It turns out, of course, that such a model of unfettered freedom is an unreachable mirage. The individual person is never so contextless, and in the end the fantasy of such freedom has culminated in the most choking of conformities. There is, to be sure, an element of truth in Enlightenment models of liberation, but such a notion is almost always insufficiently dialectical to bear upon the actual human situation.

These theological-theoretical matters may seem quite remote from the concrete task of "preaching obedience." In my judgment, however, pastor and congregation must engage these powerful (even if hidden) categories and assumptions in critical and knowing ways, in order to face the commands of

God honestly. The reason they must be faced is that they are concretely powerful, even if mostly unarticulated. It is false to take the "law/grace" dichotomy at face value, as though the creator of heaven and earth has no overriding, non-negotiable intention for God's creatures. It is equally false to accept the phony freedom of autonomy and find ourselves more deeply enmeshed in the commands of death. Only the exposure of these false articulations can permit the community of the gospel to discern and accept its true position before God, who loves, delivers, summons, and commands.

A rereading of the gospel of grace and a reconsideration of Enlightenment ideology, in my judgment, will lead to a stunning and compelling fresh awareness: Our most serious relationships, including our relationship to the God of the gospel, are, at the same time, *profoundly unconditional* and *massively conditional*. One can, I submit, test this odd claim, both in terms of our normative theological materials and in terms of our lived experience. Such a notion of course violates all of our either/or Aristotelian logic, but our most treasured relations are not subject to such an exclusionary logic.

Much Old Testament scholarship (including some of my own) has championed the notion that there are two traditions of covenant in the Old Testament, one unconditional (Abraham and David) and one conditional (Moses). While this is critically correct, our theological task is to try to understand these textual claims taken all together. The evidence to which I am drawn suggests in powerful ways that "conditional/unconditional" and "law/grace" are unworkable categories for understanding our most serious and treasured relationships. And these misguided polarities create great crises for understanding the odd dialectical character of the gospel.

We may take as emblematic of such relationships that are neither conditional nor unconditional, as do the Old Testament texts, the relations of husband-wife and parent-child. In either of these at its best, it is clear that the relationship is unconditional, that is, there is no circumstance under which the relationship will be voided. And yet in these very same relationships, there are high and insistent "expectations" of the other that shade over into demands. And when these expectations are not met, there may be woundedness, alienation, or even rejection, even though the wounded party is powerfully committed. The truth is that there is something inscrutable about such relationships that are both conditional or unconditional; or perhaps we should say neither unconditional nor conditional. If one seeks to make one term or the other final in characterizing such a relationship, we destroy the inscrutability that belongs to and defines the relationship.

It may indeed be regarded as a far leap from our experience with such relationships as husband-wife and parent-child to our relation with God. It is of course a leap made artistically and boldly in the text itself. It will, moreover, be objected that one cannot reason by analogy or metaphor about God, and yet it is the only language we have for this most serious and freighted of all relationships. Moreover, we must ask why the poets of ancient Israel chose to speak this way about God. I suggest that such images are used because the poets who have given us our primal language for God are seeking a way to voice an inscrutability that overrides our logic and is more like the inscrutability of serious relationships than it is like anything else.

The covenant God has with us, with Israel, with the world, is a command-premised relation. The covenant is based in command, and God expects to be obeyed. There are, moreover, sanctions and consequences of disobedience that cannot be avoided, even as there are gifts and joys along with obedience. The Torah is given for guidance, so that Israel (and all of Israel's belated heirs) are "clued in" to the defining expectations of this relationship. The Torah makes clear that the holy "Other" in this relationship is an Agent with will and purpose that must be taken seriously and cannot be disregarded or mocked.

Thus it is a covenantal relation that is the "underneath category" to which "grace and law," "conditional and unconditional" are subsets. The "Other" in this relation is a real, live Other who initiates, shapes, watches over, and cares about the relation. The "Other" is both mutual with us and incommensurate with us, in a way not unlike a parent is mutual and incommensurate with a child, or a teacher is mutual and incommensurate with a student. This means that the relation is endlessly open, alive, giving and demanding, and at risk. This Holy Other may on occasion act in stunning mutuality, being with and for the second party, and so draw close in mercy and compassion, in suffering and forgiveness. It is, however, this same God who may exhibit God's self in unaccommodating incommensurability with rigorous expectation and dreadfulness, when expectations are not met. It is our desperate effort to reduce or "solve" the wonder of "the Holy one in our midst" that leads to such distortions as law and grace, freedom and servitude, unconditional and conditional. No such pairing can adequately contain the inscrutability, liveliness, danger, and unsettled quality of this relationship. Israel thus knows that Torah is guidance, in order to be joyously "on the way," a way that constitutes the well-being of the relationship.

This core insight about the richness of a covenantal relation still leaves for the preacher and the congregation the demanding work of taking seriously the specific commands of this covenantal "Other." Clearly the commands and guidance of the God of Israel and of the church are not vague and fuzzy, but quite concrete in how they concern the specificities of life. Those bound with this God are summoned to act differently in every sphere of life. Indeed, obedience consists in bringing every zone of our existence under the will, purpose, and expectation of this covenantal partner. While the concrete enactments of these commands in almost every case face ambiguity and complexity, the most crucial issue for reflection and preaching is to frame the commands so that they are not alien impositions, extrinsic to our life, but belong to, and are embraced as, definitional for the very fabric of our existence.

For that purpose, I suggest two possible interpretive strategies. The first is that the commands of God are the disciplines essential to the revolution that is Yahwism. Every serious revolutionary movement requires exacting disciplines of its adherents. And while the requirements may vary, they all in substance concern single-minded devotion to the revolution, without any doubt, ambiguity, or reservation. A revolution has no chance of success unless all of its adherents are singularly committed to the vision and the project and are willing to play their assigned role with unquestioning reliability and responsiveness.

The revolution to which the biblical community is summoned is to enact in the world of social affairs a new practice of social relationships marked by justice, mercy, and peace, which touches all of life. In order to engage in such a practice, all those committed to this revolutionary vision are expected to enact the daily requirements concerning self toward God and self toward neighbor in order to "advance the revolution."

Or to change the figure slightly, Jesus and his disciples, that is, the ones under his discipline, are "on the way" as the "Kingdom of God draws near," a kingdom in which the "normalcies" of life are turned on their head. The disciples are variously summoned and dispatched to order their lives around "prayer and fasting," around empty-handed healing power, to live their lives as concrete testimony that the new realm is "at hand" and can be lived and practiced here and now.

In order to make this approach to "obedience" convincing, believers must come to see their baptism as entry into a new vision of reality, which carries with it all sorts of new possibilities that the world thinks impossible. This vision of reality is an oddity in the world, at odds with all the conventional orderings of society-political, economic, and social. This "signing on" is not an "extra" added to a normal life, but entails a reordering of all of one's life from the ground up. The specificities of obedience must constantly be seen as derivative from, and in the service of, the larger revolution. It is clear that Moses imagined a whole new way of being in the world, a way ordered as covenant, and the commands of Sinai provide the guidance for that new way. And in like fashion, it is clear that the movement around Jesus evoked such hostility and resistance precisely because his movement subverted all conventional practices and forms in the world. No doubt such demands and disciplines became "legalistic" when the concrete requirement was no longer understood to derive from a larger revolutionary intention.

I am aware that such a notion of "revolutionary discipline" will not be easily compelling for most of us in excessively complacent establishment Christianity. I do imagine, however, that for many persons (especially young people), such a notion may indeed be a powerful attraction, for it is an enactment of a powerful hope for newness amid an increasingly failed and despairing society. In any case, I suggest a second strategy for "preaching obedience." It is this: Believers are those who love God with their whole heart, or more colloquially for Christians, "love the Lord Jesus." Such "love" is to be understood in all its rich implication, both as agape and eros, as true heart's desire. This is imagery not often utilized in our Calvinist inheritance, beset as we are with a heavy sense of duty. But alongside duty, in any serious relationship are desire and delight, the energetic will to be with the one loved, to please the one loved, to find in the joy of the one loved one's own true joy. Thus one in love is constantly asking in the most exaggerated way, "What else can I do in order to delight the beloved?" In such a context, one does not count the cost, but anticipates that when the beloved is moved in joy, it will be one's own true joy as well. Indeed, in such a condition, one can find joy only in the joy of the beloved, and not apart from the joy of the beloved.

It is my judgment that we live in a moment in the U.S. church that requires a serious and explicit rethinking of the meaning of faithful obedience. At the core of evangelical faith is the claim that faith knows some things that matter for genuine life, which are now urgent for our society. Such an explicit rethinking that is the work of the whole congregation may operate with these affirmations:

- The Enlightenment's offer of unfettered freedom without accountability is an unreachable mirage, an illusion never available to us.

- The neat and conventional antithesis between law and grace is a distortion of faith, because there are no unconditional or conditional relationships in the gospel, but only relationships of fidelity that prize both freedom and accountability, the two always intertwined and to be negotiated.

- Baptism is induction into the revolution of the coming rule of God. Like every revolution, this one has demanding disciplines that distinguish its adherents from all others.

- Baptism is an acknowledgment of our true desire, our eagerness to be with, commune with, delight in, and delight through glad obedience to this life-giving holy Other.

- It is precisely in our most primary zones of sexuality and economics that the demands and desires of this alternative life are most demanding and most satisfying. Those demands and desires consist not in the voiced demands of conventional morality nor in the self-indulgence that is an alternative to the flat demand, but in the struggle for the interface of freedom and faithfulness that requires endless interpretive work and reflection.

- Rejection of disciplines of the revolution and the distortion of our true desire may take place either through flat, one-dimensional traditionalism or through self-indulgence. Such rejection and distortion constitute a betrayal of baptism and an attempt to live at least some of our life outside this coming rule and according to the rules of the kingdom of death.

- Willingness to join the revolution or to practice this core desire can never be coerced. Such engagement is possible only by those who perceive their true identity in this coming rule. And then the disciplines and desire are winsome, joyous, and life-giving, not at all burdensome.

In Mark 10:17-22, Jesus does "pastoral care" for a person who seeks for "meaning" in his life. Jew that he is, Jesus responds to the man by asserting that the assurance he is seeking is found in full obedience to Israel's core commandments. Jesus assumes the man already knows the commandments. Beyond the commands, Jesus moves to "second level" obedience: "Go, sell what you own, and give the money to the poor .. . Come, follow me." It is as though the commandments are elemental, "first level" access to the revolution, but serious pastoral care moves to a more radical reorientation of life.

We observe three items in this narrative:

- Jesus does not impose the commandments upon the man. The commands are not Jesus' idea. They are already there and already known at the beginning of the exchange. They are a premise of the conversation, to which Jesus can make appeal. Jesus credits the man with knowing them, so that there is not a cubit of coercion in the response Jesus makes to the man's serious enquiry. Nonetheless, the response of Jesus is indeed a serious one. A good future is to be shaped by what is known of who God is and what God desires.

- Jesus loved the man (v. 21). Good pastoral care depends upon such a positive disposition toward the subject. Such love, however, does not lead to the romantic easiness of unconditional acceptance. It leads rather to truth-telling that concerns obedience. Nothing imposed, nothing harsh, nothing quarrelsome, only uncompromising truth-telling about the shape of well-being, spoken in love.

- Jesus' love, plus the assumption of the commandments, led to a startling new demand, a demand too heavy for the questioner. The man decided not to join the revolution and decided to hold to his other "desire" of great possessions.

There is no anger or scolding in this meeting. We are not told that Jesus loved him any the less for his decision. But Jesus' love toward him, like that of Moses, is obedience-shaped. Jesus was clearly not much committed to "membership growth" in his little flock under revolutionary discipline. The difficulty, of course, is that truth-telling about well-being in a promiscuous society declares our common desires to be deathly. Obedience thus takes the form of alternative desire. When the Holy One is supremely desired, is the "joy of loving hearts," obedience becomes joy, and duty becomes delight. Such a claim is difficult in the midst of misperceived Enlightenment freedom and in distorted "free grace." But that in itself is no reason to doubt its life-giving truth.

Israel knew that obedience is the path to genuine life. The commands are a mode of God's grace:

The law of the Lord is perfect,

reviving the soul;

the decrees of the Lord are sure,

making wise the simple;

the precepts of the Lord are right,

rejoicing the heart;

the commandment of the Lord is clear,

enlightening the eyes;

the fear of the Lord is pure,

enduring forever;

the ordinances of the Lord are true

and righteous altogether.

More to be desired are they than gold,

even much fine gold;

sweeter also than honey,

and drippings of the honeycomb.

(Psalm 19:7-10)

EXCERPTED FROM

Remember the Poor

by Joerg Rieger

❖❖❖

"Those who change the course of history are usually those who pose a new set of questions rather than those who offer solutions."

Gustavo Gutierrez

A new theological vision for the twenty-first century is imperative for various reasons. Most theologians today are sensitive to broad shifts on the level of ideas and worldviews that send us back to our drawing boards. Ever since the Enlightenment, theology has tried to keep up with this flow. Lately, the transition from modernity to postmodernity has taken up much of our theological energies.

Underlying these shifts, however, is an even bigger crisis that often does not reach the theological consciousness. Despite the much celebrated "victory of capitalism" in the 1990s, the situation of those who do not share in this victory, people pushed to the underside of history, has worsened, even in "first world" countries. Statistics show that poverty levels have risen not only in faraway places but at home as well. If nothing else, the increasing poverty of children even in the United States and the death of 35,000 children every day throughout the world from preventable causes must serve as a wake-up call. As people of my generation in Germany have asked our parents and grandparents about their relation to the deaths of six million Jewish people, future generations will ask us about the deaths of nearly twelve million children each year, and even well-meaning theologians will not be spared. This time, however, it will be virtually impossible to respond that we did not know. At this point we have not even touched the pain and suffering inflicted along the fault lines of gender and race, and other manifestations of the underside of history that are relevant for the topic of this book.

How does theology deal with this situation? At present there is a growing awareness that theology that responds to God's embrace of all of creation will have to learn to pay attention no longer just to the flow of ideas but to other aspects of reality as well, all the way to a new understanding of the forces of the economy. Theology dealing with all aspects of life will need to investigate, furthermore, how all these things come together. Yet while broadening the theological perspective in these ways, we also need to explore how those whose pain interrupts our well-ordered reflections are becoming part of the theological enterprise as a whole. That is the overarching challenge that I will address in this book.

The Underside of History

In order to understand the potential contribution of people on the underside to theological reflection, we need to see what role they have played so far. While modern theology has generated a new concern for the "signs of the times," to use the famous expression that permeated the Second Vatican Council, few have had the courage to deal with the underside of those signs.

Even though everybody knows that there are now a growing number of theologies that have to do with poor, oppressed, and marginalized people, the extent of the challenge of these groups to theology as a whole is still little understood. This paradox points to a major blind spot in contemporary theology and requires a closer look at where we are. How well are the standard paradigms of contemporary theology equipped to deal with this challenge? The camps of mainline theology today seem to be reflected in two general interpretive frameworks whose force fields even extend to some theologies at the margins. In response to the challenge posed by people on the underside, one version tries to elevate them to a prominent place of authority and control, not unlike the place occupied by the modern self in much of modern theology. The other version makes them into recipients of charity and well-meaning support from those who are better off. In both cases, however, people at the margins are merely integrated into existing theological frameworks. Both camps of mainline theology in their various manifestations have not yet understood that precisely at this point their binary logic has reached an impasse. Theological encounters with the underside call for the paradigm shift and new theological categories.

More aware of this problem than anyone else, many liberation theologians have explored new ways of listening to people at the margins that neither patronize them nor romanticize them by putting them in the place of ultimate authority. Nevertheless, the new vision unfolds only gradually and remains a continuing challenge for the future. In the world of late capitalism and its widening gaps through which more and more people are falling, this question becomes the ultimate challenge for any theology.

Alternative Theology

The new vision does not quite fit any of the major paradigms of contemporary theology. Many of the "first world" labels that have been used to describe theologies from the underside such as "situational theology," "contextual theology," "social gospel," "orthopraxis," "political theology," and even "theology from below" fail to convey the difference introduced by the perspective of the underside of history since they work with existing theological frameworks, typically of liberal provenience. As initial encounters with the underside in theology have indicated, taking seriously the role of the marginalized leads to new ways of dealing with the two fulcrums that have alternatively served as the Archimedean points of much of modern theological thought: the modern self and the texts of the tradition (including the Bible).

Although listening to marginalized people leads back to interactions with both the modern self and the traditional texts, the new theological vision that emerges at this point cannot be understood exclusively in terms of one or the other. How strong the theological pull of those two alternatives still is can be seen in the fact that most interpreters of current theologies from the underside have tried to understand the phenomenon either in terms of one central doctrine (text) or in terms of a new theological agent (self) assuming control. Yet neither a reading on the level of the authority of texts of the church alone (dogmatics) not a reading on the level of the authority of the human self (systematics) can fully grasp the contribution of the underside to theological reflection. In the encounter with the marginalized other before God, both the concern for the texts of the church and the concern for the human self are transformed.

The irruption of the underside of history into theology reminds theologians that even our best intentions can fail. Encountering the reality of marginalization, poverty, and oppression, the way into the theological future can no longer afford to start with lofty ideals and dreams. Theologians in touch with the underside have set the course when they remind us that we need to shift from "theologizing about an ideal church" to "analyzing the actual church." The new theological vision cannot grow out of well-meaning charities, utopian dreams, stout political activism, or moralistic guilt trips. A self-critical look at theology and the church in actual solidarity with the victims will help to clear the view.

Such analysis will broaden the field of theological reflection. For example, theology done together with people on the underside cannot help but notice the intersections of theological authority and power. Where theological authority is reconsidered in the encounter with the underside, we can begin to map the connections between the production of theological authority and the prevailing structures of power in actual historical settings, and develop new blueprints for the future.

In one of his last notes Herzog reminds us that "only if we change ourselves in view of these 'invisible' people, will we become aware of the 'invisible God.' Here anchors our theological future." Let me add that without new encounters with the other at the margins, claims of encounters with the Otherness of God can be dangerous illusions, an insight that can be traced all the way back to the biblical texts.

This book deals with the following questions: In light of the growth of marginalization and suffering that we encounter today, how can those at the margins help theology to become more aware of, and accountable to, what God is doing? How can we create more space for God's work, which seems to be under constant tutelage in much of contemporary theology as it identifies ultimate theological authority alternatively either with the modern self or the traditional texts of the church rather than with Godself?

Despite necessary differences, theology as a whole will benefit from the ongoing attempt to rethink the movement of God's praxis in relation to Christian praxis and the underside of history. The theological task is to draw together, in light of the Gospel and the traditions of the church, the implications of the eruption of people on the underside and God's irruption.

———————— EXCERPTED FROM ————————

Co-opted by the System

by Sister Marie Augusta Neal

❖❖❖

In recent years the prophetic voice in the Judaeo-Christian tradition has merged increasingly with the voices of the old and the new left. The Popes have followed the old left in calling for a redistribution of wealth and the new left in calling for the redistribution of power.

The Medellin conference of Latin American bishops, bent on implementing the decrees of Vatican II, adopted in 1968 a policy directive of prophetic dimensions. It was derived from the pedagogical methods used in Brazil, Chile and elsewhere in Latin America, methods aimed at rapid basic education of peasants not only in literacy but also in social, economic, and political awareness. This educational process, which came to be called "conscientization," refers to "learning to perceive social, political, and economic contradictions and to take action against the oppressive elements of reality" (Freire, 1970, p. 19). The method was originally named and made popular through the action-reflection program of Paulo Freire, the brilliant scholar and teacher exiled from Brazil, and of his sponsor and friend Dom Helder Camara, then the archbishop of Recife in northeast Brazil. Both were held in disrepute by their government, which later co-opted the program in its own interests.

From the point of view of those who have control over the established system – labor, industry, trade, the unknown, and the uses of violence – the message of the prophets is potentially destructive. To the degree that priests celebrate the system – performing the rites that bless established interests and focus the psychic energy of the people on their appointed tasks – they and the prophets will be opponents. Those in power, fighting for their own interests and believing they have a right to do so, will provide the means for the destruction of the prophet. What is more, with the support and blessing of the priests, they will be convinced that, in doing so, justice and truth are on their side.

Established churches perform two different social functions: (1) reinforcing commitment when self-interest, unrest, loneliness, dissatisfaction, disappointment, anger, and other distractions pull people away from the common effort of staying alive and developing their potentials; (2) providing an environment for dissociating affections from the system in time of needed social change. It is because the church gathering focuses on human destiny and purpose – on our common destiny rather than individual advantage or disadvantage – that established society needs a celebrating church in its midst to restore the energies of the members and proclaim the legitimacy of its ways. (It is this function of religion that Durkheim analyzes in *Elementary Forms of the Religious Life*.) By its ritual of celebrating life and expressing love and hope by threatening punishment for those who sin, and by linking sin with violations of existing law and order, the church reinforces the social purposes of the group, confirming the goodness of the status quo. It can affirm in an unreflecting way the goodness of conformity to law and order. Prayers for national leaders or for the success of national, state or local projects and encouragement to participate in the national endeavor provide the establishment with an affirmation that is affectively reinforced whenever the worshiping community meets. The very regularity and ritual quality of the worship service guarantee that its affirmation is relatively unreflective and that what gets affirmed is the established structure.

But when a church continues this function during periods when established authorities are responsible for manifest injustice on a large scale, it plays a major role in reinforcing the evil. The injustice may affect members of a single society or, in the case of war or trade or other agreements among powerful nations, it may affect powerless peoples the world over. If the worshiping community regularly prays for the leaders of church and state but its ritual expresses no concern for migrant workers, students, black inner-city dwellers, Appalachian miners, prison inmates, or victims of disasters, war and exploitation, not only are the exploited given no reason to rejoice but church members who remember the original Gospel and are aware of current forms of oppression will find their participation less meaningful.

In many cases, churchgoers, not wanting to admit that the church has been co-opted, simply stop coming, stop caring. Those who remain–predominantly those who want the system to continue–so lack the vital drive for renewal that the church becomes a relic, contradicting its essential role of celebrating God's will, which is interpreted as being the good of humanity (Kung).

One channel of modern prophecy has chosen to focus on eliminating the causes of poverty rather than on alleviating the results. Marx was the preeminent representative of this tradition in the nineteenth century. As established interests translated his message, it came to mean that he advocated the overthrow of capitalism by violent revolution and the rejection of religion because it was the opium of the people. The result was that those with secure power were long lulled into ignoring the problem he addressed – the increasing oppression of people caused by the established division of labor.

Theoretically, Christianity stands with the poor of the world against all established interests that work to the manifest advantage of the rich man seeking to get through the eye of the needle. Historically, then, it should always be in judgmental tension with societal systems, especially as these systems have come in time to institutionalize the interests of advantaged segments of the society. Such, however, has not been the case. When Christianity remains true to its scriptural base, it is prophetic with respect to institutionalized exploitation. Membership, then, in organizations defined as Christian – that is, churches or mentalities that are distinctly Christian – should provide people with an affiliation alternate to their citizenship groups, in order to assure space for psychic solidarity that is not either easily co-opted into citizenship enthusiasm or repressed as defying the law.

The idea of civil religion is popular today because, for any nation to assert its right to program the world economy in its interests, those in power need the assurance of a naïve, spontaneous, uncritical, "religious" celebration – in Durkheim's term, an "effervescence" – to mask the mass exploitation that such a program requires. Religious enthusiasm uncritically expressed and charismatically released is one of the most effective ways of delaying the deluge.

Winner–Take–All Politics

by Jacob Hacker and Paul Pierson

◆◆◆

For those working on Wall Street, 2009 was a very good year. At the thirty-eight biggest companies, investors and executives earned a staggering $140 billion in all – the highest number on record. The venerable investment firm Goldman Sachs paid its employees nearly a half million dollars each, capping off one of the best years since its founding in 1869. The sums, while astounding, were hardly unprecedented. Unfettered pay had become the norm on Wall Street over the prior generation, as it had in American boardrooms more broadly. The CEO of Goldman Sachs, Lloyd C. Blankfein, had taken home $68 million in 2007. That same year, the top twenty-five hedge fund managers raked in $892 million on average, according to *Alpha* magazine's annual ranking of the highest earners – Wall Street's equivalent of *People* magazine's most beautiful people.

What made the 2009 payouts so shocking wasn't the numbers themselves. It was what they said about the American economy – and American government. The Wall Street of well-heeled bankers was thriving, while the Main Street of ordinary workers struggled amid the worst economic downturn since the Great Depression. And Wall Street was thriving because less than two years before it had received hundreds of billions in federal bailout money, along with less visible but far more massive indirect assistance from the Federal Reserve. In the wake of the financial crisis – a crisis prompted in no small part by banks' reckless practices – government had shoveled cash in the front doors of the nation's leading financial institutions to avert catastrophe. Now Goldman and other big firms were, in essence, discreetly but steadily shoveling a large share of that cash out the back doors into employees' private accounts.

For the very top earners, the payouts were actually less ostentatious than usual, lest they make more conspicuous the scale of the unexpected riches.

Big paychecks looked bad, after all, when the rest of the economy was staggering, and when Wall Street lobbyists were ferociously battling proposed reforms of the financial system to clip the banks' wings and forestall another bailout. Out, for the most part, were seven- and eight-figure bonuses. In were complicated "stock options" and "deferred compensation" that promised equally big returns down the road. As the New York Times helpfully explained, "Wall Street is confronting a dilemma of riches: How to wrap its eye-popping paychecks in a mantle of moderation."

This was not exactly the dilemma faced by most Americans. While the money spigot flowed freely on Wall Street, the "real economy" remained trapped under the debris of the financial implosion of 2007. Even as Blankfein insisted that Goldman was doing "God's work" – apparently missing the passage in the Bible about how hard it is for a rich man to enter heaven – tens of millions of homeowners were still reeling from the real estate crash that firms like his had helped create through heedless speculation in securities underwritten by subprime loans. Nationwide, home prices had plummeted, wiping out nearly 40 percent of American families' home equity between December 2006 and December 2008. The unemployment rate hovered around 10 percent. For every job opening there were six job seekers. State and local governments faced with unprecedented budget deficits were slashing gaping holes in the safety net, raising taxes, and threatening to lay off hundreds of thousands of teachers. Leading economists suggested it would be years before the country returned to full employment. The human toll – in shattered careers, disrupted families, and lost security – was incalculable.

These two starkly divergent tales of 2009 represent just the most recent and painful chapter of a longer story. Over the last generation, more and more of the rewards of growth have gone to the rich and superrich. The rest of America, from the poor through the upper middle class, has fallen further and further behind. Like Wall Street's deep-pocketed denizens in 2009, the very richest of Americans have shot into the economic stratosphere, leaving middle- and working-class Americans to watch their fortunate fellowmen's ascent while remaining firmly planted on economic terra firma. In the phrase that leads this book's title, the American economy has become "winner-take-all."

Consider the astonishing statistics. From 1979 until the eve of the Great Recession, the top one percent received 36 percent of all gains in household income – even after taking into account the value of employer-sponsored health insurance, all federal taxes, and all government benefits. (We will examine this "DNA evidence," which provides irrefutable proof of the hyperconcentration of economic gains at the top, in the next chapter.) Economic growth was even more skewed between 2001 and 2006, during which the share of income gains going to the top one percent was over 53 percent. That's right: More than 50 cents of every dollar in additional income pocketed by Americans over this half decade accrued to the richest 1 in 100 households.

Even more striking, the top 0.1 percent – one out of every thousand house-holds – received over 20 percent of all after-tax income gains between 1979 and 2005, compared with the 13.5 percent enjoyed by the bottom 60 percent of households. If the total income growth of these years were a pie, in other words, the slice enjoyed by the roughly 300,000 people in the top tenth of 1 percent would be half again as large as the slice enjoyed by the roughly *180 million* in the bottom 60 percent. Little wonder that the share of Americans who see the United States as divided between "haves" and "have nots" has risen sharply over the past two decades – although, as we will see, the economic winners are more accurately portrayed as the "have-it-alls," so concentrated have the gains been at the very, very top.

These mind-boggling differences have no precedent in the forty years of shared prosperity that marked the U.S. economy before the late 1970s. Nor do they have any real parallel elsewhere in the advanced industrial world. A generation ago, the United States was a recognizable, if somewhat more unequal, member of the cluster of affluent democracies known as mixed economies, where fast growth was widely shared. No more. Since around 1980, we have drifted away from that mixed-economy cluster, and traveled a considerable distance toward another: the capitalist oligarchies, like Brazil,

Mexico, and Russia, with their much greater concentration of economic bounty. Of course, the United States is far richer than these oligarchic nations. But, contrary to the rhetoric of inequality's apologists, it has not grown consistently more quickly than other rich democracies that have seen little or no tilt toward winner-take-all. America's runaway rewards for the affluent have not unleashed an economic miracle whose rewards have generously filtered down to the poor and middle class.

Quite the opposite. Like a raging fever that announces a more serious underlying disease, rising inequality is only the clearest indicator of an economic transformation that has touched virtually every aspect of American's standard of living. From the erosion of job security to the declining reach of health insurance, from the rising toll of home foreclosures to the growing numbers of personal bankruptcies, from the stagnation of upward social mobility to the skyrocketing of personal debt, the American economy that has delivered so much to the fortunate has worked much less well for most Americans. And this has been true not just over the past three years or thirteen years, but over the past thirty years. Winner-take-all has become the defining feature of American economic life.

How has this happened? If most commentators are to be believed, the answer lies in inevitable shifts in our economy driven by global, universal pressures. Like a doctor forced to dispense difficult truths to a patient in denial, these economic diagnosticians tell us that the shared prosperity of the postwar generation was rooted in a sheltered, low-tech economy that is not coming back. A technological revolution has rendered the world "flat," sweeping away differences rooted in culture and politics and policy. In today's highly globalized and competitive environment, educational achievements and workplace skills are economic destiny, and deep economic cleavages based on those achievements and skills are all but inevitable.

This diagnosis has its distinctive ideological spins, of course: On the one side, liberal economic doctors call for massive investments in education to give more people a shot at entering the winner's circle. On the other side, conservative economic doctors call for more tax cuts and deregulation to unleash the competitive economy still further, with promises that, at some point soon, the gains will "trickle down." But whatever the prescription, the diagnosis ultimately points to the same constellation of factors. Globalization, skill shifts, technological transformation, economic change – the list is familiar from the seemingly endless autopsies that crunch the numbers and report, to use James Carville's famous catchphrase, It's the economy, stupid.

Winner-Take-All Politics offers a very different diagnosis, one rooted in a very different sort of exploration. Rather than doctors dispensing difficult truths, we see ourselves as investigators uncovering buried clues that point to culprits beyond the usual suspects most analysts have fingered. The truths that we find share little in common with the familiar nostrums about the natural course of the American economy. Yet, in some respects, they offer an even more disturbing assessment. They strip away the aura of economic destiny surrounding runaway inequality. But they replace the certainty of a false economic diagnosis with discomforting conclusions – along with a new set of puzzles – about how, and for whom, American politics works.

The puzzles are all around us. How can hedge-fund managers who are pulling down billions sometimes pay a lower tax rate than do their secretaries? And why, in an era of increased economic uncertainty, is it so hard for their secretaries to form or join a union? How have corporate managers – who, along with Wall Street bigwigs, make up more than half of the top 0.1 percent – ascend from pay levels twenty to thirty times that of a typical worker to levels two to three hundred times as great? And why, over a generation in which most Americans have experienced modest economic gains, have politicians slashed taxes on the rich even as the riches of the rich have exploded?

To answer these questions, we need to adopt a perspective that is both broader and deeper than that commonly on offer – to see the big changes in the landscape of American politics that are too often missed or taken for granted, to look inside the black box of government policies that are too often treated as immaterial or uninteresting (but which turn out to be neither). We need to travel down neglected byways of American political and economic life that lead to the heart of the winner-take-all economy, to find the forgotten stories that help us see the profound changes in American democracy that have unfolded in our time. Along the way, we will meet sometimes-little-known figures who helped engineer hidden but profound organizational changes – in American politics and through those political shifts, in the American economy.

Winner-Take-All Politics is not another of the many book-length indictments of our nation's present economic wrongs, with their familiar finger-pointing at the greed or incompetence of public or private figures. Our current crisis certainly bears emphasis, in part because it so clearly reveals the sources and costs of the winner-take-all economy. And by the end of our investigation, the roots and realities of contemporary discontents will indeed be apparent. But, as will become clear, our current crisis is merely the latest in a long struggle rooted in the interplay of American democracy and American capitalism. This struggle has not unfolded overnight. Nor is it a simple linear tale of sweeping, inevitable change. The advancing tide of the winner-take-all economy sometimes feels like a force of nature. (Certainly, it is convenient for its beneficiaries to describe it that way.) Yet America's slow, steady slide toward economic oligarchy has been neither beyond human control nor bereft of resistance.

We tell the story of a thirty-year war. Marked by bitter conflict, it has involved more than flash-in-the-pan personalities or fleeting electoral victories. Step by step and debate by debate, America's public officials have rewritten the rules of American politics and the American economy in ways that have benefited the few at the expense of the many. Not all have been as candid about what they were doing as former Democratic Senator John Breaux when he joked that his vote could not be bought but could be "rented" by the highest bidder. Nor have many been as rhapsodic as Republican Senator Phil Gramm, who described Wall Street as a "holy place." But, for reasons we shall explain and with consequences we will unveil, all of America's political class have felt the increasing pull of the winner-take-all economy.

Our story unfolds in three parts. Part 1 delves into the mystery of the winner-take-all economy. We come face-to-face with what has really happened in the American marketplace over the last generation: who's won and who's lost in the thirty-year war, and how government has played an integral role in creating these new economic realities. Here, we crunch the economic numbers – the *right* numbers, the numbers that truly get to the heart of what has happened to our economy over the last generation. But we also take our investigation where the right numbers lead and, in doing so, enter surprisingly uncharted territory. To uncover the path to winner-take-all requires seeing the transformation of American government over the last generation, a transformation that has fundamentally changed what government does, and whom it does it for.

But resolving our first mystery only reveals a deeper one: If government has played a central part, how could this happen? In a country where public officials must regularly face the judgment of citizens at the polls, how could their efforts come to so persistently favor the very few? In our search for clues, we show that this is an age-old question, and that the thirty-year war has parallels in our nation's past – in the great debates over government's place in a dynamic, increasingly unequal economy that took place in the first half of the last century.

Part 2 takes us down to the subterranean roots of the winner-take-all economy, which lie, against common expectations, in the political transformations of the 1970s. The seventies are the forgotten decade of American political history. Received wisdom seeks the wellspring of our polarized and confrontational politics in the cultural clashes and electoral upheavals of the 1960s. Casting liberal movements against conservative political reactions, this familiar story-line misses the true timing and character of the shifts that have generated our deeper crisis – and overlooks some of the central political movements that reshaped the battlefield of combat.

In part 3, we provide a portrait of the new world of American politics forged in this crucible – the world of "Winner-Take-All Politics." We do so through the prism of the nation's two political parties, showing how Republicans and Democrats have both responded, in different ways, to the political pull of America's superrich. Here we see the full causes and consequences of the political transformations of the era. Here we also see the daunting challenges that President Obama has had to grapple with in the latest and most epic battle in the thirty-year war.

We would have liked to end our book by declaring the end of winner-take-all politics. But the effects of a thirty-year war are not wiped away overnight. The hurdles to renewal, rooted in the story we tell, are formidable. Yet, as high as they are, they do not lead us to counsel despair. For the obstacles are not irresistible forces of nature but man-made forces of politics. And they are obstacles that our nation has faced before. The gap between the ideals of American democracy and the realities of American politics has yawned in the past. Reformers have dramatically narrowed this gap in the past as well. Nothing in this history suggests today's barriers will be easily cleared. But there is much to instill determination that they can and must be.

From Believing to Following

by George Johnson

◆◆◆

I don't know who – or what – put the question; I don't know when it was put.
I don't even remember answering. But at some moment I did answer yes to
someone – or something – and from that hour I was certain that existence is
meaningful and that, therefore, my life, in self-surrender, had a goal. From
that moment I have known what it means "not to look back," and "to take no
thought for the morrow."

Dag Hammarskjold
UN General Secretary

When new members are received into our churches, we seldom ask them if they have responded to the call to follow Jesus Christ. We ask them about their beliefs. "Do you believe in Jesus?" No new member has questioned me as to what it means to believe. Most find it easy to say they believe in God and in Jesus. As Bonhoeffer says, "we haven't asked any awkward questions."

In the Sunday morning service some stand and recite a Confession of Faith. "We believe in God the Father Almighty...in Jesus Christ...in the Holy Spirit." Would it make a difference if we stood and said, "I am a follower of Jesus, who was executed because of his subversive love for me and for my neighbor" or, "I have decided to follow Jesus this coming week in all I say, do, or think"?

Could it be that in our desire to keep the gospel pure, and be clear on salvation as a gift, we have failed to extend the call to follow Jesus Christ as it is given in the scriptures? Have we been too afraid of the role of decision on our part? Isn't coming to a decision a work of the Spirit also?

Jim Wallis, in his book *Call to Conversion*, says that neither evangelicals nor liberals have grasped the meaning of conversion for these times. It is his contention that any conversion (repentance and faith) that is removed from social and political reality is simply not biblical. His book lays out a strong argument for the recovery of an emphasis on conversion in the church in order for the church to be able to respond to a suffering world.

Such a conversion emphasis necessitates believing and following Jesus. Many people who have moved beyond the trap of guilt and powerlessness talk about their conversion, sometimes their second or third conversion. By this they mean a turnaround in their lives, a new mindset, a new perspective. Such conversions do not negate our baptismal covenant but rather awaken us to what Martin Luther calls the daily death and resurrection meaning of our baptism. Every day we answer the call to believe and follow. Dorothee Soelle reminds us that in saying yes to Jesus there is a decisive no also involved; for example, a no to the royal empires of today that call for our primary allegiance.

In the prologue to his book *Jesus – A Revolutionary Biography*, John Dominic Crossan reminds the reader that there is more to being a follower of Jesus than facts and beliefs. He gives an imaginary dialogue with the historical Jesus who says, "I read your book, Dominic, and it's quite good. So now are you ready to live by my vision and join me in my program?" "I don't think I have the courage, Jesus, but I did describe it quite well didn't I, and the method was especially good, wasn't it?" "Thank you Dominic, for not falsifying the message to suit your own incapacity. That at least is something." "Is it enough, Jesus?" "No, Dominic, it is not."

Other Voices

Are You Following Jesus or Believing in Christ?

It began innocently enough – a friend recommending a book, *Christology at the Crossroads* by Jon Sobrino. The Salvadoran Jesuit blew most of my theological ducks out of the water. He threw a hat down on my Scrabble board and messed up many of my combinations. He forced me to contend for the ground I had claimed. The question that Jon Sobrino put to me I must share with you: Are you following Jesus, or believing in Christ?

Plunge into the Gospels anywhere and you will likely find Jesus asking someone to follow. The verb is *akaloutheo*. It represents a dominant motif. Why, then, do we hear so little about following Jesus in the church today? I've been in, with, and around the church for more than 50 years, and no one has ever asked me, "Are you following Jesus?" Not when I was in the communicant's class; not when I joined the church; not when I became a candidate for the ministry; not when I was ordained; and never in any of my services of installation. Always the questions have dealt with belief: Do you believe in God – Father, Son and Spirit? Do you believe in the veracity of the Scriptures and the Westminster Confession? Do you believe in the unity and purity of the church?

It is as though we held the notion that following Jesus was "in" until the crucifixion and went out with the resurrection – that we can take up with Jesus on easier terms on the other side of Easter.

Do you believe in Christ? It isn't so hard to answer that. What is wanted is an affirmative response to treasured propositions about the second person of the Trinity. But when someone asks, "Are you following Jesus?" this can get to be expensive. This question has to do with my lifestyle, my attitudes, my values, my surrender.

If I'm following Jesus, why am I such a good insurance risk? If I'm following Jesus, why, when I have done my giving, have I so much left over for myself? If I'm following Jesus, why do my closets bulge when so many are unclothed? If I'm following Jesus, why do I have so many friends among the affluent and so few among the poor? If I'm following Jesus, why do I have so much privacy in a world that is starved for love? If I'm following Jesus, why am I tempted to overeat in a world where so many beg for bread? If I'm following Jesus, why am I getting on so well in a world that marked him out for death?

Are you following Jesus or believing in Christ? Unfair you say: The two are inseparable.

Theoretically, yes, but pragmatically, no. We separate them all the time. If we must err, let us err on the side of following. *For one can believe without following, but one cannot follow without believing.*

Ernest Campbell, Riverside Church, New York

CHAPTER TWENTY

We have gathered like eagles round the carcass of cheap grace, and there we have drunk of the poison that has killed the life of following Christ. We have given away the Word and sacraments wholesale; we baptized, confirmed and absolved a whole nation without asking awkward questions or insisting on strict conditions. Our humanitarian sentiment made us give that which was holy to the scornful and unbelieving. We poured forth unending streams of grace. But the call to follow Jesus was hardly ever heard.

Dietrich Bonhoeffer

Spiritual Renewal that Empowers

Please don't think I'm a real "fundie." That's not my background at all. For the past 10 or 15 years I've been working to inform, inform, inform and motivate, motivate, motivate and I've come to the conclusion that all the information and motivation goes just so far. My husband and I are in the midst of a very radical change in our ministry and lifestyle. We feel joyful and thankful and pray that we are being more faithful to our Lord. This is only possible because of a spiritual renewal in our lives that is empowering us to change. I feel so strongly that the whole world needs to change, especially the United States. Our external world will never change unless/until our internal/spiritual selves are renewed. That's the starting point.

Deborah Peters, Montana Hunger Advocate

Then Jesus told his disciples, "If any man would come after me, let him deny himself and take up his cross and follow me. For whoever would save his life will lose it, and whoever loses his life for my sake will find it."

Matthew 16:24-25

Reflection Action

• Think through the Hammarskjold quote. Has there ever been a moment when you said yes? Have there been any mini- or maxi-conversions in your life? How did your perspective change?

• Why is it easier to think about believing in Jesus than to think about following Jesus? How do you understand the difference?

• Discuss the Bonhoeffer quote.

In a Culture of
Ecological Crisis
and Greed

I have fond memories of living on a farm in Minnesota when I was a young boy in elementary school. During the summer months of my high school and college years I would earn money by working on a farm. I remember milking cows by hand, shocking grain and mowing hay with a team of horses. On Saturday nights we took cream to the town's creamery and eggs to the market. I still love to visit farms.

One of the things I have learned over the years is that farmers are not only producers of food but also caretakers of our land and its resources. A repeated refrain in this chapter will remind us that we all are involved in agriculture and responsible for the care of the earth and its creatures. We are at a critical moment today because unless we begin to think differently about ecology and care of creation we may find future survival on this planet difficult.

The image of the banquet table is often used to describe the abundant life. Sallie McFague, a theologian who taught for years at Vanderbilt, calls our attention to the fact that every creature deserves a place at the table, not just humans. Articles in this chapter alert us to what is happening to creation at alarming rates because care of creation has not been central to gospel proclamation in most churches.

My brother-in-law, a farmer in Iowa, tells about a Sunday in his rural church just after a heavy rainfall on the preceding Saturday. The young pastor in his sermon that Sunday talked about the top soil he saw in the ditches running to the sea. Then he thanked the farmers who were practicing responsible conservation of the earth. During the coffee hour hang out in the basement of the church after the service my brother-in-law heard one farmer saying . . . "Why doesn't the pastor stick to the Bible?" Thinking differently is needed in so many areas of our lives and theology.

Wendel Berry, the poet-farmer, urges us to think differently because ecological health is paramount to the health of humans. Maybe it is time to sit up and notice what is happening and our role in it.

George S. Johnson

—————— EXCERPTED FROM ——————

New Climate for Theology

by Sallie McFague

❖❖❖

Is there any hope for us – we middle-class North American Christians? Can we at least be honest, if not good? It might help if we could keep our "wild space" intact. Being a Christian, even a middle-class North American one – as I envision it – involves having a wild space. That wild space is the shocking suggestion – even if only a suspicion – that all really are invited to the banquet, that every creature deserves a place at the table. This is not the hegemonic view of our society or of the church; it is counter-cultural and counter-church. It is a different vision of the good life, but wild as it may seem, it is not necessarily wrong or impossible. Its two key principles are mundane ones: justice and sustainability. Could the wild space become the whole space – the household of planet earth where each of us takes only our share, cleans up after ourselves, and keeps the house in good repair for future dwellers? I do not know, but perhaps we Christians could at least admit what life abundant truly should be, terrifying as it may be.

And here we are eight years later, facing a vision of dystopia from global warming that is as far removed as possible from what we want: the vision of the banquet where all are invited to the table, the abundant life of justice and sustainability, the deep desire within each of us – our wild space – that tells us a different world is possible. So what is the "next" thing I must do as a theologian? I want to suggest that theology within the context of climate change must focus on deconstructing and reconstructing two key doctrines: who we are and who God is. The interpretation of the God-world relationship is a critical issue. If theologians, who are some of the keepers and interpreters of this deep knowledge, allow false, inappropriate, unhelpful, and dangerous notions of God and ourselves to continue as our society's assumptions, we are not doing our job. A primary task of theologians is to guard and encourage right thinking about God and ourselves. This, of course, is but one small task needed for the planetary agenda to change. Other people – doctors, car manufacturers, teachers, parents, corporate leaders, lawyers, politicians, agriculturalists, and so on – also have important offerings to make in our struggle against climate change. The particular task of theologians is prior to our action; it is at its roots. It is a limited task and mainly a linguistic one: suggesting different language for talking about God and ourselves – with the hope that different action may follow. The limitations of this task and its possibilities are perhaps best seen in the negative: if we do not change our basic assumptions about God and ourselves from an individualistic to a communitarian view, can we expect people to change their behavior? If we know nothing else, do we have a choice?

Given this assignment, I begin in part one with the science of global warming, followed by a chapter on its significance for theology. These two chapters provide the groundwork for the rest of the book. It is critical, I believe, that theology be done within the contemporary scientific worldview; therefore, a careful reading of our empirical situation is the necessary beginning point. It is also important, I think, for theology to attend to the specific task for which it is responsible: theos-logia, words about God. To many people, it is not obvious that theology has anything to do with issues such as climate change. Why should it? My answer is that theology must deal with global warming because one of the basic marks of the church is its ecological catholicity, which must be lived out in a political context. In other words, Christian faith is concerned with a just and sustainable existence for all of God's creation.

Is a Different World Possible? Human Dignity and the Integrity of Creation

For I am about to create new heavens
And a new earth;
The former things shall not be remembered
Or come to mind.
But be glad and rejoice forever
In what I am creating:
For I am about to create Jerusalem as a joy,

And its people as a delight . . .
No more shall the sound of weeping be heard in it,
Or the cry of distress.
No more shall there be in it
An infant that lives but a few days,
Or an old person who does not live out a lifetime . . .
For like the days of a tree shall the days of my people be,
And my chosen shall long enjoy the work of their hands.
They shall not labor in vain,
Or bear children for calamity;
For they shall be offspring blessed by the Lord...
Before they call I will answer,
While they are yet speaking I will hear.
The wolf and the lamb shall feed together,
The lion shall eat straw like the ox . . .
They shall not hurt or destroy
On all my holy mountain,
Says the Lord.

Isa. 65:17-25

Reading this passage makes us weep – weep for our world, our poor, sorry world. The world we want, that we ache for, is a world where children get to grow up and live to old age, where people have food and houses and enjoyable work, where animals and plants and human beings live together on the earth in harmony, where none "shall hurt or destroy." This is our dream, our deepest desire, the image we cannot let go of. This vision of the good life makes us unwilling to settle for the unjust, unsustainable, and indeed cruel and horrendous world we have. Global warming seems like the last straw: "Things are not supposed to be this way. A different world is possible." Isaiah's hymn to a new creation and Jesus' parables of the reign of God touch this deepest desire in each of us for a different, better world. It would be a world in which human dignity and the integrity of creation are central, a world in which the intrinsic value of all human beings and of the creation ognized and appreciated. Human dignity and the integrity of creation lie at the heart of the biblical vision of the good life, and at the heart of our contemporary vision as well. Do we have any hope for a different, better world? Given the situation we face at the beginning of the twenty-first century of war, violence, AIDS, capitalist greed, and now the specter of global warming, it seems absurd to even bother with such a question. And yet we read in the Isaiah passage that in the midst of painting this wonderful picture of life beyond our wildest dreams, God says, "Before they call I will answer, while they are yet speaking I will hear." *While they are yet speaking*" – we have only to ask for God to answer! But we must ask with our whole being; a better world must become our deepest desire. And this means, of course, we must work at it; we must give our whole selves to it.

First, let us look at the kind of destruction that our world is presently undergoing – this will be an analysis of what is wrong. Then we will consider what we need to do to turn things around; in other words, our preliminary work so that God may answer.

Since September 11, 2001, terrorism appears to many people as the major kind of destruction we face. Terrorist acts are sharp, clear, and horrible: we all react instinctively to them with fear and loathing. Terrorist acts encourage us to see ourselves as good and the destroyers as evil; they provide us with an enemy for our world's troubles that is not ourselves. Of course, when we dig deeper and look at the roots of terrorism – things such as poverty, racism, market greed, the struggle for arable land and clean water – a whole different picture emerges of who is to blame. But our current popular analysis of acts of terror does not encourage this kind of thinking. Rather, it tells us that the terrorists are evil and that we, on the other hand, are basically good, or at least okay.

But there is another kind of destruction that is slower, deeper, and involves us more clearly, epitomized by climate change. Here it is more difficult to escape the root analysis that, as with terrorism, we are somehow involved – our understanding of who we are and how we should be acting is part of the world we see before us. More people, including children, die in a world being destroyed by climate change than from terrorist acts; the dying is slower and for the most part out of our sight. As such, it allows for our denial and indifference; in other words, for sins of omission. Unlike terrorists, we don't actually have to commit evil acts to participate in the evil of climate change: our very existence as well-off North Americans living the good consumer life assures that we are involved. Even when we try to hide our heads, saying that we don't yet have all the facts about climate change, we know we are rationalizing. We know we would rather focus on the terrorists and their blatant evil acts than on ourselves and our less obvious but more damaging acts of omission and indifference. More people and plant life die from our neglect and our overconsumption than from acts of terror.

So where does this leave us? Burdened with guilt but helpless? Sorry for what we are doing but not knowing what else to do? Yes, all of these things, but something else also comes to mind: repentance. The first step in behaving differently is admitting that we have not really and truly been asking God for a better world, not asking with our whole heart. Do we have the willingness to turn around, to change, to see ourselves and the world differently? This is an enormous question and would take a lifetime to answer, for we would have to live it, not just think it. But let us at least begin to think differently with the hope that we might also begin to live differently.

Throughout this book we have been asking the basic anthropological question: Who are we, and where do we fit in the scheme of things? It is time now to summarize our findings on this issue as they relate to action. Who are we? Where do we fit on planet Earth? How do we get there?

Who Are We?

The Earth Charter, the United Nations document that emerged from a decade-long, worldwide, cross-cultural conversation about common goals and shared values, suggests a picture of who we are. It is a statement of fundamental principles for building a just, sustainable, and peaceful global society. It includes sixteen major principles, the first one being the most important: "Respect Earth and life in all its diversity." Spelled out in more detail, it advises,

"Recognize that all beings are interdependent and every form of life has value regardless of its worth to human beings. Affirm faith in the inherent dignity of all human beings and in the intellectual, artistic, ethical, and spiritual potential of humanity." As I read these two sentences, they claim that all life, human and nonhuman, is valuable *as such*. There is here no separation of good and evil beings, nor the suggestion that some are worthwhile only because they are useful to others. The value of all life and the dignity of human beings comprise the first and most important principle in the Earth Charter. We have seen this same insistence on the intrinsic value of all life at the heart of the first creation story in the book of Genesis. What many remember from that story is that the text tells human beings to subdue and dominate the rest of creation, but while that command is given once, what is central to the story are the seven times God says, "It is good." After each act of creation – the sun, moon, stars, oceans, plants, animals, and finally human beings – God says, "It is good," ending with "It is very good." This is amazing – God appears to have an aesthetic appreciation for every scrap and tidbit of creation. God loves things for themselves, simply because they are. I think the philosopher Iris Murdoch was trying to express something similar when she wrote, "Love is the extremely difficult realization that something other than oneself is real. Love…is the discovery of reality." What the Earth Charter, Genesis, and Iris Murdoch are suggesting is that the dignity of human beings and the integrity of creation rest on seeing everyone and everything as valuable, on seeing everything as "good" as God does. We want to see some people as good and some as bad, some parts of creation as useful to us and other parts as less useful. We want to think in dualisms, not continuities. But this new picture of who we are says that God loves – this is, recognizes the value of – each and every piece of creation.

If we were to begin to think this way about ourselves and other creatures, what might the consequences be? Recently, I have been reading and teaching about some of the people we call saints – people such as the Dalai Lama, Jean Vanier, Dorothy Day, Nelson Mandela, and Bishop Tutu. One outstanding characteristic of these people is their universal love – love that seems to know no bounds. It does not stop with their own family, tribe, race, country, or even species. All life is honored just because it exists. John Woolman, the eighteenth-century

American Quaker and early abolitionist, describes his conversion experience in these terms. He writes that true religion consists in loving God the creator and willing justice and goodness to all people and even to "brute creatures," for he claims, "To say we love God as unseen, and at the same time exercise cruelty toward the least creature moving by [God's] life...is a contradiction in itself." In other words, one cannot love God without loving all that God has made – to do otherwise is a contradiction. His conversion to what he calls "true religion" consists in a deepening love of God that results in the increase of "universal love to my fellow-creatures."

Another example is that of the Holocaust rescuers. Studies done on these people reveal that they did not hide and save Jews because they had any special preference for Jews; rather, they did so simply because they felt that every human being has the right to live. Nor did they think that they did anything special: they thought that anyone in their position would have done the same thing. Of course, not everyone did. Not all people do see themselves and all other human beings, as well as creation itself, as valuable in and of themselves. Not everyone is truly a democrat when it comes to existence, as God is in Genesis.

The first movement we need to make in our commitment to think and act differently, then, is at the most fundamental level of who we think we are. The dignity of human beings and the integrity of creation rest, first of all, on our willingness to affirm the value of all life, not just our own or that of our own tribe or religion or country or class or species. Like the saints, we need to practice developing a universal love that knows no bounds, a love that becomes more and more inclusive. How far can it go? Jesus suggests that the stretch must include the enemy that is certainly an interesting proposal.

We have seen that human dignity and the integrity of creation rest on a sensibility that respects the other, whether that other in a human being or a nonhuman aspect of creation. The most basic stance that we must take in order to live differently in the world is appreciation for something other than ourselves and our own interests. Like God, we need to be able to look at the world and say, "It is good." Period.

Where Do We Fit?

But a second movement is equally important and is in fact part of the first: all individuals, whether human beings, tigers, mountains, dandelions, apples, slugs, atoms, or elephants, exist only because of other things. In contrast to the Western belief that human beings are individuals who live *on* the earth, we in fact live *in* it. Moreover, we do not decide *when* we want to form relationships with other people and the earth, for we are in the most intimate and complex relationships from before our birth until after our death. Hence, the appreciation for each and every creature in creation – for its particularity and specialness and difference – does not mean a doctrine of "individualism" such as we see in our present Western culture. Just the opposite: individuals exist only in networks of interrelationship and interdependence.

This is one of the most important shifts needed in our view of ourselves if we are to make some progress in living appropriately in our time of climate change. Let us consider two insights about who we are and where we fit that come from the centrality of interrelationship. First, interrelationship says that everything is on a continuum. Since we and everything else in the universe evolved together from the Big Bang billions of years ago, we are all related – we are distant cousins to the stars, to oak leaves, and to deer. This means that we are like and unlike these others in mysterious and interesting ways. We want to think that humans are totally different from animals and plants – by thinking in terms of dualisms, we can use and misuse others. But nature operates in terms of continuities. Thinking on a continuum has profound implications for both human dignity and the integrity of creation: it means that all humans are intimately related to one another, whether they be male or female, black or white or brown, straight or gay, rich or poor, able-bodied or physically challenged, Muslim or Christian. The centrality of interrelationship means that regardless of whether other human beings are like us or not, and whether we like them or not, they *are* our relatives, our closest relatives, our nuclear family, if you will. It means that all other creatures are our relatives as well, even if distant cousins. The continuum also means that some people are not good and others evil, some are right and others wrong, some are healthy and others sick – we exist together in various shades and gradations.

The edges are fuzzy that separate us from one another, and it is at these fuzzy edges that we often stretch out and touch each other.

It is with acceptance of the continuum of life that empathy develops. The saint's growing sense of universal love, love for all without exception, is not a momentary or mysterious insight. Rather, it develops in tandem with loving God; it is an extension of seeing God everywhere. As Woolman notes, one can't love God without loving all that God has made. The continuum of life is a reflection of the oneness of creation: we are called by God's love to universal love for all, a possibility that is based on the interdependence of all life. Hence, profound empathy with all forms of life is not a romantic fantasy; rather, it is based on the empirical evidence that *we are all interconnected and interdependent.*

The second insight about ourselves that emerges from the centrality of relationship concerns how the individual fits into the whole. It is easy for this to go wrong: for an individual to dominate the whole (as in totalitarianism) or for the whole to suffocate the individual (as in some fundamentalist cults). How can genuine individuality and radical relationship exist together? In the United States, the image of the melting pot unites all individuals into a somewhat bland similarity, whereas in Canada the mosaic allows individuals to be nicely differentiated but not very united. Ecological unity – the unity in which individuals exist in relationships and only in relationships – says that the whole is made up of the differences among individuals. In other words, individuality and unity depend on each other: an old-growth forest consists of millions of different plants and trees, insects and animals, each doing its job in order for the whole to be sustained. The whole is nothing but the healthy functioning of all the parts; hence, each and every part is valuable and necessary. Needless to say, this understanding of the whole and the parts has important implications for global economics as well as environmental standards. Justice and sustainability belong together: all of the parts must have the necessities of existence in order for the whole to survive. Justice to individuals – feeding people and sustaining plants – is not a choice that well-off people might make in a spirit of charity. Again, we see a correlation between ecology and saintly insight. The saint's universal love for all is a necessity: it is based on the simple but radical insight that others beside myself exist. What appears to be a radical stance – inclusive love for all beings – is at one level simply good planetary economics. Justice at the level of the basics needed for the health of individuals, human and nonhuman, is a necessity: the whole cannot be sustained apart from the health of the parts. This sobering fact calls for a radical change in the behavior of those of us presently taking more than our share and, hence, causing other people and life-forms to deteriorate for lack of nourishment.

If we accept this picture of interrelationship and interdependence – the picture that puts us on a continuum with all other creatures and that claims that the whole can be healthy only if the parts are fed – then we have a very different understanding of ourselves than that depicted in our consumer culture and its consequence, climate change. That culture basically says that each of us human individuals has the right to all we can legally acquire – in fact, we owe it to ourselves to have the very best.

Once again, the saints have a very different view. In his Christmas sermon in 1967, Martin Luther King wrote, "As nations and individuals, we are interde-pendent . . . all caught up in an inescapable network of mutuality, tied into a single garment of human destiny." We do not want to admit this truth, be-cause acknowledging it demands too much of us. And yet King's view is what contemporary science is also telling us about our world. It is not just Christian piety that claims relationships are central, as in the Great Commandment to love God and neighbor. As Iris Murdoch puts it, "Love . . . is the discovery of reality." What a wonderful assertion that is! It tells us that loving others is not a sentimental religious teaching; rather, it is an objective statement about our world and where we fit into it. The individualistic view of capitalist consumer-ism is outmoded: it came from the eighteenth century, which discovered the importance of the individual (and for that we are grateful) but did not realize that individuals exist only in relationship.

We are beginning to see, perhaps, how the postmodern ecological view of who we are overlaps in crucial ways with the most profound insights from religion. Christianity is one of many religions that teaches love, empathy, compassion, and indeed sacrifice for the well-being of others. Both religion and ecology recognize the basic interconnection and interdependence of all life. Therefore, love toward others is the way things should be because it is based on the way things are. We need each other. What climate change is telling us loud and clear is that the days of radical individualism and its consumer culture are over; it is time to return to the roots of religion and the roots of life: *we are, all of us, in this together*.

My Cherry Tree

The spring of 2000 was my last semester at Vanderbilt Divinity School after thirty years of teaching. I was selling my house and leaving my children and grandchildren, as well as my country and the job I loved, in order to join my partner in Vancouver, British Columbia. All of this change was disorienting and difficult, but most difficult of all was the death of my wonderful ninety-five-year-old mother. Moreover, I was ill with a then-undiagnosed immune disease that made me constantly tired and prone to respiratory infections. It was a challenging time for me personally, and I had many dark days.

But in the backyard of my house in Nashville was a cherry tree, a thing of rare beauty. I wrote about it in my journal:

March 19, 2000

My cherry tree is in full bloom and it is raining – a good, solid, penetrating rain that all the wonderful new buds need. It is Sunday; I am alone, still under the influence of an awful cold, but happy to have a quiet day.

I look at that cherry tree and feel "touched by God." It is a glorious thing and tells of God's glory. Only a cherry tree, *this* cherry tree, can tell of the particular aspect of divine beauty that it alone embodies. It "incarnates" God (as each and every creature and thing does), but in its own special way. There is only one Jesus of Nazareth, but there is also only one cherry tree in the backyard of 3703 Meadowbrook Avenue, Nashville, Tennessee. We are all touched by God, stamped and sealed with some aspect of God. What a different and wonderful way to understand reality: everything is itself as it tells of God. The delicate, irregular limbs and blossoms of this cherry tree, swaying in the breeze, shimmering in the sun: a hymn to God's glory in every twig.

God is not far off, but the near God, nearer to me than my own breath. God is in the cherry tree – oh, yes, especially in my cherry tree! Every time I look at that beautiful creature, I see it shouting out the glory of God. It would not be so beautiful, or so transparent to God, if it were not for the breeze. The filmy white blossoms on the irregular, fragile limbs move in the wind, in the breath of the Holy Spirit, calling me to deeper appreciation of its loveliness. It is saying, "See me speak of God, of a tiny bit of the divine glory, the bit that I can image." I *do* see and I thank you, my cherry tree, for telling me of God. I wish I might do the same. Can any of us be as fine an image of God as a cherry tree?

Few of us can be as fine an image of God as that cherry tree. But each of us is called to be, to do, what we can. During these past eight years since writing *Life Abundant*, I have come to believe that each of us reflects a unique aspect of God's glory – and it is this that we are called to become. We are not expected to save the world or become someone or something else: just ourselves. We become ourselves by acknowledging our radical dependence on God and on our planet: we find our place to be within God, and with and for other creatures. This is who we are. Freed from having to save ourselves or our world, we rest in God, whose body, the world, supports, delights, and calls for our help. To give this help, we have a place in which to stand: within God for the earth. And now we can get to work.

EXCERPTED FROM

Destroying Small Farmers

by Vandana Shiva

◆◆◆

From *Earth Democracy: Justice, Sustainability, and Peace,* Copyright © 2005, reproduced with permission of South End Press via Copyright Clearance Center.

Imperialistic globalization is emerging as the worst form of genocide in our times. It is turning the vast majority of the human race into threatened species. Small farmers and peasants – two thirds of humanity – are endangered species in the agenda of globalized, corporatized agriculture. Women – half of humanity – are also becoming a threatened species as subtle changes in societal arrangements introduce imbalance and the patriarchal biases of traditional cultures converge with patriarchal biases of global capitalism to render women disposable.

Lee Kyung Hae martyred himself while wearing a sign reading "WTO kills farmers" at the Cancun WTO ministerial to attract attention to one of the worst genocides of our times – the genocide of small farmers through the rules of globalization. His suicide is merely the most public of the tens of thousands of farmers who have been driven to kill themselves. Thirty thousand farmers have been killed by globalization policies in India over a decade. According to India's National Crime Bureau, 16,000 farmers in India committed suicide during 2004. During one six-month span in 2004, there were 1,860 suicides by farmers in the state of Andhra Pradesh alone.

Farmer suicide emerged in India in 1997. The policies of corporate-driven globalized and industrialized agriculture deliberately destroy small farms, dispossess small farmers, and render them disposable.

The Indian peasantry, the largest body of surviving small farmers in the world, today faces a crisis of extinction. Two-thirds of India makes its living from the land. In this country of a billion, that has farmed this land for more than 5,000 years, the earth is the most generous employer. However, as farming is delinked from the earth, the soil, the climate, and biodiversity, and is instead linked to global corporations and global markets, and as the generosity of the earth is replaced by the greed of corporations, the viability of small farmers and small farms is destroyed. Farmer suicides are the most tragic and dramatic symptom of the crisis of survival faced by Indian peasants.

Rapid increase in indebtedness is at the root of farmers' taking their lives. Debt is a reflection of a negative economy. Two factors have transformed agriculture from a positive economy into a negative economy for peasants – the rising costs of production and the falling prices of farm commodities. Both these factors are rooted in the policies of trade liberalization and corporate globalization.

In 1998, the World Bank's structural adjustment policies forced India to open up its seed sector to global corporations like Cargill, Monsanto, and Syngenta. The global corporations changed the input economy overnight. Farm-saved seeds were replaced by corporate seeds, which need fertilizers and pesticides and cannot be saved.

Corporations prevent seed savings through patents and by engineering seeds with nonrenewable traits. As a result, poor peasants have to buy new seeds for every planting season and what was a traditionally free resource, available by putting aside a small portion of the crop, becomes a commodity. This new expense increases poverty and leads to indebtedness.

The shift from saved seed to a corporate monopoly of the seed supply also represents a shift from biodiversity to monoculture in agriculture. The district of Warangal in Andhra Pradesh used to grow diverse legumes, millets, and oilseeds. Now the imposition of cotton monocultures has led to the loss of the wealth of farmer's breeding and nature's evolution.

Monocultures and uniformity increase the risks of crop failure, as diverse seeds adapted to diverse ecosystems are replaced by the rushed introduction of uniform and often untested seeds into the market. When Monsanto first introduced Bt cotton in India in 2002, the farmers lost 1 billion rupees due to crop failure. Instead of 1,500 kilos per acre as promised by the company, the harvest was as low as 200 kilos per acre. Instead of incomes of 10,000 rupees an acre, farmers ran into losses of 6,400 rupees an acre. In the state of

Bihar, when farm-saved corn seed was displaced by Monsanto's hybrid corn, the entire crop failed, creating 4 billion rupees in losses and increased poverty for desperately poor farmers. Poor peasants of the South cannot survive seed monopolies. The crisis of suicides shows how the survival of small farmers is incompatible with the seed monopolies of global corporations.

The second pressure Indian farmers are facing is the dramatic fall in prices of farm produce as a result of the WTO's free trade policies. The WTO rules for trade in agriculture are, in essence, rules for dumping. They have allowed wealthy countries to increase agribusiness subsidies while preventing other countries from protecting their farmers from artificially cheap imported produce. Four hundred billion dollars in subsidies combined with the forced removal of import restrictions is a ready-made-recipe for farmer suicide. Global wheat prices have dropped from $216 a ton in 1995 to $133 a ton in 2001; cotton prices from $98.2 a ton in 1995 to $49.1 a ton in 2001; soya bean prices from $273 a ton in 1995 to $178 a ton. This reduction is due not to a change in productivity, but to an increase in subsidies and an increase in market monopolies controlled by a handful of agribusiness corporations.

The US government pays $193 per ton to US soya farmers, which artificially lowers the price of soya on the world market. In India, due to the removal of quotas and the lowering of tariffs, cheap soya has destroyed the livelihoods of not only soya growers but also other farmers who grow oil-producing crops, including coconut, mustard, sesame, and groundnut.

Similarly, cotton producers in the US are given a subsidy of $4 billion annually. This has artificially brought down cotton prices, allowing the US to capture world markets previously accessible to poor African countries such as Burkina Faso, Benin, and Mali. This subsidy of $230 per acre in the US is untenable for the African farmers. African cotton farmers are losing $250 million every year. That is why small African countries walked out of the Cancun negotiations, leading to the collapse of the WTO ministerial.

The rigged prices of globally traded agriculture commodities steal from poor peasants of the South. A study carried out by the Research Foundation for

Science, Technology and Ecology (RFSTE) shows that due to falling farm prices, Indian peasants are losing $26 billion annually. This is a burden their poverty does not allow them to bear. As debts increase – unpayable from farm proceeds – farmers are compelled to sell a kidney or even commit suicide. Seed saving gives farmers life. Seed monopolies rob farmers of life.

The use of the word suicide obscures the social cause of this act. When viewed as the actions of individual farmers, these are suicides. When the 16,000 Indian farmer suicides in 2004 are viewed as the result of economic policy, this is not suicide; it is genocide.

The WTO rules on agriculture are a deliberately designed policy to destroy small farmers and shift agriculture into the hands of agribusiness. The trade rules inflict on our small farmers conditions of life calculated to bring about their physical destruction as sovereign producers. WTO policies are, hence, a genocide on small farmers.

It is necessary to stop this war against small farmers. It is necessary to rewrite the rules of trade in agriculture. It is necessary to change our paradigms of food production. Feeding humanity should not depend on the extinction of farmers and extinction of species. Another agriculture is possible and necessary – an agriculture that protects farmers' livelihoods, the earth, its biodiversity, and our public health.

EXCERPTED FROM

One War We Will Never Win

by Wendell Berry

◆◆◆

Henry David Thoreau wrote somewhere that hundreds are hacking at the branches for every one who is striking at the root. He meant this as a metaphor, but it applies literally to modern agriculture and to the science of modern agriculture. As it has become more and more industrialized, agriculture increasingly has been understood as an enterprise established upon the surface of the ground. Most people nowadays lack even a superficial knowledge of agriculture, and most who do know something about it are paying little or no attention to what is happening under the surface.

The scientists at The Land Institute in Salina, Kansas, on the contrary, are striking at the root. Their study of the root and the roots of our agricultural problems has produced a radical criticism, leading to a proposed solution that is radical.

Their criticism is made radical by one crucial choice – the adoption of the natural ecosystem as the first standard of agricultural performance, having priority over the standard of productivity and certainly over the delusional and dangerous industrial standard of "efficiency." That single change makes a momentous difference, one that is historical and cultural as well as scientific.

By the standard of the natural or the healthy ecosystem, we see as if suddenly the shortcomings, not only of industrial agriculture but of agriculture itself, insofar as agriculture has consisted of annual monocultures. To those of us who are devoted to agriculture in any of its historical forms, such criticism is inevitably painful. And yet we may see its justice and accept it, understanding how much is at stake. To others, who have founded their careers or their businesses precisely upon the shortcomings of agriculture as we now have it, their criticism will perhaps be even more painful, and no doubt they will resist with all the great power we know they have.

Even so, this is a criticism for which the time is ripe. A rational denial of its justice is no longer possible. There are many reasons for this, but the main one, I think, is the virtual meltdown of the old boundaries of specialist thought in agriculture – a meltdown that I hope foretells the same fate for the boundaries of all specialist thought.

The justifying assumptions of the industrial agriculture that we now have are based on a reductive science working within strictly bounded specializations. This agriculture, an agglomeration of specialties, appeared perfectly rational and salutary so long as it was assumable that efficiency and productivity were adequate standards, that husbandry was safely reducible to science, and fertility to chemistry, that organisms are merely machines, that agriculture is under no obligation to nature, that it has only agricultural results, and that it can be confidently based upon "cheap" fossil fuels.

The inventors of this agriculture assumed, in short, that the human will is sovereign in the universe, that the only laws are the laws of mechanics, and that the material world and its "natural resources" are without limit. These are the assumptions that, acknowledged or not, underlie the "war" by which we humans have undertaken to "conquer" nature, and which is the dominant myth of modern intellectual life.

In the days of human darkness and ignorance, now supposedly past, we found ways to acknowledge the sanctity of nature and to honor her as the common mother of all creatures, including ourselves. We conducted our relations with her by prayer, propitiation, skilled work, thrift, caution, and care. Our concern about that relationship produced the concepts of usufruct and stewardship. A few lines from the "Two Cantos of Mutability" that Edmund Spenser placed at the end of The Faerie Queene will suffice to give a sense of our ancient veneration:

> Then forth issewed (great goddesse) great dame Nature,
> With goodly port and gracious Majesty;
> Being far greater and more tall of stature
> Than any of the gods or Powers on hie . . .

This great Grandmother of all creatures bred
Great Nature, ever young yet full of eld,
Still moving, yet unmoved from her sted;
Unseen of any, yet of all beheld . . .

Thus, though he was a Christian, Spenser still saw fit at the end of the sixteenth century to present Nature as the genius of the sublunary world, a figure of the greatest majesty, mystery, and power, the source of all earthly life. He addressed her, in addition, as the supreme judge of all her creatures, ruling by standards that we would now call ecological:

Who Right to all dost deal indifferently.
Damning all Wrong and tortious Injurie,
Which any of thy creatures do to other
(Oppressing them with power, unequally)
Sith of them all thou art the equall mother,
And knittest each to each, as brother unto brother.

And then, at about Spenser's time or a little after, we set forth in our "war against nature" with the purpose of conquering her and wringing her powerful and lucrative secrets from her by various forms of "tortious Injurie." This we have thought of as our "enlightenment" and as "progress." But in the event this war, like most wars, has turned out to be a trickier business than we expected. We must now face two shocking surprises. The first surprise is that if we say and believe that we are at war with nature, then we are in the fullest sense at war: That is, we are both opposing and being opposed, and the costs to both sides are extremely high.

The second surprise is that we are not winning. On the evidence now available, we have to conclude that we are losing – and, moreover, that there was never a chance that we could win. Despite the immense power and violence that we have deployed against her, nature is handing us one defeat after another. Even in our most grievous offenses against her – as in the present epidemic of habitat destruction and species extinction – we are being defeated, for in the long run we can less afford the losses than nature can. And we have to look upon soil erosion and the spread of exotic diseases, weeds, and pests as nature's direct reprisals for our violations of her laws. Sometimes she seems terrifyingly serene in her triumphs over us, as when, simply by refusing to absorb our pollutants, she forces us to live in our mess.

Thus she has forced us to recognize that the context of American agriculture is not merely fields and farms or the free market or the economy, but it is also the polluted Mississippi River, the hypoxic zone in the Gulf of Mexico, all the small towns whose drinking water contains pesticides and nitrates, the pumped-down aquifers and the no-longer-flowing rivers, and all the lands that we have scalped, gouged, poisoned, or destroyed utterly for "cheap" fuels and raw materials.

Thus she is forcing us to believe what the great teachers and prophets have always told us and what the ecologists are telling us again: things are connected; the context of everything is everything else. By now, many of us know, and more are learning, that if you want to evaluate the agriculture of a region, you must begin not with a balance sheet, but with the local water. How continuously do the small streams flow? How clear is the water? How much sediment and how many pollutants are carried in the runoff? Are the ponds and creeks and rivers fit for swimming? Can you eat the fish?

We know, or we are learning, that from the questions about water we go naturally to questions about the soil. Is it staying in place? What is its water-holding capacity? Does it drain well? How much humus is in it? What of its biological health? How often and for how long is it exposed to the weather? How deep in it do the roots go?

Such are the questions that trouble and urge and inspire the scientists at The Land Institute, for everything depends upon the answers. The answers, as these scientists know, will reveal not only the state of the health of the landscape, but also the state of the culture of the people who inhabit and use the landscape. Is it a culture of respect, thrift, and seemly skills, or a culture of indifference and mechanical force? A culture of life, or a culture of death?

And beyond those questions are questions insistently practical and economic, questions of accounting. What is the worth, to us humans with our now insupportable health care industry, of ecological health? Is our health in any way separable from the health of our economic landscapes? Must not the health of water and soil be accounted an economic asset? Will not this greater health support, sustain, and in the long run cheapen the productivity of our farms?

If our war against nature destroys the health of water and soil, and thus inevitably the health of agriculture and our own health, and can only lead to our economic ruin, then we need to try another possibility. And there is only one: If we cannot establish an enduring or even a humanly bearable economy by our attempt to defeat nature, then we will have try living in harmony and cooperation with her.

By its adoption of the healthy ecosystem as the appropriate standard of agricultural performance, The Land Institute has rejected competition as the fundamental principle of economics, and therefore the applied sciences, and has replaced it with the principle of harmony. In doing so, it has placed its work within a lineage and tradition that predate both industrialism and modern science. The theme of a human and even an economic harmony with nature goes back many hundreds of years in the literary record. Its age in the prehistoric cultures can only be conjectured, but we may confidently assume that it is ancient, probably as old as the human race. In the early twentieth century this theme was applied explicitly to agriculture by writers such as F. H. King, Liberty Hyde Bailey, J. Russell Smith, Sir Albert Howard, and Aldo Leopold, Howard being the one who gave it the soundest and most elaborate scientific underpinning. This modern lineage was interrupted by the juggernaut of industrial agriculture following World War II. But, in the 1970s, when Wes Jackson began thinking about the Kansas prairie as a standard and model for Kansas farming, he took up the old theme at about where Howard had left it, doing so remarkably without previous knowledge of Howard.

And so, in espousing the principle and the goal of harmony, The Land Institute acquired an old and honorable ancestry. It acquired at the same time, in the same way, a working principle also old and honorable: that of art as imitation of nature. The initiating question was this: If, so to speak, you place a Kansas wheatfield beside a surviving patch of the native Kansas prairie, what is the difference?

Well, the primary difference, obvious to any observer, is that, whereas the wheatfield is a monoculture of annuals, the plant community of the prairie is highly diverse and perennial. There are many implications in that difference, not all of which are agricultural, but five of which are of immediate and urgent agricultural interest: The prairie's loss of soil to erosion is minimal; it is highly efficient in its ability to absorb, store, and use water; it makes the maximum use of every year's sunlight; it builds and preserves its own fertility; and it protects itself against pests and diseases.

The next question, the practical one, follows logically and naturally from the first: How might we contrive, let us say, a Kansas farm in imitation of a Kansas prairie, acquiring for agriculture the several ecological services of the prairie along with the economic benefit of a sufficient harvest of edible seeds? And so we come to the great project of The Land Institute.

I lack the technical proficiency to comment at much length on this work. I would like to end simply by saying how I believe the science now in practice at The Land Institute differs from the science of industrial agriculture.

We are living in an age of technological innovation. Our preoccupation with invention and novelty has begun, by this late day, to look rather absurd, especially in our strict avoidance of cost accounting. What invention, after all, has done more net good or given more net pleasure than soap? And who invented soap? It is all too easy, under the circumstances, to imagine a media publicist snatching at The Land Institute's project as "innovation on an epic scale" or "the next revolution in agriculture" or "the new scientific frontier."

But these scientists are contemplating no such thing. Their vision and their work do not arise from or lead to any mechanical or chemical breakthrough; they do not depend on any newly discovered fuel. The innovation they have in mind is something old under the sun: a better adaptation of the human organism to its natural habitat. They are not seeking to implement a technological revolution or a revolution of any kind. They are interested merely in improving our fundamental relationship to the earth, changing the kind of roots we put down and deepening the depth we put them down to. This is not revolutionary, because it is merely a part of a long job that we have not finished, that we have tried for a little while to finish in the wrong way, but one that we will never finish if we do it the right way. Harmony between our human economy and the natural world – local adaptation – is a perfection we will never finally achieve but must continuously try for. There is never a finality to it because it involves living creatures who change. The soil has living creatures in it. It has live roots in it, perennial roots if it is lucky. If it is the soil of the right kind of farm, it has a farm family growing out of it. The work of adaptation must go on because the world changes; our places change and we change; we change our places and our places change us. The science of adaptation, then, is unending. Anybody who undertakes to adapt agriculture to a place – or, in J. Russell Smith's words, to fit the farming to the farm – will never run out of problems or want for intellectual stimulation.

The science of The Land Institute promptly exposes the weakness of the annual thought of agricultural industrialism because it measures its work by the standard of the natural ecosystem, which gives pride of place to perennials. It exposes also the weakness of the top-down thought of technological innovation by proceeding from the roots up, and by aiming not at universality or uniformity, but at local adaptation. It would deepen the formal limits of agricultural practice many feet below the roots of the annual grain crops, but it would draw in the limits of concern to the local watershed, ecosystem, farm, and field. This is by definition a science of place, operating within a world of acknowledged limits – of space, time, energy, soil, water, and human intelligence. It is a science facing, in the most local and intimate terms, a world of daunting formal complexity and of an ultimately impenetrable mystery – exactly the world that the reductive sciences of industrial agriculture have sought to oversimplify and thus ignore. This new science, in its ancient quest, demands the acceptance of human ignorance as the ever-present starting point of human work, and it requires the use of all the intelligence we have.

——————— EXCERPTED FROM ———————

Down to Earth Economy
by David Korten

From "What Would Nature Do?" the Winter 2013 Issue of *YES!* magazine

With proper care and respect, Earth can provide a high quality of life for all people in perpetuity. Yet we devastate productive lands and waters for a quick profit, a few temporary jobs, or a one-time resource fix.

Our current expansion of tar sands oil extraction, deep-sea oil drilling, hydraulic fracturing natural gas extraction, and mountaintop-removal coal mining are but examples of this insanity. These highly profitable choices deepen our economic dependence on rapidly diminishing, nonrenewable fossil-energy reserves, disrupt the generative capacity of Earth's living systems, and accelerate climate disruption.

A global economy dependent on this nonsense is already failing and its ultimate collapse is only a matter of time. For a surprisingly long time, we humans have successfully maintained the illusion that we are outside of, superior to, and not subject to the rules of nature. We do so, however, at a huge cost, and payment is coming due.

To secure the health and happiness of future generations, we must embrace life as our defining value, recognize that competition is but a subtext of life's deeper narrative of cooperation, and restructure our institutions to conform to life's favored organizing principle of radically decentralized, localized decision making and self-organization. This work begins with recognizing what nature has learned about the organization of complex living systems over billions of years.

Our Original Instructions

Some indigenous people speak of the "original instructions." Chief Oren Lyons, of the Onondaga Nation, summarizes the rules in "Listening to Natural Law" in the anthology *Original Instructions*:

"Our instructions, and I'm talking about for all human beings, are to get along ... with [nature's] laws, and support them and work with them. We were told a long time ago that if you do that, life is endless. It just continues on and on in great cycles of regeneration ... If you want to tinker with that regeneration, if you want to interrupt it, that's your choice, but the results that come back can be very severe because ... the laws are absolute."

Modern neuroscience affirms that the human brain evolved to reward cooperation and service. In other words, nature has hard-wired the original instructions into our brain. Extreme individualism, greed, and violence are pathological and a sign of physical, developmental, cultural, and/or institutional system failure. Caring relationships are the foundation of healthy families, communities, and life itself.

We are living out the consequences of our collective human failure to adhere to the original instructions – the organizing principles of healthy living systems readily discernible through observation of nature at work. These are the principles by which we must rethink and reorganize human economies.

So how would nature design an economy? An economy is nothing more than a system for allocating resources to productive activity – presumably in support of life. In fact, nature is an economy, with material and information exchange, saving, investment, production, and consumption – all functions we associate with economic activity. Absent human intervention, as Lyons says, "It just continues on and on in great cycles of regeneration."

Nature surrounds us with expressions of the organizing principles that make possible life's exceptional resilience, capacity for adaptation, creative innovation, and vibrant abundance. Earth's biosphere and the human body are two magnificent examples.

The Economy of the Biosphere

Earth's exquisitely complex, resilient, and continuously evolving band of life – the biosphere – demonstrates on a grand scale the creative potential of the distributed intelligence of many trillions of individual self-organizing, choice-making living organisms. Acting in concert, they continuously regenerate soils, rivers, aquifers, fisheries, forests, and grasslands while maintaining climatic balance and the composition of the atmosphere to serve the needs of Earth's widely varied life forms. So long as humans honor the original instructions, the biosphere has an extraordinary capacity to optimize the capture, organization, and sharing of Earth's energy, water, and nutrients in support of life – including human life.

In nature, species and individuals earn a right to a share in the bounty of the whole as necessary to their sustenance through their contribution to the well-being of the whole. Over the long term, those that contribute prosper, and those that do not contribute expire. The interests of the whole are protected against rogue behavior by natural limits on the ability of any individual or species to monopolize resources beyond its own need to the exclusion of the needs of others.

Individuals and species may compete for territory and sexual dominance, but the amount of territory or number of mates nature allows an individual or species to claim is local, limited, and subject to continuous challenge. Until humans began to create the imperial civilizations characteristic of our most recent 5,000 years, the idea that any species, let alone a few individual members of a species, might claim control of all of Earth's living wealth to the exclusion of all others was beyond comprehension.

The Economy of the Body

The human body is a more intimate demonstration of the creative power of life's organizing principles. The individual human body comprises tens of trillions of individual living cells, each a decision-making entity with the ability to manage and maintain its own health and integrity under changing and often stressful circumstances. At the same time, each cell faithfully discharges its responsibility to serve the needs of the entire body on which its own health and integrity depend.

Working together, these cells create and maintain a self-organizing human organism with the potential to achieve extraordinary feats of physical grace and intellectual acuity far beyond the capability of any individual cell on its own.

Each decision-making, resource-sharing cell is integral to a larger whole of which no part or system can exist on its own. Together they create regulatory mechanisms internal to the whole that work to assure that no part asserts dominance over the others or monopolizes the body's stores of energy, nutrients, and water for its exclusive use. Resources are shared based on need.

All the while, the body's cells self-organize to fight off a vast variety of viruses, cancer cells, and harmful bacteria, adapt to changing temperatures and energy needs and variations in the body's food and water intake, heal damaged tissues, and collect and provide sensory data to our conscious mind essential to our conscious choice making.

Another of the many impressive expressions of the body's capacity to self-organize is the process by which our cells continuously regenerate while maintaining the body's integrity as a unified organism. The cells lining the human stomach have a turnover of only five days. Red blood cells are replaced every 120 days or so. The surface of the skin recycles every two weeks. The cells of the body are constantly reproducing, growing, and dying.

A Human Economy Based on Nature

If nature were in charge of creating an enduring human economy, she would surely apply the same principles she applies in natural systems. Her goal would be a global system of bioregional living economies that secure a healthy, happy, productive life for every person on the planet in symbiotic balance with the non-human systems on which we humans depend for breathable air, drinkable water, fertile soils, timber, fish, grasslands, and climate stability. Each bioregional economy would meet its own needs for energy, water, nutrients, and mineral resources through sustained local capture, circular flow, utilization, and repurposing. Decision making would be local and the system would organize from the bottom up. Diversity and redundancy would support local adaptation and resilience.

This should be our goal and vision. With the biosphere as our systems model, we would design our economic institutions and rules to align with nature's rules and organizing principles. We would replace GDP as the primary measure of economic performance with a new system of living system indicators that assess economic performance against the outcomes we actually want – healthy, happy people and healthy, resilient natural systems. These indicators might be based on Bhutan's Gross National Happiness Index. We would redirect the time, talent, and money we currently devote to growing GDP, material consumption, securities bubbles, and Wall Street bonuses to producing the outcomes we really want.

We would favor local, cooperative ownership and control. Organizing from the bottom up in support of bioregional self-reliance, our economic institutions would support local decision-making in response to local needs and opportunities. Cultural and biological diversity and sharing within and between local communities would support local and global resilience and facilitate life-serving system innovation.

The result would be an economy based on a love of life that honors the original instructions and conforms to the organizing principles of nature, real markets, and true democracy. The challenge is epic in its proportion and long overdue.

We are Earth's children; she is our mother. We must honor and care for her as she loves and cares for us. Together we can forge an integral partnership grounded in the learning and deep wisdom of her 3.8 billion-year experience in nurturing life's expanding capacities for intelligent self-organization, creative innovation, and self-reflective consciousness.

———————— EXCERPTED FROM ————————

Sacramentalism and Eco-feminism

by Larry L. Rasmussen

◆◆◆

From *Earth Community, Earth Ethics,* Copyright © 1996, reproduced with permission of MaryKnoll, New York: Orbis Books

The heart of the Orthodox contribution, to return to earlier discussion, is not a stewardship cosmology and ethic, however, or even its variant of partnership. It is a sacramentalist one. Sacramentalism as a model has gained new popularity in recent years. It is rooted in diverse and archaic cosmologies from pre-Augustinian Christianity around the Mediterranean to Celtic Christianity in more northerly climes. Orthodox communions from early centuries onward have consistently understood the sacraments as dramatizations of nature's transfiguration. Humans' high calling is as "priests of 'creation,'" referring the creation back to the creator in acts of liturgical doxology. In such praise humans act as representatives for the whole creation, setting loose, in Jurgen Moltmann's words, "the dumb tongue of nature" through human thanksgiving. "So when in the 'creation' psalms thanks are offered for *the* sun and the light, *for* the heavens and the fertility of the earth, the human being is thanking God, not merely on his own behalf, but also in the name of heaven and earth and all created beings in them." This is not meant homocentrically, Moltmann explains, because "everything that has breath" praises God, and "the heavens declare the glory of God" in their own way, even without human beings and apart from them. Nature's tongue isn't wholly dumb. Yet human beings are the singers of the cosmic song and the tellers of its tale in a special way; we can represent creation and give voice to it in a cosmic liturgy of praise and transfiguration. We are mediators, then, but not the center. We intercede for the Community of Life and speak on its behalf before God. We are the *imago mundi* (image of the world) who, as also *imago dei* (image of God), voice God to creation and creation to God. Such is the Orthodox notion (and the Hasidic Jewish notion as well).

Sometimes called "panentheism," sacramentalism recognizes and celebrates the divine ine, with, and under all nature, ourselves included. The creaturely is not identified as God, however. (This is pantheism, not panentheism.) Nature and the world are thus not of themselves divine and are not worshiped. Rather, the infinite is a dimension of the finite; the transcendent is immanent; the sacred is the ordinary in another, numinous light – without any one of these terms exhausting the other. Sacraments themselves are symbols and signs that participate in the very Reality to which they point, but they are not themselves worshiped. To identify something earthly as holy and sacred is not to say it is God. Rather, it is *of* God; God is present in its presence.

The natural response to the sacramental in our midst is wonder, awe, amazement, fascination, astonishment, curiosity, and surprise. It is also a sense of being very small amidst a grand Reality. At times it is a sense of being unworthy in the face of holy wonder and the awareness that the pulse of God's energy flows through me as it does through all life. In any event, the moral posture is certainly not mastery, control, and abstracted distance. Rather, it is presence, relationship, and the care and respect due the sacred. The sacramental "emphasizes the tender elements of the world," biologist Charles Birch says, and the "spiritual unity that gives the physical its meaning." This in turn nurtures "a humbling sense that all creatures are fellow creatures and that human responsibility extends infinitely to the whole of creation." Species humility and responsibility are the proper foci of earth ethics.

At Canberra, sacramentalism was endorsed not only by the Orthodox but even more powerfully by indigenous peoples. They burst forth upon the assembly's stage, often literally dancing, and demonstrated once again in their words and actions that the primal vision of peoples of the land is invariably sacramentalist. The entire cosmos is the sacred community, and life should be lived with the respect and treatment due the sacred – it's that simple and profound.

In both the Kuala Lumpur document and the Section I report of Canberra the roll call of teachers of "a deepened understanding of creation" included indigenous peoples. Not least among the lessons learned is the easy flow of the everyday into the sacred and the refusal to desacralize any arena of life. For native peoples generally everything in nature represents transcendent power and order, and all the activities of culture – farming, hunting, cooking, eating, householding – are sacramental. They are visible signs of divine power and presence amidst daily practices.

This same lesson, now applied to environmental policy, is given voice by Wes Jackson of the Land Institute in Salina, Kansas. Jackson objects to setting aside pristine wilderness while at the same time treating the rest of the land profanely (as a commodity and utilitarian vehicle of profit only):

I do not object to either saints or wilderness, but to keep the holy isolated from the rest, to treat our wilderness as a saint and to treat Kansas or East Saint Louis otherwise, is a form of schizophrenia. Either all the earth is holy, or it is not. Either every square foot deserves our respect, or none of it does . . . The wilderness of the Sahara will disappear unless little pieces of non-wilderness become intensely loved by lots of people. In other words, Harlem and East Saint Louis and Iowa and Kansas and the rest of the world where wilderness has been destroyed will have to be loved by enough of us, or wilderness is doomed.

As with the steward model, sacramentalism is not without its distortions and moral corruption. These are rooted in the picture of society present in many sacramentalist cosmologies. The age-old sacramentalist assumption is that a harmony of social and natural interests exists somewhere just below the surface and that a soft, nurturing process will bring this precious flower to bloom. Sacramentalism's metaphors for society as well as church are thus typically "organic." (Feudalism lives on!) Or, in the Orthodox version, "symphonic." But metaphors of organisms and symphonies don't expose the unequal and corrupted power relations of life among human beings, nor between humans and other creatures. They mask the fact that struggle and conflict so often are the status quo. "Healing," rather than fundamentally reordered ecosocial relationships, thus becomes the "cure" for "sin" in much sacramentalist theology, whether of established religious traditions or quasi-religious movements

(New Age rituals, for example). It is as though earth's basic problem were illness or bad tuning, not injustice or unequal and corrupted power.

John Haught says it differently. Nature, ourselves included, is not yet what it could be, nor fully revelatory of God. Its beauty is only partial, and its fulfillment remains in the form of promise. Any orientation that is only a mystical affirmation of what is, no matter how deep the experience, falls short; and with that it fails to recognize the long and painful distance between the present state of affairs and a better earth. The sacramentalist stance, lost in wonder at what is, can easily incline to such mystical affirmation and its resident shortcomings. It can glory in what is, to the neglect of what ought to be. When it does, it sacrifices its inherent moral and ethical power.

Here again indigenous peoples brought an important contribution to Canberra. They, together with others of the poor and women from all social ranks, know that sacramental spirituality is empty as an ethic if there is no commitment to the political agenda, and that political commitment entails organized action along paths of hard resistance as well as soft ones of gentle persuasion. Healing is needed, and is itself a powerful metaphor, but so is organized force on the way to reconciliation. To make marginated peoples truly angry, steal their spirituality without joining their political struggle.

Eco-feminism has not yet found its full voice in the WCC. But it may eventually make the greatest contribution and impact of all because its potential constituency is huge and because earth consciousness and women's consciousness often go together. Furthermore, eco-feminism discloses a profound understanding of the specific social and sociopsychological causes of earth's suffering. In its Christian incarnation, eco-feminism represents the twin streams of sacramentalism and liberationism flowing together. In Canberra this development was eloquently presented in the plenary session on the council's Decade of the Churches in Solidarity with Women. The pattern of presentation was women from around the world – South Africa, Russia, Palestine, Sweden, Egypt, Nicaragua – telling their stories of women's struggles in their communities and of God's presence with them in adversity. As each finished her story, she took a branch of green and placed it in a large wooden structure resting at the rear of the stage. The structure's dead wood quietly greened as the stories of suffering and hope, death and life, punctuated the session. When all the tales were told, the women together hoisted the heavy beams upright. It was a cross become the tree of life.

The greening of the cross, it turns out, is an ancient Armenian Orthodox tradition, recalling early Christian symbolism. Here the ancient sacramentalist vision of earth nicely served many women's experiences, but only as merged with their struggles for justice, peace, and creation's integrity. Ironically, the general Orthodox intransigence on women and ministry has concealed the extraordinary parallels between Orthodox spirituality and feminist spirituality, just as it has made it so difficult to recognize common ground in creation theology. Yet there is no doubt that women in the ecumenical movement will continue to voice the sacramentalist possibilities in cosmology and ethics, even when one of their sharpest criticisms of the Orthodox, Roman Catholic, and Anglican communions is that the sacramentalism of these traditions has served to reinforce powerful linkages of patriarchy, social domination, and environmental degradation.

Both indigenous peoples and feminists, then, marry sacramental and liberation postures. They insist that our striving is amidst and about ordinary, daily activities and that the preciousness of life is found here or it is found nowhere. Either the good and the holy are at the center of what we do in our lives, or else we must change the ways of living that segregate the good and holy from the everyday. Part of this involves our very way of thinking and imagining, since, as noted, what people define and imagine as real is real in its consequences. The conclusion is that the symbols of religious traditions must be scrutinized to see whether in fact they are lodged firmly on the side of life and its fulfillment, work against such liberation and fulfillment, or are blandly oblivious to daily affairs. Process theology, to continue the survey of sacramentalist possibilities, has only recently been lofted into ecumenical orbit. But it will be influential for years to come. Not least, its earth-embracing and dynamic cosmology is highly compatible with the newly influential currents of science that in turn find affinities with sacramentalist cosmology. (More on

But it will be influential for years to come. Not least, its earth-embracing and dynamic cosmology is highly compatible with the newly influential currents of science that in turn find affinities with sacramentalist cosmology. (More on this shortly.) Perhaps the best pre-Canberra discussion of earth ethics emerged from the process theology camp – Liberating Life: Contemporary Approaches to Ecological Theology. It included a report written for the Canberra assembly. The drawback of process work is that it has been slow to link its metaphysics to sophisticated social analysis. It thus misses what many in the WCC have come to believe is a vital part of theological method itself. The aforementioned volume, however, was undertaken explicitly to bring both to bear on "justice and sustainability." Insofar as it succeeds, it does so in the persuasive way of process theology. Which is to say that God so gathers in all things that their condition affects God. When humans and other creatures are violated and their lives diminished, God's glory is dimmed and dishonored. Conversely, when life is fuller and richer, God's glory is enhanced. Justice, sustainability, and the well-being of creation are therefore intrinsically, not extrinsically, related to God and the divine life. This is the core teaching of process theology and ethics.

Song of Thanksgiving • "Micah 6:8"

God has shown you, O peo-ple what is good; And what does the Lord re-quire of you? But to do just-ice and to love mer-cy, and to walk hum-bly with your God.

In a Culture of Silence and Job Insecurity

My wife and I took Dorothee Soelle,a German theologian, out for a meal when she visited the Twin Cities for a presentation at Augsburg College. We had a wonderful conversation and she was gracious to answer our questions about Germany during WW II. She was now a professor at Union Theological Seminary in New York City. It was inspiring to sense her passion for non-violence and world peace.

Since my wife and I had recently taken our daughters on a trip through Europe and had visited the Dacau concentration camp museum, I asked her if the people in Dacau knew about what was happening at the camp just a stone's throw from the city limits. Her answer was short and poignant. "They didn't want to know."

I wonder if that is the reason why so many today are reluctant to be confronted with some of the realities of unjust structures and systems that cause the great divide between the poor and non-poor in our world. Articles in this chapter will suggest ways we have silenced the voices of those who cry out for justice and freedom from hunger because *we don't want to know.* Does not our silence plus our fear of changing our minds make us complicit in maintaining the status quo?

Silence is not on the list of Gandhi's seven deadly sins. Maybe it should be. It causes more suffering than any other human failing .Yet seldom is it lifted up in today's pulpits or included In liturgies and confession of sin.

Included in this chapter is an outstanding sermon preached by Walter Brueggemann at the Festival of Homiletics in Minneapolis in 2011. After pointing out what Jeremiah was not allowed to utter in public in Jerusalem, he lists things preachers today cannot utter from the pulpit. Congregations have a lot to do with the silence from the pulpits. Jesus continuously had to confront resistance to the prophetic word. He said to his audience, "You kill the prophets and then polish their graves." Who dares preach on that text? Does the call into pastoral ministry include a call to be a whistleblower when it is needed?

George S. Johnson

———— EXCERPTED FROM ————

Appearing Before the Authorities

by Walter Brueggemann

———— ◆◆◆ ————

I want to think with you, dear sisters and brothers who preach, about the words you dare not speak from the pulpit, and what that "not daring" does to our hearts. Because when you preach, every time you do it, it is done as you "appear before the authorities."

I.

As some of you well know, George Carlin has a list of seven words you cannot say on television. He is as hilarious about the list as he is obscene. All of his prohibited words refer to bodily or sexual functions, the kind that cause junior high boys to giggle and blush. Carlin has a debate with himself about his list, because some of the words are hyphenated and so reiterate others on the list. But when he gets the list set, he can recite it in two nano-seconds.

The reason Carlin cannot say these words on television is because the censors will not allow it, the censors being the guardians of establishment power to keep things nice and therefore safe. He cannot say these words because they remind us of bodily functions that we cannot control. We do not speak them because they remind us that we are bodies, and therefore frail and therefore mortal and therefore about to die. Arnold Toynbee has said that death is "un-American," an affront to everyone's right to life, liberty, and the pursuit of happiness. The censors prefer matters nice and safe. They prefer that people like us talk of spiritual matters and not such topics as the body or the body politic or the economics of the body politic. The list censored and disapproved concerns the smelly and unsavory, so that we do better to deny the body.

II.

Well, George Carlin is not the first to have such a list of things that could not be said in public. Already Jeremiah, in his frightened, jeopardized world, knew such a list of things not to be uttered in public in Jerusalem:

> He could not say that the divine promise to David was sheer ideology;

> He could not say that God's perpetual presence in the Jerusalem temple was a priestly hoax;

> He could not say that being chosen did not give Israel a pass on moral responsibility;

> He could not say that Nebuchadnezzar, the hated superpower, was a tool of God to bring it all down;

> He could not say that the Jerusalem network was under judgment and would not be spared or sustained;

> He could not say that God's eternity did not extend to the little human accomplishments that they loved too much with all their hearts. (Is that seven?)

He could not say these things, because he knew that saying them was inflammatory:

> I am now making my words in your mouth a fire,

> And this people wood, and the fire shall devour them.

> I am going to bring upon you a nation from far away,

> O house of Israel, says the Lord (Jeremiah 5:14-15).

He knew he had to say these words because there were so many false words that needed to be countered in Jerusalem:

> Is not my word like fire, says the Lord, and like a hammer that breaks a rock in pieces? See, therefore, I am against the prophets, says the Lord, who steal my words from one another [more than plagiarism!] See, I am against the prophets, says the Lord, who use their own tongues and say, "Says the Lord." See, I am against those who prophesy lying dreams, says the Lord, and who tell them,

and who lead my people astray by their lies and their recklessness, when I did not send them or appoint them; so they do not profit this people at all, says the Lord.

(Jeremiah 23:29-32)

It was too dangerous to say what had to be said. And he did not say it. And it tore his guts apart. He risked saying it, but at the last minute he did not. And then he gets sick for not saying it:

> For whenever I speak, I must cry out,
>
> I must shout, "Violence and destruction!"
>
> For the word of the Lord has become for me
>
> a reproach and derision all day long.
>
> If I say, "I will not mention him,
>
> or speak anymore in his name,"
>
> then within me there is something like a burning fire
>
> shut up in my bones;
>
> I am weary with holding it in, and I cannot (Jeremiah 20:8-9).

So finally he said it! He said it over and over! He was brought to trial for his words, because the "spiritual leaders," the priests, wanted him silenced for saying the prohibited words on television, uttering the unutterable. In that trial he escaped by the skin of his teeth, because of some tough old witnesses who supporter him and who stood by him (26:17-19, 24). But he was regarded as a traitor who "weakened the hand of the soldiers," that is, who "undermined the war effort" (38:4). It is no wonder that he cries out to God in pain and anguish: "You have seduced me." You have given me an impossible assignment. He prays in honesty for vengeance against his adversaries. Because he had to say what he dared not say. And all hell came upon him.

III.

Well, George Carlin is not the last one to have such a list of the unsayable. There is, for example, you, you preachers who pray and brood and study and know. And then mostly must retreat to the "nice" of denial. Or you preach your heart out; and the vestry or the session doubles the pain like a hammer, or a major donor stomps out in indignation. Or worse, you preach your heart out and the most you get is that someone reminds you that you forgot the Lord's Prayer...for God's sake! I am led to this thought by the many preachers who have told me, almost in passing as though it were normal, that they could not speak about the Iraq war in their church, or about immigration or about global warming. And I am, moreover, a member of a theological faculty that was not permitted to say something at the outset about the war because the institutional risks were too great! And my own daring preacher, on the Fourth of July Sunday, had a person walk out in a huff because he said something about US arrogance and privilege.

I have been thinking about a list of things, give or take, that a preacher cannot say. Or if said, is dismissed as a gal who never met a payroll:

> Some could not say that the war is stupid and we are expending our precious young on the folly of the National Security State;

> Some could not say that present day capitalism has failed in its excessive greed that devours the poor and now reaches into the middle class;

> Some could not say that the oil-spill is simply the token of Western technological hubris at its extreme;

> Some could not say that we have forfeited our democracy to a secret government that runs over the Constitution and shreds civil rights in order to defend the intemperate wealth of the few;

> Some could not say that the frantic rush to get a child to the next soccer practice and the next dance class is membership in the rat race that cannot be won;

CHAPTER TWENTY-SIX

Some cannot say that the technological fixes violate the neighborly fruitfulness of the creation;

Some cannot say that the immigrants are indeed sisters and brothers who come under the welcome sign;

Some cannot say that our penchant for violence is toxic for the heart of our common life;

Some cannot say that the experiment in greedy entitlement has failed, and we will have to find other ways to maintain our hummers. (Is that seven?)

Some cannot say things because the cocoon of denial claims us all, and we would rather not risk so much. Well, maybe this is not quite your list. You can adjust. All I know is that there is a lot not being said; and we all know why.

This is not a sermon about being prophetic or taking on the world or blowing the lid off the church in one loud binge. This is a pastoral reflection on what it does for us, alongside Jeremiah and George Carlin, to be silenced in ways that shrink and cramp our humanness. Such coerced silence is not benign. It makes us inordinately weary. It drives us to despair...or cynicism. It compels us to denial. It reduces us to managers and therapists and cheer leaders and entertainers and program directors. And all the while the word grinds at our guts, because we know better. What we cannot say is that the body is fragile and smelly and cannot be made otherwise. What we cannot say is that the body politic now has a smell of death about it. What we cannot say is that evangelical faith is about bodily existence in the neighborhood, bodily since the creator called it "good," bodily since God freed the slaves from their pained bodily bondage, bodily since, as we say in the creed:

For us and for our salvation

he came down from heaven,

was incarnate of the Holy Spirit and the Virgin Mary,

and became truly human.

Or as we know it more anciently, "and was made man!" Became human, fragile, vulnerable, smelly, about to die. Became man! When about to die, as "man" or as body politic or as us, then Carlin's "piss" or "fart" are not really objectionable or interesting, because such smelly regularity beyond our control belongs inescapably to our short-term creatureliness.

IV.

Well, I thought it was worth reflecting on the fix we are in. The preacher in our society is given words that cannot be uttered. And if not uttered, the preacher grows cold, plays it safe, and perhaps needs to be loved more. And as I pondered this, I am aware that not once in my life, in my tenured life, have I been in the dangerous place that many of you occupy every week. You are like the apostles in the book of Acts, sure to be called before the authorities, and examined for your testimony, to see whether your words are safe and acceptable, or as dangerous and inflammatory as those of George Carlin or Jeremiah. The authorities sit before you and conduct your trial.

But then I came to this other text given me by C. S. Song, the great Korean theologian, who has indeed been before the authorities. In Luke 21, Jesus anticipates the coming debacle. You wonder how he knew about our coming debacle: "Not one stone will be left on another." It sounds like an oil spill or an economic melt-down. They asked him, "When?" He said, "I do not know." But then he says, before whatever time line in which it will occur:

> But before all this occurs, they will arrest you and persecute you;
> they will hand you over to synagogues and prisons, and you will be
> brought before kings and governors because of my name. This will
> give you an opportunity to testify (vv. 12-13).

They will ask you to speak up. They will expect you to utter your truth. They will watch your words to see if any of your words are like those of George's list or the list of Jeremiah. Then I thought, even if Luke is anticipating the Roman destruction of the Jerusalem temple, he is making connections to our time and place and danger. Now like then, the authorities are bewildered.

They want some guidance or assurance for a dangerous time; but they do not want to do to the bed-rock faith of these witnesses. So what do you have to tell us, Ms. Apostle, of the truth and nothing but? What have you got for us, Reverend?

And then Jesus says – or Luke says, or the Jesus Seminar says – these most stunning words:

> **So make up your minds not to prepare your defense in advance; for I will give you words and a wisdom that none of your opponents will be able to withstand or contradict. (vv. 14-15)**

Don't work it out logically and carefully or anxiously or with too much calculated caution, because that venue presses you beyond that. Trust the spirit of Jesus, he says, and receive wisdom that will admit you to new freedom. Imagine, on hard issues of the day before the Roman authorities, Jesus will be close at hand with a word. What he says is, "I will give you mouth."

And then he says two things to his followers:

-First, this truth-telling will get you into a lot of trouble:

You will be betrayed even by parents and brothers, by relatives and friends; and they will put some of you to death. You will be hated by all because of my name (vv. 16-17).

-Second, you will be safe:

But not a hair of your head will perish. By your endurance you will gain your souls (vv. 18-19).

Big trouble . . . and you will gain your soul, your identifiable center of vitality. You will get yourself back in the process of telling the truth before the authorities. You likely will find allies among tough old witnesses. But for sure, you will have yourself in all your vocational freedom.

I do not give you advice. I give you only a text. I do know about the risk of the church budget, and about the risk to one's family (I am a PK!), and about being without tenure, and the danger to one's pension and medical coverage. Of course!

But I also know about the diminishment of self through coerced silence and the loss of freedom and courage and vitality and energy and joy. I crave for you an edge of freedom that will let you witness to the full truth that has entrusted to you. Jeremiah discovered, through his much anguish, that he had allies as he ran risks, that he was kept safe in ways he could not have imagined. He could not know that before he bore witness. I have thought about what it means for us to walk close to the gospel. There is no doubt that greater freedom for the word is needed among us. It is needed by those who need to hear. But it is also needed by those who are called to speak. This is a gospel time. This is a time when the old reliances have failed, when autonomous, arrogant ways of life, in many manifestations, have been shown to be empty. This is a moment to line out an alternative. We have that alternative and it must be uttered for the sake of the body politic.

The utterance is not only for the sake of the body politic. It is also for the sake of our souls. Imagine what it will be like to break out of fatigue and despair and resignation and gentle denial to be one's self with the truth of the gospel. You do not need to be Jim Forbes, and I do not need to be Tony Campollo with their bravado. We need only be ourselves with the word entrusted to us, with God's word given us, with news that sets us free from heart burn or ulcers or anger with Jeremiah.

The word we will be given in gospel freedom is not a nice word about a nice world. It is rather a true word about our bodies and our body politic, the bodies infused with God's truth, but nonetheless temporary, passing, fragile, mortal.

All of us in his gathering are in it together. So I thought, let us together hold this moment precious. Let us think about the truth entrusted to us, the truth of God, God from God, true God from true God, the word that "was made man," suffered and died, and was indeed raised to new life and new freedom.

It is not a wonder that Jeremiah, at the end of his struggle with speech and silence, finally, in verse 13, breaks out in doxology:

> Sing to the Lord;
>
> Praise the Lord!
>
> For he has delivered the life of the needy
>
> from the hands of evil doers (20:13).

He comes to joy by breaking his silence. I do not urge you to say more than you can say. I do not urge you to run risks in dangerous places that you cannot run. I do not lay a guilt trip on you. Rather I invite you to take stock of the truth you have been given, and to ponder what it would be like for you to move to greater freedom. Finger your head; check your hairs. Imagine them all counted and guarded and kept safe. Imagine the way the hairs on your head are safe and the way in which the freedom for your mouth is connected to the safety of our hairs. And then imagine, as your silence is broken, "Free at last, free at last, thank God almighty, free at last!"

EXCERPTED FROM

Yesterday's Victims Forgotten
by Elie Wiesel

◆◆◆

From "Yesterday's Victims Forgotten Struggle" by Elie Wiesel

A letter arrives from Buenos Aires. A woman whose son is numbered among those who have disappeared asks me, "Is there really nothing to be done?" Have I knocked on all the doors, mobilized all my friends in high places? I'm afraid so, I reply. I've done everything I can. Unfortunately, my all is not enough.

I met her last year in a secret meeting place somewhere in the Argentine capital. I had come to Buenos Aires in an attempt to free a Jewish publisher being held under house arrest. In the course of that mission I discovered still more persecutions, more forms of oppression.

There are now many hundreds of mothers and wives in Argentina whose husbands and children have been taken away by members of the present regime's secret police. Men and women have disappeared without a trace. The government advises the relatives left behind to consider the victims dead . . . "for practical and humanitarian reasons."

These men and women were never tried and condemned before a public tribunal. Nothing is known of their agony, and nothing will be known of their end. Not so long ago, in the time of Europe's great darkness, these clandestine disappearances in the night had a name that made people tremble: *Nacht und Nebel* – night and fog!

Will the past never cease to haunt us?

A chilling account comes to me from Bangkok. A friend tells me of the fate of the Cambodian refugees whom we had visited shortly before this spring. They are now being moved from camp to camp; everyone wants them out of the way. This human burden is more than we can bear; if only these people would just disappear so that we could sleep in peace again!

In the meantime, hunger continues to ravage the emaciated bodies of starving children, while poverty and wretchedness darken their horizon.

Last February I asked myself the question, Can an entire people die? Now I would formulate it differently, Will we stand by and let them die? We spend billions of dollars on nuclear arms and billions more on cosmetics; we kneel before the sacred shrine of all-holy Oil and make fine-sounding speeches for the entertainment and delectation of the peanut gallery in the United Nations. We sink into hyprocrisy and indifference. And all the while in the poor nations the shadow of poverty lengthens from day to day. And the shadow of fear as well.

I would never have imagined that I should one day feel compelled to vent my rage against the present as I have against the past.

From Paris, a series of images: Starving men and women somewhere in Uganda. Bodies so emaciated that they are almost transparent. Shriveled children expiring in the arms of mothers who will die in their turn only a few hours later. "You have to shout; you have to raise a cry of outrage," says my friend who sent me the documents.

And so I shout. I bellow. I alert my journalist comrades. I call up senators and high-level functionaries. We haven't the right to keep silent! An entire people – once again – is stepping down into darkness before our very eyes; if we do nothing to save them, we shall have been accomplices in their deaths!

But – and I am ashamed to say it – people are tired. Tired of fighting for yet another cause. Tired of throwing themselves into yet another struggle. Biafra, Bangladesh, the Congo, Cambodia, and now Uganda. There is a limit to human comprehension! A time comes when people avert their eyes out of an instinct for self-preservation.

Nevertheless, we have no choice. Indifference is a crime. Not to choose is in itself a choice, as Camus said. To do nothing is to let death do everything.

As for myself, I have seen too much in my life to stand by and watch. It may not be in our power to evade our own suffering, but it is within our power to give our suffering some meaning. And it is in combating the suffering of others that we find meaning in our own.

If I struggle for today's victims, it is because yesterday's were forgotten, abandoned, handed over to the enemy without protest. It is my recollection of the past that gives me the strength to do whatever I can to save our common future.

That future is in danger. One has to belong to a traumatized generation such as mine in order to be aware of just how much danger. Too much hate is building up in too many places. Too many fingers are poised over the nuclear button. Don't tell me that the unthinkable is impossible. Today more than yesterday – and even because of yesterday – the unthinkable and the impossible swiftly become realities.

I ask myself one final question. Have we who survived the Holocaust done so only to see our witness fall upon deaf ears?

EXCERPTED FROM

Letter from a Birmingham Jail

by *Martin Luther King, Jr.*

◆◆◆

16 April 1963
My Dear Fellow Clergymen:

I think I should indicate why I am here in Birmingham, since you have been influenced by the view which argues against "outsiders coming in." Basically, I am in Birmingham because injustice is here. Just as the prophets of the eighth century B.C. left their villages and carried their "thus saith the Lord" far beyond the boundaries of their home towns, and just as the Apostle Paul left his village of Tarsus and carried the gospel of Jesus Christ to the far corners of the Greco Roman world, so am I compelled to carry the gospel of freedom beyond my own home town. Like Paul, I must constantly respond to the Macedonian call for aid.

Moreover, I am cognizant of the interrelatedness of all communities and states. I cannot sit idly by in Atlanta and not be concerned about what happens in Birmingham. Injustice anywhere is a threat to justice everywhere. We are caught in an inescapable network of mutuality, tied in a single garment of destiny. Whatever affects one directly, affects all indirectly. Never again can we afford to live with the narrow, provincial "outside agitator" idea. Anyone who lives inside the United States can never be considered an outsider anywhere within its bounds.

You deplore the demonstrations taking place in Birmingham. But your statement, I am sorry to say, fails to express a similar concern for the conditions that brought about the demonstrations. I am sure that none of you would want to rest content with the superficial kind of social analysis that deals merely with effects and does not grapple with underlying causes. It is unfortunate that demonstrations are taking place in Birmingham, but it is even more unfortunate that the city's white power structure left the Negro community with no alternative.

You may well ask: "Why direct action? Why sit ins, marches and so forth? Isn't negotiation a better path?" You are quite right in calling for negotiation. Indeed, this is the very purpose of direct action. Nonviolent direct action seeks to create such a crisis and foster such a tension that a community which has constantly refused to negotiate is forced to confront the issue. It seeks so to dramatize the issue that it can no longer be ignored. My citing the creation of tension as part of the work of the nonviolent resister may sound rather shocking. But I must confess that I am not afraid of the word "tension." I have earnestly opposed violent tension, but there is a type of constructive, nonviolent tension which is necessary for growth. Just as Socrates felt that it was necessary to create a tension in the mind so that individuals could rise from the bondage of myths and half truths to the unfettered realm of creative analysis and objective appraisal, so must we see the need for nonviolent gadflies to create the kind of tension in society that will help men rise from the dark depths of prejudice and racism to the majestic heights of under-standing and brotherhood. The purpose of our direct action program is to create a situation so crisis packed that it will inevitably open the door to negotiation. I therefore concur with you in your call for negotiation. Too long has our beloved Southland been bogged down in a tragic effort to live in monologue rather than dialogue.

One of the basic points in your statement is that the action that I and my as-sociates have taken in Birmingham is untimely. Some have asked: "Why didn't you give the new city administration time to act?" My friends, I must say to you that we have not made a single gain in civil rights without determined legal and nonviolent pressure. Lamentably, it is an historical fact that privi-leged groups seldom give up their privileges voluntarily. Individuals may see the moral light and voluntarily give up their unjust posture; but, as Reinhold Niebuhr has reminded us, groups tend to be more immoral than individuals.

We know through painful experience that freedom is never voluntarily given by the oppressor; it must be demanded by the oppressed. Frankly, I have yet to engage in a direct action campaign that was "well timed" in the view of those who have not suffered unduly from the disease of segregation. For years now I have heard the word "Wait!" It rings in the ear of every Negro with piercing familiarity. This "Wait" has almost always meant "Never." We must come to see, with one of our distinguished jurists, that "justice too long delayed is justice denied."

We have waited for more than 340 years for our constitutional and God given rights. The nations of Asia and Africa are moving with jetlike speed toward gaining political independence, but we still creep at horse and buggy pace toward gaining a cup of coffee at a lunch counter. Perhaps it is easy for those who have never felt the stinging darts of segregation to say, "Wait." But when you have seen vicious mobs lynch your mothers and fathers at will and drown your sisters and brothers at whim; when you have seen hate filled policemen curse, kick and even kill your black brothers and sisters; when you see the vast majority of your twenty million Negro brothers smothering in an airtight cage of poverty in the midst of an affluent society; when you suddenly find your tongue twisted and your speech stammering as you seek to explain to your six year old daughter why she can't go to the public amusement park that has just been advertised on television, and see tears welling up in her eyes when she is told that Funtown is closed to colored children, and see ominous clouds of inferiority beginning to form in her little mental sky, and see her beginning to distort her personality by developing an unconscious bitterness toward white people. There comes a time when the cup of endurance runs over, and men are no longer willing to be plunged into the abyss of despair. I hope, sirs, you can understand our legitimate and unavoidable impatience. You express a great deal of anxiety over our willingness to break laws. This is certainly a legitimate concern. Since we so diligently urge people to obey the Supreme Court's decision of 1954 outlawing segregation in the public schools, at first glance it may seem rather paradoxical for us consciously to break laws. One may well ask: "How can you advocate breaking some laws and obeying others?" The answer lies in the fact that there are two types of laws: just and unjust. I would be the first to advocate obeying just laws. One has not only a legal but a moral responsibility to obey just laws. Conversely, one has a moral responsibility to disobey unjust laws. I would agree with St. Augustine that "an unjust law is no law at all."

Of course, there is nothing new about this kind of civil disobedience. It was evidenced sublimely in the refusal of Shadrach, Meshach and Abednego to obey the laws of Nebuchadnezzar, on the ground that a higher moral law was at stake. It was practiced superbly by the early Christians, who were willing to face hungry lions and the excruciating pain of chopping blocks rather than submit to certain unjust laws of the Roman Empire. To a degree, academic freedom is a reality today because Socrates practiced civil disobedience. In our own nation, the Boston Tea Party represented a massive act of civil disobedience.

We should never forget that everything Adolf Hitler did in Germany was "legal" and everything the Hungarian freedom fighters did in Hungary was "illegal." It was "illegal" to aid and comfort a Jew in Hitler's Germany. Even so, I am sure that, had I lived in Germany at the time, I would have aided and comforted my Jewish brothers. If today I lived in a Communist country where certain principles dear to the Christian faith are suppressed, I would openly advocate disobeying that country's antireligious laws.

I must make two honest confessions to you, my Christian and Jewish brothers. First, I must confess that over the past few years I have been gravely disappointed with the white moderate. I have almost reached the regrettable conclusion that the Negro's great stumbling block in his stride toward freedom is not the White Citizen's Counciler or the Ku Klux Klanner, but the white moderate, who is more devoted to "order" than to justice; who prefers a negative peace which is the absence of tension to a positive peace which is the presence of justice; who constantly says: "I agree with you in the goal you seek, but I cannot agree with your methods of direct action"; who paternalistically believes he can set the timetable for another man's freedom; who lives by a mythical concept of time and who constantly advises the Negro to wait for a "more convenient season." Shallow understanding from people of good will is more frustrating than absolute misunderstanding from people of ill will. Lukewarm acceptance is much more bewildering than outright rejection.

I had hoped that the white moderate would understand that law and order exist for the purpose of establishing justice and that when they fail in this purpose they become the dangerously structured dams that block the flow of social progress. I had hoped that the white moderate would understand that the present tension in the South is a necessary phase of the transition from an obnoxious negative peace, in which the Negro passively accepted his unjust plight, to a substantive and positive peace, in which all men will respect the dignity and worth of human personality. Actually, we who engage in non-violent direct action are not the creators of tension. We merely bring to the surface the hidden tension that is already alive. We bring it out in the open, where it can be seen and dealt with. Like a boil that can never be cured so long as it is covered up but must be opened with all its ugliness to the natural medicines of air and light, injustice must be exposed, with all the tension its exposure creates, to the light of human conscience and the air of national opinion before it can be cured.

In your statement you assert that our actions, even though peaceful, must be condemned because they precipitate violence. But is this a logical assertion? Isn't this like condemning a robbed man because his possession of money precipitated the evil act of robbery? Isn't this like condemning Socrates because his unswerving commitment to truth and his philosophical inquiries precipitated the act by the misguided populace in which they made him drink hemlock? Isn't this like condemning Jesus because his unique God consciousness and never ceasing devotion to God's will precipitated the evil act of crucifixion? We will have to repent in this generation not merely for the hateful words and actions of the bad people but for the appalling silence of the good people. Human progress never rolls in on wheels of inevitability; it comes through the tireless efforts of men willing to be co workers with God, and without this hard work, time itself becomes an ally of the forces of social stagnation. We must use time creatively, in the knowledge that the time is always ripe to do right. Now is the time to make real the promise of democracy and transform our pending national elegy into a creative psalm of brotherhood. Now is the time to lift our national policy from the quicksand of racial injustice to the solid rock of human dignity.

Oppressed people cannot remain oppressed forever. The yearning for freedom eventually manifests itself, and that is what has happened to the American

Negro. Something within has reminded him of his birthright of freedom, and something without has reminded him that it can be gained. Consciously or unconsciously, he has been caught up by the Zeitgeist, and with his black brothers of Africa and his brown and yellow brothers of Asia, South America and the Caribbean, the United States Negro is moving with a sense of great urgency toward the promised land of racial justice. If one recognizes this vital urge that has engulfed the Negro community, one should readily understand why public demonstrations are taking place. The Negro has many pent up resentments and latent frustrations, and he must release them. So let him march; let him make prayer pilgrimages to the city hall; let him go on freedom rides – and try to understand why he must do so. If his repressed emotions are not released in nonviolent ways, they will seek expression through violence; this is not a threat but a fact of history. So I have not said to my people: "Get rid of your discontent." Rather, I have tried to say that this normal and healthy discontent can be channeled into the creative outlet of nonviolent direct action. And now this approach is being termed extremist. But though I was initially disappointed at being categorized as an extremist, as I continued to think about the matter I gradually gained a measure of satisfaction from the label. Was not Jesus an extremist for love: "Love your enemies, bless them that curse you, do good to them that hate you, and pray for them which despitefully use you, and persecute you." Was not Amos an extremist for justice: "Let justice roll down like waters and righteousness like an ever flowing stream." Was not Paul an extremist for the Christian gospel: "I bear in my body the marks of the Lord Jesus." Was not Martin Luther an extremist: "Here I stand; I cannot do otherwise, so help me God." And John Bunyan: "I will stay in jail to the end of my days before I make a butchery of my conscience." And Abraham Lincoln: "This nation cannot survive half slave and half free." And Thomas Jefferson: "We hold these truths to be self evident, that all men are created equal . . ." So the question is not whether we will be extremists, but what kind of extremists we will be.

I had hoped that the white moderate would see this need. Perhaps I was too optimistic; perhaps I expected too much. I suppose I should have realized that few members of the oppressor race can understand the deep groans and passionate yearnings of the oppressed race, and still fewer have the vision to see that injustice must be rooted out by strong, persistent and determined action. I am thankful, however, that some of our white brothers in the South have grasped the meaning of this social revolution and committed themselves to it. They are still all too few in quantity, but they are big in quality. Let me take note of my other major disappointment. I have been so greatly disappointed with the white church and its leadership. Of course, there are some notable exceptions. I am not unmindful of the fact that each of you has taken some significant stands on this issue. I commend you, Reverend Stallings, for your Christian stand on this past Sunday, in welcoming Negroes to your worship service on a nonsegregated basis. I commend the Catholic leaders of this state for integrating Spring Hill College several years ago.

But despite these notable exceptions, I must honestly reiterate that I have been disappointed with the church. I do not say this as one of those negative critics who can always find something wrong with the church. I say this as a minister of the gospel, who loves the church; who was nurtured in its bosom; who has been sustained by its spiritual blessings and who will remain true to it as long as the cord of life shall lengthen.

When I was suddenly catapulted into the leadership of the bus protest in Montgomery, Alabama, a few years ago, I felt we would be supported by the white church. I felt that the white ministers, priests and rabbis of the South would be among our strongest allies. Instead, some have been outright opponents, refusing to understand the freedom movement and misrepresenting its leaders; all too many others have been more cautious than courageous and have remained silent behind the anesthetizing security of stained glass windows.

I have heard numerous southern religious leaders admonish their worshipers to comply with a desegregation decision because it is the law, but I have longed to hear white ministers declare: "Follow this decree because integration is morally right and because the Negro is your brother." In the midst of blatant injustices inflicted upon the Negro, I have watched white churchmen stand on the sideline and mouth pious irrelevancies and sanctimonious trivialities. In the midst of a mighty struggle to rid our nation of racial and economic injustice, I have heard many ministers say: "Those are social issues, with which the gospel has no real concern." And I have watched many churches commit themselves to a completely other worldly religion which makes a strange, un-Biblical distinction between body and soul, between the sacred and the secular.

In deep disappointment I have wept over the laxity of the church. But be assured that my tears have been tears of love. There can be no deep disappointment where there is not deep love. Yes, I love the church. How could I do otherwise? I am in the rather unique position of being the son, the grandson and the great grandson of preachers. Yes, I see the church as the body of Christ. But, oh! How we have blemished and scarred that body through social neglect and through fear of being nonconformists.

But the judgment of God is upon the church as never before. If today's church does not recapture the sacrificial spirit of the early church, it will lose its authenticity, forfeit the loyalty of millions, and be dismissed as an irrelevant social club with no meaning for the twentieth century. Every day I meet young people whose disappointment with the church has turned into outright disgust.

Perhaps I have once again been too optimistic. Is organized religion too inextricably bound to the status quo to save our nation and the world? Perhaps I must turn my faith to the inner spiritual church, the church within the church, as the true ekklesia and the hope of the world. But again I am thankful to God that some noble souls from the ranks of organized religion have broken loose from the paralyzing chains of conformity and joined us as active partners in the struggle for freedom. They have left their secure congregations and walked the streets of Albany, Georgia, with us. They have gone down the highways of the South on tortuous rides for freedom. Yes, they have gone to jail with us. Some have been dismissed from their churches, have lost the support of their bishops and fellow ministers. But they have acted in the faith that right defeated is stronger than evil triumphant. Their witness has been the spiritual salt that has preserved the true meaning of the gospel in these troubled times. They have carved a tunnel of hope through the dark mountain of disappointment. I hope the church as a whole will meet the challenge of this decisive hour. But even if the church does not come to the aid of justice, I have no despair about the future. I have no fear about the outcome of our struggle in Birmingham, even if our motives are at present misunderstood. We will reach the goal of freedom in Birmingham and all over the nation, because the goal of America is freedom. Abused and scorned though we may be, our destiny is tied up with America's destiny.

If I have said anything in this letter that overstates the truth and indicates an unreasonable impatience, I beg you to forgive me. If I have said anything that understates the truth and indicates my having a patience that allows me to settle for anything less than brotherhood, I beg God to forgive me.

I hope this letter finds you strong in the faith. I also hope that circumstances will soon make it possible for me to meet each of you, not as an integrationist or a civil-rights leader but as a fellow clergyman and a Christian brother. Let us all hope that the dark clouds of racial prejudice will soon pass away and the deep fog of misunderstanding will be lifted from our fear drenched communities, and in some not too distant tomorrow the radiant stars of love and brotherhood will shine over our great nation with all their scintillating beauty.

Yours for the cause of Peace and Brotherhood,

Martin Luther King, Jr.

EXCERPTED FROM

The Cross and the Lynching Tree

by James H. Cone

◆◆◆

They put him to death by hanging him on a tree.
Acts 10:39

Hundreds of Kodaks clicked all morning at the scene of the lynching. People in automobiles and carriages came from miles around to view the corpse dangling from the end of a rope... Picture cards photographers installed a portable printing plant at the bridge and reaped a harvest in selling the postcard showing a photograph of the lynched Negro. Women and children were there by the score. At a number of country schools the day's routine was delayed until boy and girl pupils could get back from viewing the lynched man. "*The Crisis* 10, no.2, June 1915, on the lynching of Thomas Brooks in Fayette County, Tennessee."

The cross and the lynching tree are separated by nearly 2,000 years. One is the universal symbol of Christian faith; the other is the quintessential symbol of black oppression in America. Though both are symbols of death, one represents a message of hope and salvation, while the other signifies the negation of that message by white supremacy. Despite the obvious similarities between Jesus' death on a cross and the death of thousands of black men and women strung up to die on a lamppost or tree, relatively few people, apart from black poets, novelists, and other reality-seeing artists, have explored the symbolic connections. Yet, I believe this is a challenge we must face. What is at stake is the credibility and promise of the Christian gospel and the hope that we may heal the wounds of racial violence that continue to divide our churches and our society.

In its heyday, the lynching of black Americans was no secret. It was a public spectacle, often announced in advance in newspapers and over radios, attracting crowds of up to twenty thousand people. An unspeakable crime, it is a memory that most white Americans would prefer to forget. For African Americans the memory of disfigured black bodies "swinging in the southern breeze" is so painful that they, too, try to keep these horrors buried deep down in their consciousness, until, like a dormant volcano, they erupt uncontrollably, causing profound agony and pain. But as with the evils of chattel slavery and Jim Crow segregation, blacks and whites and other Americans who want to understand the true meaning of the American experience need to remember lynching. To forget this atrocity leaves us with a fraudulent perspective of this society and of the meaning of the Christian gospel for this nation.

While the lynching tree is seldom discussed or depicted, the cross is one of the most visible symbols of America's Christian origins. Many Christians embrace the conviction that Jesus died on the cross to redeem humankind from sin. Taking our place, Jesus suffered on the cross and gave "his life a ransom for many" (Mark 10:45). We are "now justified by [God's] grace as a gift, through the redemption that is in Christ Jesus, whom God put forward as a sacrifice of atonement by his blood, effective through faith" (Rom 3:24-25). The cross is the great symbol of the Christian narrative of salvation.

Unfortunately, during the course of 2,000 years of Christian history, this symbol of salvation has been detached from any reference to the ongoing suffering and oppression of human beings – those whom Ignacio Ellacuria, the Salvadoran martyr, called "the crucified peoples of history." The cross has been transformed into a harmless, non-offensive ornament that Christians wear around their necks. Rather than reminding us of the "cost of discipleship," it has become a form of "cheap grace," an easy way to salvation that doesn't force us to confront the power of Christ's message and mission. Until we can see the cross and the lynching tree together, until we can identify Christ with a "recrucified" black body hanging from a lynching tree, there can be no genuine understanding of Christian identity in America, and no deliverance from the brutal legacy of slavery and white supremacy.

I was born in Arkansas, a lynching state. During my childhood, white supremacy ruled supreme. White people were virtually free to do anything to blacks with impunity. The violent crosses of the Ku Klux Klan were a familiar reality, and white racists preached a dehumanizing segregated gospel in the name of Jesus' cross every Sunday. And yet in rural black churches I heard a different message, as preachers proclaimed the message of the suffering Jesus and the salvation accomplished in his death on the cross. I noticed how the passion and energy of the preacher increased whenever he talked about the cross, and the congregation responded with outbursts of "Amen" and "Hallelujah" that equaled the intensity of the sermon oration. People shouted, clapped their hands, and stomped their feet, as if a powerful, living reality of God's Spirit had transformed them from nobodies in white society to somebodies in the black church. This black religious experience, with all its tragedy and hope, was the reality in which I was born and raised. Its paradoxes and incongruities have shaped everything I have said and done. If I have anything to say to the Christian community in America and around the world, it is rooted in the tragic and hopeful reality that sustains and empowers black people to resist the forces that seem designed to destroy every ounce of dignity in their souls and bodies.

This work is a continuation and culmination of all my previous books, each of them, in different ways, motivated by a central question: how to reconcile the gospel message of liberation with the reality of black oppression. But in many ways this book is particularly personal. Its subject brings me back to my first memories of hearing the gospel, as well as back to primal memories of terror and violence that were part of the reality of growing up in the Jim Crow South. As a child, I watched my mother and father deal with segregation and the threats of lynching and was deeply affected by their examples, and by the sacrifices they made to keep their children safe.

Through the black religious experience I caught a vision of my possibility, entered the Christian ministry in the African Methodist Episcopal Church, made my way to college and seminary, and received a Ph.D. in theology at Garrett Biblical Institute (now Garrett-Evangelical Theological Seminary) and Northwestern University in 1965. My journey was long and hard, but I was determined to be more than what America had intended for me. Just as books kept Richard Wright alive and gave him "vague glimpses of life's possibilities," the black church and theological texts kept me wrestling with life and faith, trying to find meaning in a society and an intellectual discourse that did not even acknowledge that I existed. How could I find meaning in a world that ignored black people? I decided that I had to say something about that contradiction.

My first theological cry burst forth with the publication of Black Theology and Black Power in 1969. I found my voice in the social, political, religious, and cultural context of the civil rights and black power movements in the 1960s. The Newark and Detroit riots in July 1967 and the assassination of Martin Luther King Jr. in April 1968 were the events that shook me out of my theological complacency, forcing me to realize the bankruptcy of any theology in America that did not engage the religious meaning of the African American struggle for justice. What I studied in graduate school ignored white supremacy and black resistance against it, as if they had nothing to do with the Christian gospel and the discipline of theology. Silence on both white supremacy and the black struggle against racial segregation made me angry with a fiery rage that had to find expression. How could any theologian explain the meaning of Christian identity in America and fail to engage white supremacy, its primary negation?

I concluded that it was my responsibility to address the great contradiction white supremacy poses for Christianity in America. Published three months before I arrived at Union Theological Seminary in New York, Black Theology and Black Power was followed by A Black Theology of Liberation (1970), The Spirituals and the Blues (1972), and God of the Oppressed (1975). In my next work, Martin & Malcolm & America: A Dream or a Nightmare (1991), I returned explicitly to the two figures whose influence had combined implicitly to shape the theme and style of black liberation theology. Most people rejected one and embraced the other – seeing Martin and Malcolm as rivals, nemeses, representing oppositional categories of Christian and black, integration and separation, nonviolence and violence, love and hate. I embraced them both because I saw them advocating different methods that corrected and complemented each other, as they worked for the same goal – the liberation of black people from white supremacy. Just as I could not separate Martin from Malcolm, neither could I separate my Christian identity from my blackness. I was black before I was Christian. My initial challenge was to develop a liberation theology that could be both black and Christian – at the same time and in one voice. That was not easy because even in the black community the public meaning of Christianity was white. Martin King and Malcolm X gave me intellectual resources and the spiritual courage to attack white supremacy.

In earlier reflections on the Christian faith and white supremacy, I had focused on the social evils of slavery and segregation. How could whites confess and live the Christian faith and also impose three-and-a-half centuries of slavery and segregation upon black people? Self-interest and power corrupted their understanding of the Christian gospel How could powerless blacks endure and resist the brutality of white supremacy in nearly every aspect of their lives and still keep their sanity? I concluded that an immanent presence of the transcendent revelation, confirming for blacks that they were more than what whites said about them, gave them an inner spiritual strength to cope with anything that came their way. I wrote because words were my weapons to resist, to affirm black humanity, and to defend it.

And yet through all this time I avoided dealing directly with the reality of lynching. As a southern black, the subject brought back such painful feelings. But finally I had no choice. The subject chose me. This symbol of white supremacy was like a wild beast that had seized me by the neck, trying to kill me, and I had to fight it before I could fully live. Reading and writing about the lynching nightmare, looking at many images of tortured black bodies, has been my deepest challenge and the most painful experience I have had as a theologian. At times it was almost too heavy for me to bear. The more I read about and looked at what whites did to powerless blacks, the angrier I became. Paradoxically, anger soon gave way to a profound feeling of liberation. Being able to write about lynching liberated me from being confined by it. The cross helped me to deal with the brutal legacy of the lynching tree, and the lynching tree helped me to understand the tragic meaning of the cross.

In writing this book, my primary concern is to give voice to black victims, to let them and their families and communities speak to us, exploring the question: how did ordinary blacks, like my mother and father, survive the lynching atrocity and still keep together their families, their communities, and not lose their sanity? How could they live meaningful lives, knowing that they could be lynched for any small violation of what Richard Wright called "the ethics of living Jim Crow"? I wrestle with questions about black dignity in a world of white supremacy because I believe that the cultural and religious resources in the black experience could help all Americans cope with the legacy of white supremacy and also deal more effectively with what is called "the war on terror." If white Americans could look at the terror they inflicted on their own black population – slavery, segregation, and lynching – then they might be able to understand what is coming at them from others. Black people know something about terror because we have been dealing with legal and extralegal white terror for several centuries. Nothing was more terrifying than the lynching tree.

I do not write this book as the last word about the cross and the lynching tree. I write it in order to start a conversation so we can explore the many ways to heal the deep wounds lynching has inflicted upon us. The cross can heal and hurt; it can be empowering and liberating but also enslaving and oppressive. There is no one way in which the cross can be interpreted. I offer my reflections because I believe that the cross placed alongside the lynching tree can help us to see Jesus in America in a new light, and thereby empower people who claim to follow him to take a stand against white supremacy and every kind of injustice.

EXCERPTED FROM

Being Prophetic Takes Courage
by Leonardo Boff

✦✦✦

From *The Church as Prophet: When theology listens to the poor,* Copyright © 1988, reproduced with permission of Harper Collins

The presence of sin as a destructive historical force is manifest in the thousands of crosses human beings prepare for one another. The crucified are legion. Nearly every human being on the face of the Earth hangs on some cross. This cross is wicked, and an abomination to God. A horrible, persistent cross hunches the shoulders of Latin America's subjugated black and Amerindian cultures. This cross is an injustice, and has produced a veritable demographic hecatomb. According to Cook-Simpson, in 1519 there were 11,000,000 Indians living in Mexico; by 1607 the number had fallen to 2,014,000. Wars, disease, and incredibly barbarous oppressions had decimated the dominated population. Nor has this process ever been reversed. Millions upon millions of the downtrodden in Latin America continue to eke out their crucified existence, subsisting on starvation wages, struggling in working conditions that cut their lives off in their youth, languishing in hygienic situations that slaughter some forty million persons annually. Other persons and groups writhe on the cross of discrimination simply because they happen to be female, or sick, or poor, or black, or homosexual, or Marxist, or by reason of some other criterion of exclusion and social death.

In his proclamations, as in his practice, Jesus makes a preferential option for all of these outcasts. Through him is inaugurated the Reign of God, which is to be a regime of the liberation of the oppressed. Be they oppressed by blindness, by imprisonment, or by the threat of death (cf. Luke 4:17-21, Matt. 11:2-6), these are the privileged members of the Reign. There is no denying that the historical Jesus made this preferential option for the very neediest. His option is the reason for his holy wrath against the injustices of this world. His option involves an act of political love Jesus sees that the reality around him contradicts his Father's plan. If this reality is overcome, this is a sign that the Reign of God is in our midst (Luke 7:22). And so he hurls his invectives against the perpetrators of the injustices – the rich (Luke 6:24), the greedy (Luke 12:15), those who fail in solidarity (Matt. 25:33-46). His option translates into a practice of liberation, beginning with a focus on life's infrastructure: hunger is slain, diseases are healed, the dead are raised, and a new social relationship is established. Now the ties that knit society will no longer be based on the interests of power, but on gift and universal acceptance. Now we shall have a society that accepts all persons on an equal footing, even the "least ones," even our enemies (Luke 6:35-36).

What does it mean to preach death and the cross in this context? It means that we must become prophets. It means proclamation and denunciation – *anuncio e denuncia*. We must proclaim the judgment of God that tears the mask from the face of this antireality, this disorder masquerading as order, this "social balance" that is the sheer dominance of one class, which uses the apparatus of state to realize its interests while the underclasses foot the bill. We must denounce injustice as cruelty, poverty as a process of impoverishment of the people, and wealth as possessions heaped up on the backs of the masses. There are times when Christian leaders should be more prophets than shepherds. Pastors, shepherds, see to the mediations, saving where they can, balancing the forces in tension, comforting and aiding the bleeding sheep, going in search of the one that is lost, and taking care lest fat sheep gobble up the fodder intended for the thin ones. Prophets live two radical fidelities at once. One is to God, in whose name they proclaim and denounce. The other is to the people, the poor, on whose behalf they raise their voices and utter their cry. Prophets smite the wolves with their crooks, denouncing their ruses and telling the whole truth, despite its stinging like salt on a raw wound. But bishops are not only pastors, not only shepherds. Bishops are prophets, as well – teachers of the full truth. Theirs is the duty to proclaim not only the truth about God, Christ, the Church, and human beings, but the truth about poverty as well, the truth about the spoliation of the people and the imposition of authoritarian, antipopular regimes. The crosses that martyrize the lowly and defenseless must be denounced and condemned. God abominates them, Christ struggled against them, and those with a sense of humanity reject them. Bishops will be found on the same side.

There is an attitude, a way of proclaiming death and the cross, that must be avoided at all costs. There is a preaching of the cross which, without any such intent on the part of the preachers, ends by legitimating abominations, or representing them as a providence of the will of God. This is fatalism. Fatalism maintains that there is simply no escaping the suffering and death that pervade our history. The lethal flaw of fatalism lies in its abstraction and insensitivity. If fails to distinguish between that suffering and death that are part and parcel of life – the suffering and death that we considered earlier, issuing from the finite structure of existence – and a suffering and death needlessly, wickedly inflicted by the strong on the weak. Furthermore, fatalism removes all hope. It freezes history. For fatalism, history can only be the endless repetition of the same. And so the human being is reduced to helplessness and impotency. The mighty are great lovers of fatalism. The permanence of the status quo is to their benefit, of course, because it is they who control history. It is they who prevent the poor from shaking off their chains and becoming the agents of a more worthy destiny.

Another attitude tending to legitimate death and the cross consists in pessimism and cynicism. Cynics and pessimists are the hard-hearted enemies of their own humanity, refusing to believe in the possibility of overpowering dehumanizing relationships. They ridicule Christian believers, and even manage to cite passages from the Bible in their efforts to disarm the libertarian spirit. They love to quote the saying of Jesus "The poor you always have with you" (John 12:8). As we know, Jesus' meaning here is not that there will always be poor, let alone that God wills their poverty, but that we must never neglect the interests of the poor, that we must never turn our backs on the challenge to join the battle against poverty.

Finally, no less mistaken and pernicious is the attitude that exalts death and the cross as fonts of new life and light in themselves. The champions of this view are likely to repeat, without due reference to mediation and context, the declaration in Hebrews that "without the shedding of blood there is no forgiveness" (Heb. 9:22). There are those who would blasphemously conclude that people must therefore be killed in order that they or others may have life, or that suffering is pleasing to God. Jesus had to die, we hear (cf. John 18:14, Luke 24:26), in virtue of the Father's eternal dispensation. But statements such as these in Scripture have a very precise meaning, which we shall presently discuss, and it is not legitimate to make use of them to manufacture a cult of pain and death, or to perpetuate the crucifixions by which we offend God and render the already painful journey of the humiliated and the wronged of our history more excruciating still. Death and the cross are not directly willed or loved by God. They are not directly pleasing to him. On the contrary, of themselves they represent a cancellation of his project of life, the negation of his will to exalt the meaning of creation.

DEATH AND THE CROSS EMBRACED AS THE PRICE OF THEIR DEFEAT

A prophet arises, proclaims the demands of the Reign of God, and denounces the injustice, the crosses, the violent death, meted out by the agents of sin. That prophet can count on persecution, curses, imprisonment, torture, and death. No prophet, yesterday or today, is likely to die in bed. Prophet here need not mean an individual. It may mean an entire institution, such as the Church that has emerged from Medellin and Puebla. An institution, too, can prophetically denounce the antievangelical character of the poverty and misery in which so many millions of our sisters and brothers in Latin America are forced to live out their lives. In all serenity, such an institution will recognize that the stance it has taken is bound to entail incomprehension on the part of the ruling classes, and the whole national security state, and thus occasion a vicious persecution.

In a Culture of Empire and Civil Religion

It was Memorial Day weekend. After watching 60 Minutes that honored veterans returning from Iraq and Afghanistan my wife, Vivian, turned to me and asked, "George, do you love your country?" Did she need to ask that question? Of course I love my country. What followed was a provocative conversation about patriotism, nationalism and the direction our country seems to be going.

James Cone, an African American theologian who teaches at Union Seminary, suggests that there needs to be a willingness to acknowledge and face the atrocities that our country tolerated when thousands of black American men and women were lynched after the Civil War. Dorothee Soelle, in her article, *Don't Forget the Best*, on page 268, also believes it is important to remember the dark holes in our history if we are ever going to bring healing to what is broken.

In this chapter you will be challenged to think about things that we haven't thought much about. The whole concept of American Empire carries a negative feeling. We don't want to think that our country exploits or dominates other nations. Miguel De La Torre, a professor at Iliff School of Theology in Denver, shows how the rise of neocolonialism has allowed multi-national corporations to control economics worldwide. The question, who has power, is critical to our thinking differently.

One hears the phrase *American Exceptionalism* more and more these days. In what way do we want to think of ourselves as exceptional? Authors in this chapter call for a critical analysis of the concept from a biblical perspective, and raise good questions about capitalism and current economic trends. They suggest that we look to the scriptures if we want to know the source of socialism and distribution of wealth. Courage to think differently includes a look at the language we use and the things we associate with certain words.

Sister Marie Augusta Neal, a professor of sociology at Emmanuel College in Boston, reminds us that any country that wants their economic system to be in control over others must have within its citizenship a kind of religion that will not only support it but also remain silent when such systems oppress others. To think differently means being aware of the ways religion can be used to silence protest and keep politics out of our prophetic voices.

I wrote the article *Was Jesus Subversive?* for our Lutheran magazine to remind Christians that the Lenten season is not just about Jesus dying for our sins (which can be a form of civil religion) but a time to remember that Jesus died because of what he said and did. Maybe we need to examine our atonement language.

George S. Johnson

EXCERPTED FROM

It's Not Class Warfare

by Susan Brooks Thistlethwaite

From the weekly column "On Faith" online section in the *Washington Post*,
Copyright © 2011, reproduced with permission of the author and *Washington Post*,
http://www.washingtonpost.com/national/on-faith

President Obama just drew the economic battlelines more clearly in his call to raise $1.5 trillion in new revenue primarily through increased taxes on the wealthy, letting the Bush tax cuts expire, and closing tax loopholes.

"Class warfare!" countered the opponents.

Americans sharing more equally in the burden of pulling our country out of massive debt, and using tax revenue to stimulate the economy and create jobs isn't "class warfare," it's actually Christianity at work.

Many Christians are starting to find the increasing concentration of wealth in the hands of a few very rich people to be an enormous moral and ethical problem. Catholic theologians and ethicists took pains recently to challenge Speaker Boehner on Catholic values in regard to his views particularly on the economy.

But not all Christians agree with those perspectives. Today, not only is economics a political battleground, it is a faith battleground particularly in Christianity. According to some Christian conservatives, unregulated capitalism, with all its inherent inequalities of wealth, is God's plan.

"Christian Capitalism" in their view, isn't an oxymoron, it's God's will as revealed in the Bible. God wants you to own property and make money, and if some make a lot more money than others, that's okay. In fact, it's God's will too.

These competing views are very influential in our current public debates. The Christian conservative viewpoint, however, has been more instrumental in shaping our political shift to the right in recent years, not only on social issues, but also on economic issues. You can see this display in the "God Hates Taxes" signs carried at Tea Party rallies.

Let me be clear as I can be. We need to understand the so-called "Christian" underpinnings of the anti-tax, anti-government, anti-the-poor, "let him die" approach to economics and public policy today as completely un-Christian, as well as un-American. What we need to do is re-establish our national values of fairness, equality and opportunity for all, values that I believe are actually the core of the Christian faith, (as well as of other religious traditions and of humanist values).

First, in order to do that, we need to understand how we got to the place where the "ownership of private property" and amassing wealth is accepted by many as the "biblical perspective," and taking care of each other through shared sacrifice, is dismissed as secular humanism. Nothing against humanists here, but the Bible is all about taking care of each other, including taking care of each other by sharing what we have, not through amassing wealth.

Part of the way we got here is by Christian conservatives ignoring a lot of what the Bible says on wealth and poverty, and being highly selective in what they call "biblical." In all these references to the "Bible," the self-styled Christian capitalists don't ever seem to recall that in the Book of Acts, the early disciples "shared all things in common." The early church is Glenn Beck's worst nightmare because it was socialist.

This is what the Bible actually says about the economic practices of Jesus' followers: "Now the company of those who believed were of one heart and soul, and no one said that any of the things which he possessed was his own, but they had everything in common… There was not a needy person among them, for as many as were possessors of lands or houses sold them, and brought the proceeds of what was sold and laid it at the apostles feet; and distribution was made to each as any had need." Acts 4:32-35.

Glenn Beck's attacks on the Reverend Jim Wallis, an evangelical Christian who works on poverty issues from a biblical perspective, is illustrative of the need of the far right to discredit biblically based anti-poverty political work.

But as I, and Jim Wallis and others have shown over and over and over, the biblical practices on justice for the poor are far more radically egalitarian than anything being proposed in terms of economics today by Democrats.

Not only do we need to understand that "Christian Capitalism" isn't Christian, we need to understand how it is distorting capitalism. The "ultracapitalism" of some people is often called "market fundamentalism" and it is the nearly unshakeable faith held by its true believers that the best economic results are obtained when the market is allowed to function without the restraints of regulation. Just reduce taxes and let the "job creators" do their thing. Remember "trickle down economics" from the Reagan years? This is the belief system that launched the Reagan Revolution in the U.S. and started the decades long reduction in real wages of the American middle class and the rise in American poverty levels.

"Market fundamentalism" isn't good, it's the economic theory that is rotten to its core, and as Kevin Phillips argues, "bad" for our economy. Phillips, in his book *Bad Money: Reckless Finance, Failed Politics, and the Global Crisis of American Capitalism* shows exactly how it is that the Christian conservative view that unregulated capitalism is God's will props up, or enables, the bad economic theory of unfettered, "reckless" capitalism. In his book, Phillips connects the dots on how conservative religion and market fundamentalism mutually reinforce one another, to the great detriment of the country and the world. He calls Christian fundamentalism the "enabler" of market fundamentalism and shows how conservative Christianity provided the cultural shift necessary so that ordinary Americans would become anesthetized to their previous suspicion of unregulated capitalism born in the 1930s.

Phillips observes that the complete breakdown in the United States these days of realistic thinking about how markets and financial systems actually do work has three sources: "homage to financial assets...market efficiency" and "evangelical, fundamentalist Christianity, infused with a millennial preoccupation with terrorism, evil, and Islam..." These are the three legs of the stool that caused the "de facto anesthetizing, over the last twenty years, of onetime populist southern and western" regions.

"Anesthetizing" is a great metaphor for what's happening in our public square about the economy because you have to be nearly unconscious not to realize that "Christian capitalism" is neither good Christianity nor good capitalism.

It's not "Christian" because it ignores the central teachings of Jesus on the moral imperative of taking care of the poor in the Sermon on the Mount, and it dismisses the actual economic practice of the disciples as described in the Book of Acts.

It is also lousy capitalism. Capitalism is an economic system where the means of production are privately owned and operated for profit in a competitive market. The capitalist system relies on self-interest, not "stewardship" to actually run. Theories of markets actually assume that people will act according to their self-love, and never talk to them of our own necessities but of their advantage.

Capitalism isn't "God's Plan," it's an economic system that runs on the human desire for more, our own self-interest. This is not necessarily evil. It can actually be a very productive system, but it is not beneficent. In order for there to be good values in our economic life, capitalism needs to be regulated so it does not wreck the whole ship with unfettered greed (as happened in the banking industry starting in 2008), and it needs to be supplemented with social safety nets and tax policy to achieve an approximate (not absolute) "freedom from want" as in Franklin Roosevelt's wonderful phrase. It was Roosevelt who translated "freedom from want" into a series of government programs to make it a reality such as Social Security, unemployment insurance, aid to dependent children, the minimum wage, housing, stock market regulation, and federal deposit insurance for banks.

The Christian approach to economics is to be the conscience of the nation and to insist that we regulate capitalism so it does not become reckless and destructive. Christians must call on the nation's politicians to have us share the burdens and the sacrifices, in order get to the "freedom from want" that is in our democratic values and our faith values.

We do this because the Christian conscience is driven by duty to "love God with your whole heart and your neighbor as yourself."

That's in the Bible. Luke 10:27. Look it up.

EXCERPTED FROM

Global Exploitation

by Miguel A. De La Torre

◆◆◆

The cultural influences of the Greek empire, the imperial might of the Roman empire, the religious supremacy of the Holy Roman Empire, and the global reach of the British all pale in comparison with the cultural dominance, the military might, the capitalist zeal, and the global influence of the U.S. empire. The term "empire" can no longer be narrowly defined as the physical possession of foreign lands that must pay tribute. Empire is understood today as a globalized economy that provides economic benefits to multinational corporations whose influences are secured through the military might of one superpower.

Indeed, the sun never sets today on the dominating influence of the United States. At no other time in human history has one nation enjoyed such supremacy of power. While empires of old relied on brute force, the U.S. empire relies mainly on economic force. Through its economic might, the United States dictates terms of trade with other nations, guaranteeing that benefits flow to the United States and the elite of countries that agree to the trade agreements. Take corn, for example, a staple of life in many parts of he world.

While Mexican farmers cultivate corn the way they have for centuries by using plows pulled by burros on small plots of land and relying on rain for irrigation, their U.S. counterparts operate heavily mechanized mega-farms that rely on satellite images to mete out water and fertilizer. Because corn grown in the U.S. is heavily subsidized, it is cheaper for Mexicans to buy what is exported from the U.S. than their home-grown crops. According to the Institute for Agriculture and Trade Policy, U.S. corn sells for 25 percent less than what local Mexican growers earn, meaning that those growers lose money with every acre they plant. Today, subsidized U.S. corn accounts for almost half of the world's stock, setting a world price so low that it eliminates all indigenous competition. It effectively robs three-quarters of the world's poor who live in rural areas (the poor are mostly farmers) and depend on exporting their crops for their livelihood.

Originally, the NAFTA agreement set a fifteen-year period for gradually raising the amount of U.S. corn that could enter Mexico without tariffs; however, Mexico willingly lifted the quotas in fewer than three years to assist its chicken and pork industries. According to Mexican NAFTA negotiators, the suspension of quotas directly benefitted fellow negotiator Eduardo Bours, whose family owns Mexico's largest chicken producer. Although the lifting of quotas rewarded his family business, Mexico lost some $2 billion in tariffs while half a million corn farmers abandoned their lands and moved to the cities in hope of finding a new livelihood. And the flow of cheaper U.S. corn did not translate into cheaper food prices for Mexicans. Quite the contrary. Price controls were lifted on tortillas and tortilla flour, causing their prices to triple. Not surprisingly, while the World Bank continues to sing the praises of NAFTA, a study conducted by the Carnegie Endowment for International Peace has concluded that a decade of NAFTA has failed to generate substantial job growth in Mexico and has brought hardship to hundreds of thousands of subsistence farmers. Real wages in Mexico are lower in 2004 (adjusted for inflation) than they were when NAFTA was adopted in 1994. Additional income inequality is greater and immigration to the United States continues to soar.

In the early part of 2002, the United States Congress passed a bill signed by President George W. Bush authorizing $100 billion in farm subsidies over an eight-year period. By 2003, the world's wealthiest nations were giving their farmers more than $300 billion in subsidies. These subsidies privilege industrial-size farms that produce more acres of crops than are needed for domestic consumption and sell the surplus overseas at prices lower than indigenous farmers require. Even James D. Wolfensohn, president of the World Bank, accuses wealthy nations of "squandering" $1 billion a day on farm subsidies that have devastating effects on impoverished countries. Ian Goldin, the World Bank's vice-president stated it clearly: "Reducing these subsidies and removing agricultural trade barriers is one of the most important things rich countries can do for millions of people to escape poverty all over the world." Every rural peasant forced to leave the land means another producer who is forced to migrate to the city, becoming, along with a family, one more consumer. This migration greatly contributes to the perpetual need for future food aid (George 1987:8).

THE RISE OF NEOLIBERALISM

The rise of the U.S. empire was neither an accident nor the result of luck. At the close of World War II, the Bretton Woods Conference (1944) attempted to create an economic order that would rebuild Europe so as to prevent any further world wars. Free trade was perceived as the means by which to bring stability to the global order. Although the original intentions may have been noble, in the end, the new economic order promoted the development of first-world banks and institutions (the World Bank and the International Monetary Fund [IMF] were both created at Bretton Woods), and transnational corporations. The United States and its Western European allies developed their economic wealth at the expense of the peripheral nations, which provided raw materials and cheap labor. Underdevelopment of the periphery became a by product of development of the center. What was once accepted as colonialism, where world powers directly occupied the lands of others to extract their national resources and human labor, was replaced with a more modern form of global exploitation, often termed neoliberalism. Underdevelopment will continue to persist so long as neoliberalism continues to privilege the nations that have placed themselves at the world's center. This is why any Christian ethical response to global injustices must start with a comprehension of neoliberalism.

Neoliberalism is a relatively new economic term. It was coined in the late 1990s to describe the social and moral implications of the free-trade policies of global capitalism (liberalism) since the collapse of the Eastern Bloc (neo-, meaning new or recent). Critics maintain that neoliberalism is responsible for the increasing disparity in global wealth and that it has created a parasitic relationship where the poor of the world sacrifice their humanity to serve the needs, wants, and desires of a privileged few. It provides the few with the right to determine what will be produced, who (nation-state or group of individuals) will produce it, under what conditions will production take place, what will be paid for the finished product, what will the profits amount to, and who will benefit from the profits. In spite of foreign aid programs designed by rich nations to assist so-called underdeveloped nations, more of the world's wealth, in the form of raw materials, natural resources, and cheap labor, is extracted through unfair trade agreements than is returned under the guise of humanitarianism or charity. The first world continues to appropriate the resources of weaker nations through the open market, causing internal scarcities in basic living needs required to maintain any type of humane living standard.

Insuring stable political systems, regardless of how repressive they may be, is a prerequisite for the economic marketplace to function. Political stability, which is needed to insure the steady and profitable flow of goods, supersedes the need for freedom and liberty. Thus, a history exists of U.S. pressure to topple democratically elected governments and install tyrants who secured stability (as has happened with the governments of Abenz in Guatemala, Allende in Chile, and Mossadegh in Iran). Ironically, supporters of the continuing expansion of neoliberalism often confuse this economic structure with democratic virtues like liberty. Hence, raising questions about ethics of the present economic structure can be construed as an attack on democracy itself (George 1999).

To some degree, neoliberalism can be understood as a movement within the World Bank akin to that of religion. According to economic development experts Susan George and Fabrizio Sabelli, the World Bank is "[a] supranational, non-democratic institution [that] functions very much like the Church, in fact the medieval Church. It has a doctrine, a rigidly structured hierarchy preaching and imposing this doctrine [of neoliberalism] and a quasi-religious mode of self-justification" (1994:5).

For theologians Clodovis Boff and George Pixley, "The theological status of [neoliberalism] today is precisely that of a vast idolatrous cult of the great god Capital, creator and father of so many lesser gods: money, the free market, and so on" (1989:144). Like most religious beliefs, the economic pronouncements expounded by the World Bank or IMF can be neither validated nor invalidated, but are usually accepted on faith. Ironically, the ethics employed by these institutions are not based on concepts of morality, but on interpreted principles of economics and the power amassed by the institution. This point is best illustrated by a statement of Brian Griffiths, vice-chairman of Goldman Sachs International and member of the British House of Lords: "What should be the Christian response to poverty? First, to support global capitalism by encouraging the governments of developing countries to privatize state-owned industries, open up their economies to trade and investment and allow competitive markets to grow" (2003:171).

For neoliberalism, market forces are more important than ethics, even when the market causes widespread hunger and poverty. Economist Milton Friedman once said, "Indeed, a major aim of the liberal [market] is to leave the ethical problem for individuals to wrestle with. The 'really' important ethical problems are those that face an individual in a free society – what he should do with his freedom" (1962:12).

Any focus on *individual and personal issues* of faith and redemption poses problems for Christian ethicists, especially those working on the margins. Daniel Bell best captures this new neoliberal attitude toward ethics in the words, "Capitalism has put a new twist on Augustine's famous dictum, 'Love and do as you please.' Now it is, 'Produce for the market and do as you please'" (2001:18). The pursuit of gain for the few most often creates scarcity for the many. Liberation theologians such as Peruvian Gustavo Gutierrez insist that "In the Bible, material poverty is a subhuman situation, the fruit of injustice and sin" (1984:54). Here then is the crux of the conflict between neoliberalism and the gospel message of liberation: neoliberalism lacks a global ethical perspective because it reduces ethics to the sphere of individualism.

The dichotomy between communal and personal ethics – or between market forces and human development – allows Christians to accept the market as a "good." The market, then, determines the fate of humanity and humans exist for the market. Maximization of wealth becomes a virtue in and of itself, as well as a reason for being, and competition separates the sheep from the goats. Economic "losers" result from a lack of personal ethics to manage their own lives properly. Failure in being employable indicates a collapse of moral duty to maximize one's potential in the labor marketplace.

Transnational corporations also compete by eliminating competitors through mergers and acquisitions, which usually result in job losses. As technological advances reduce the need for manual labor, humans become dispensable, nonessential units that are rendered superfluous. Although raw material remains in high demand, the populations of the two-thirds world are no longer needed.

Neoliberalism tends to encompass and dictate every aspect of human existence. Nothing can exist outside the market. Even nations are reduced to "companies" with which the transnationals form alliances. Every thing and body is reduced to a consumer good. If a nation is unable to compete in the global marketplace, then a process of financial prioritizing, known as "structural adjustments" or "austerity programs" takes place so that the nation can become a stronger player, usually at the expense of their populations, whose living conditions worsen.

Those who question neoliberalism are not necessarily opposed to globalization, which has become a reality of modern life. Rather, they are against how globalization has come to be defined. The new political, social, and economic order that neoliberalism represents negatively impacts all humanity, especially the marginalized. Nevertheless, the good news is that God traditionally sides against the empires of history. In closing, consider the words of former Brazilian Archbishop Helder Camera: "When I feed the hungry, they call me a saint, when I ask why they are hungry, they call me a Communist." Any ethical praxis geared to dismantling global injustices must begin here – by asking why people are hungry. We cannot begin to deal with the liberation of the world's marginalized unless we first deal with the root cause of all their misery and suffering – economic injustice. The next three chapters will briefly explore three consequences of neoliberalism: global poverty, war, and the environment.

John Darkow, cartoonist. Reproduced with permission.

————— EXCERPTED FROM —————

America the Exceptional

by Brian McLaren

What kind of nation are we called to be: arrogantly superior or humbly exemplary?

Thomas Jefferson repeatedly spoke of the United States as a unique – or exceptional – historical phenomenon. As a democratic republic, it differed from Europe, and all the nations of the past. Since then, of course, scores of nations have followed our example in forming democratic republics, so what was exceptional in Jefferson's time has now, we might say, become the norm. Does that make us "the nation formerly known as exceptional," but now typical?

Alexis de Tocqueville, perhaps the best-loved (and certainly the most-quoted) Frenchman in U.S. history, also detailed certain features in which the U.S. was exceptional. But they're not exactly the attributes candidates are referring to today. For example, he said that Americans were so focused on making money that they didn't pay attention to "science, literature, and the arts" as Europeans did, yet somehow Americans had so far avoided "relapsing into barbarism." (He spoke before the era of TV shows such as *Married with Children* and *Jersey Shore.*) Our preoccupation with money even made Americans disregard religion, he said, except "from time to time," when we shoot "a transient and distracted glance to heaven." This money-focused turn of character, de Tocqueville concluded, made America exceptional – but not in an exemplary way.

The first historical record of the precise term "American exceptionalism" actually comes (this is embarrassing) from Joseph Stalin, who complained that American Communists thought themselves an exception to the normal rules of Marxist economic evolution. They were guilty, he said, of "the heresy of American exceptionalism."

Between de Tocqueville and Stalin, the idea of American exceptionalism became deeply associated with the doctrine of Manifest Destiny, the idea that God had chosen Americans, as God chose the ancient Israelites, for a special divine purpose on Earth. This belief was based on a passage in the Book of Genesis:

And the Lord said to Abraham, I will bless you and make your name great. I will make you a great nation and all nations will submit to your exceptional status. They will kow-tow to your interests, submit to your invasions, and defer to your economic policies. You will act unilaterally and lead, not cooperate with, unexceptional nations. You will use and abuse the alien and stranger among you as you please, for they are not my chosen people blessed by manifest destiny. And if other nations curse you by failing to acknowledge your exceptional status, you will smite them in my name. For I am the Lord who shows favoritism to whom he will, and you are my chosen people.

Oops! That is not Genesis 12 – but it might as well have been, based on projects and attitudes promoted via the doctrine of Manifest Destiny.

In a September 2011 speech at the Reagan Library in Simi Valley, California, New Jersey Gov. Chris Christie seemed to agree with Palin – to a degree. He defined the term as meaning, "…we are different and, yes, better." But then he raised a warning: "Unfortunately, through our own domestic political conduct of late, we have failed to live up to our own tradition of exceptionalism. Today, our role and ability to effect change has been diminished because of our own problems and our inability to effectively deal with them . . . "

He returned to the theme later in his speech: "Today, the biggest challenge we must meet is the one we present to ourselves. To not become a nation that places entitlement ahead of accomplishment. To not become a country that places comfortable lies ahead of difficult truths. To not become a people that thinks so little of ourselves that we demand no sacrifice from each other. We are a better people than that; and we must demand a better nation than that."

The question raised by Christie's words is, of course, "Of whom do we demand a better nation?" For many, the answer will be their party or their candidate. But the only realistic answer would be that we demand of ourselves the commitment to face the challenges Christie named – to put accomplishment ahead of entitlement (including the entitlements associated with being an exceptional nation), to face the difficult truths about ourselves, our past, and our future (including truths about the ways we have been negatively exceptional and not exceptional at all), and to demand sacrifice of each other... and so to be better people and a better nation.

It is one thing to strive to become a better nation – better than we have been in the past, and better than we are at this moment. It's a very different thing to assume we already are better than all other nations in all important ways. The former describes a vibrant and hopeful nation; the latter an arrogant and self-deceived one. And that difference should be in our minds each time we hear the term "American exceptionalism" echoing across the fruited plain.

In what ways do we want to be exceptional – not in the sense of being different for difference's sake, and certainly not in the sense of being granted exceptions to normal standards of decency, but in the sense of being exemplary? In what ways do we want to lead?

Would we like to lead in resource consumption and environmental irresponsibility? Would we like to lead in wealth inequality, incarceration rates, and capital punishment? Would we like to lead in political polarization and partisan brinksmanship? Would we like to lead in unmitigated unsustainability – whether in the realm of national debt, personal debt, or environmental degradation? Would we like to lead in our refusal to demand sacrifices of the rich while demanding sacrifices of the poor and middle class? Would we like to lead military expenditures, drone strikes, weapons sales, toppled regimes, and occupations?

Next to nobody really wants to be exceptional in any of these ways.

At our best moments – whether we're Brits or Greeks or Argentines or Papua New Guineans or Americans – the kind of exceptionalism we really want is not arrogant superiority. What we want is to be a good and distinct people, the best possible version of ourselves, not merely fulfilling (and exploiting) some national myth of manifest destiny, but instead creating a national legacy for our children and grandchildren, a great nation among other great nations, through wisdom, justice, freedom, compassion, and action.

And that, I think, is the only kind of exceptionalism that is theologically justified.

In the Hebrew scriptures, the idea of being chosen or exceptional is highly problematic. It was used to justify horrific acts (see Deuteronomy 7:1-5). But even in the same disturbing passages that command behavior we would call genocidal, God goes out of God's way to remind the people that they were not chosen for their size or superiority, but for their smallness and weakness (Deuteronomy 7:6-7). God warns them not to "exalt themselves" in times of plenty. He commands them to remember that every blessing they will ever enjoy is a gift of God – not an attainment of their "power and the might of (their) own right hand" (8:12-18).

Even more striking, just as they are reminded that "the LORD set his heart in love on your ancestors alone and chose you, their descendants after them, out of all the peoples," they are further reminded that because God "loves the strangers... You shall also love the strangers" (10:15-19).

And if the chosen people are tempted to presume upon their status, throughout Deuteronomy God solemnly promises them that their exceptionalism is conditional. If they don't fulfill the responsibilities (including caring for the poor – Deuteronomy 15) that go along with blessings they have received, their blessings will turn into curses (28:15 ff). The choice is theirs (30:11 ff).

So it turns out that President Obama had it right: People can feel exceptional without being exclusive about it, as the prophet Amos similarly affirms: "Are you not like the Ethiopians to me, O people of Israel? says the Lord. Did I not bring Israel up from the land of Egypt, and the Philistines from Caphtor and the Arameans from Kir?" (9:7).

In the New Testament, Paul challenges the whole idea of seeking the first place. Don't think more highly of yourselves than you should, he says, "but have sober judgment" (Romans 12:3). "Be of the same mind, having the same love, being in full accord and of one mind. Do nothing from selfish ambition or conceit, but in humility regard others as better than yourselves" (Philippians 2:2-3). It's hard to imagine that on a bumper sticker: "We're Not Number One!" Our example isn't the emperor (or a contemporary politician) who claws his way to the top: It's the Lord who serves his way to the bottom (2:5 ff). There is the paradoxical exceptionalism of the Kingdom of God, as Christ commanded:

> **You know that the rulers of the Gentiles lord it over them, and their great ones are tyrants over them. It will not be so among you; but whoever wishes to be great among you must be your servant, and whoever wishes to be first among you must be your slave, just as the Chosen One came not to be served but to serve, and to give his life as a ransom for many."**
>
> *(Matthew 20:25-28)*

Subtle choices are being made in addition to the obvious ones. We're not only choosing who will next lead our nation; we're also choosing what kind of nation our next president will lead: a nation more in the tradition of "the rulers of the Gentiles," or one more in line with the way of Jesus. Mediocre or excellent, arrogantly superior or humbly exemplary, exceptional in domination or exceptional in service, exceptionally regressive or exceptionally eager to "excel in doing good" – we are choosing not just whether or not to continue a historical tradition of "American exceptionalism," but more important, what kind of exceptionalism is worth desiring in the America of the future.

Brian D. McLaren is an author, speaker, and activist based in southwest Florida. His new book is *Jesus, Moses, the Buddha, and Mohammed Walk into a Bar: Christian Identity in a Multi-Faith World.*

——————— EXCERPTED FROM ———————

Israel, Palestine and Iran

by Rabbi Michael Lerner

◆◆◆

From *Iran, Israel and Obama*, Volume 27, no. 3, pp. 6-9, 52-53, Copyright © 2012, reproduced with permission of Duke University Press, www.dukeupress.edu.

Iran, Israel, and Obama

The mainstream media have frequently framed their discussions about U.S. and Israeli policy toward Iran as a debate between U.S. President Barack Obama and Israeli Prime Minister Benjamin Netanyahu about whether to strike Iran immediately or to wait to see if sanctions work. This narrative has set the framework for a march toward war by excluding from the discourse the nonviolent option: that we not use coercion to achieve our ends.

The Obama administration has done little to disrupt this troubling narrative. Following in the path of George W. Bush, Obama has instead helped to legitimize the notion of a preemptive U.S. military strike against Iran – a nation that has never taken direct military action against the United States.

Indeed Ben-Dror Yemini, the opinion editor for the Israeli daily newspaper *Ma'ariv*, said this March that Obama couldn't have been much clearer in his commitment to make a military strike against Iran unless sanctions deterred Iran from developing a nuclear weapon. "He didn't say he would vote for the Likud. But aside from that, one should pay attention, he sounded almost like the Likud leader," Yemini said.

The Legitimization of Preemptive Strikes

In truth, President Clinton already blazed the path to preemptive strikes in his attempts to save the people of Bosnia from the genocide that was being carried out by Serbia. And the legitimacy of attacking a nation for a reason other than self-defense was again affirmed when the United States intervened as a silent but strong partner in the NATO intervention to stop Muammar el-Qaddafi from murdering the Libyan citizens who had rebelled against his regime.

The argument for military intervention is stronger in humanitarian cases such as these, which involve the clear and present suffering and deaths of civilians.

Far weaker is the argument that an intervention can be justified whenever one is able to offer a worrisome hypothesis about what any given regime may do at some future point. This approach leads us to a world in which statements from extremists inside or outside the government of a rival state give the powerful free license to use military strikes or even start wars to preempt the feared evil of the other side.

If we go too far down that path, we get into arguments like those heard about Iran, with those who favor a preemptive strike saying, "Well, Iran's president and Ayatollah both have made statements calling for Iran to eliminate the Jewish state," and those who oppose the strike saying, "No, that's a mistranslation. Iran's leaders did not pledge to do this; they just said they wished the current Zionist expansionist regime would disappear into the dustbin of history. That is a wish shared by many Israelis who want a secure Israel but don't necessarily want it to be tied to the Occupation of the West Bank and Gaza."

From the standpoint of those of us who want a peaceful world, Obama's legitimization of preemptive warfare in principle is a big victory for the warmakers of the future. It's a terrible development that could be as destructive as his decision to sign into law the part of the National Defense Appropriation legislation that authorizes the president to imprison for life and without trial any U.S. citizen suspected of supporting terrorists. And it rivals the current administration's development of drones used for "targeted assassinations" that frequently kill other human beings in the vicinity.

Israelis listening to President Obama's speech to the American Israel Public Affairs Committee (AIPAC) conference in Washington, D.C., on March 4 were almost unanimous in acknowledging just how far he had gone to satisfy the militarists in Israel and the Jewish community worldwide. Here is the part of Obama's talk that satisfied the Israeli hawks most:

> I have said that when it comes to preventing Iran from obtaining a nuclear weapon, I will take no options off the table, and I mean what

I say. That includes all elements of American power: a political effort aimed at isolating Iran, a diplomatic effort to sustain our coalition and ensure that the Iranian program is monitored, an economic effort that imposes crippling sanctions and, yes, a military effort to be prepared for any contingency. Iran's leaders should understand that I do not have a policy of containment; I have a policy to prevent Iran from obtaining a nuclear weapon. And as I have made clear time and again during the course of my presidency, I will not hesitate to use force when it is necessary to defend the United States and its interests . . . Rest assured that the Iranian government will know our resolve and that our coordination with Israel will continue.

A Peaceful Path to Non-Proliferation

We at Tikkun also want Israel (and all nations, for that matter) to be safe from nuclear threats. But we do not believe that the path outlined by Obama is the correct one, even if it succeeds in keeping Iran from developing nuclear weapons capacity in the short run.

We hope that Iran will, by the time this magazine is printed, already have agreed to stop any development of nuclear weapons and to open all its suspected development sites to international inspection. But such a pledge may be a hard sell to Iranian nationalists who could easily argue that militaristic threats from Obama and Netanyahu underscore the dangers Iran faces unless it has the nuclear capacity to defend itself.

A far more effective way to stop proliferation would be for the United States and all other nuclear states (including Israel) to disarm their nuclear military power and thus show that they were not simply seeking to retain their own power by insisting that others refrain from doing what they themselves are already doing. Media in Arab and Muslim states have frequently made a point of the hypocrisy of Israel, which refused to sign the Nuclear Non-Proliferation Treaty precisely to avoid having its nuclear weapons' capacities revealed to the world, now preaching to Iran about the need for Iranians to never equally arm themselves. A nuclear-free world would be a far better gift to the human race than an Iran bombed by Israel and/or the United States.

Part of our view was stated in the advocacy ad we managed to place in the New York Times on March 7, while Netanyahu and the AIPAC crowd were beating the drums of war among congressional representatives eager to show their right-wing Jewish and Christian Zionist constituencies that they could be counted on to support whatever Israel decided to do. We were able to run the ad thanks to the help of more than 3,000 signatories and donors (mostly Tikkun subscribers and members of the Network of Spiritual Progressives) and thanks to the co-sponsorship of the Shalom Center. The content of the ad is reprinted below.

No, Mr. Netanyahu, No, President Obama: No War on Iran and No First Strike

Some of us who signed this ad believe that even a nuclear Iran – faced with the certainty that its first aggressive use of nuclear weapons would engender a massive retaliation sufficient to kill most of the people of Iran – would not dare take a first nuclear strike against Israel or the United States. Americans once perceived the Soviet Union to be equally evil, irrational, and driven by ideological fundamentalism – yet the Soviet Union, armed to the teeth with nuclear weapons, was constrained by the possibility of mutually assured destruction. The same is likely to be true of Iran should its ideologically driven fundamentalist leaders ever decide to develop nuclear weapons.

Some of us fear that electoral pressures have pushed President Obama and many Democrats in Congress to abandon the strategy of containment used with all the other nuclear powers and instead to coerce Iran into not developing nukes.

We agree with the goal of non-proliferation, but believe that the only way to restrain the development of nukes by other states like Iran, Brazil, Saudi Arabia, and Egypt is for the current nuclear powers – including the United States, the United Kingdom, France, Russia, China, North Korea, India, Pakistan, and Israel – to disarm their own nuclear weapons. President Obama: show some leadership by making dramatic advances in negotiating the universal elimination of nuclear weapons contained in the Nuclear Non-Proliferation Treaty instead of only taking seriously the parts of that treaty calling for others to not obtain such weapons!

Unfortunately, President Obama made clear when he spoke to AIPAC on March 4 that he and Netanyahu only disagree about how long to use economic coercion (creating suffering for ordinary Iranians) before they revert to military attacks. Yet many of us who signed this ad believe that coercion is not in the best interests of the U.S., Israel, the Jewish people, or world peace. The only path to peace is a path of peace and nonviolence. Our means must be as holy as our ends. President Obama: please show some leadership by affirming the value of nonviolence even when dealing with a state like Iran. Break the cycles of violence that have physically, ethically, and spiritually wounded the human race for so much of its history. We know the outcome of the strategy of domination and violence. It's time to use a fundamentally different approach.

Some of us believe that Israel could actually work out peaceful relations with Iran and enhance its own security and U.S. security by ending the Occupation of the West Bank and Gaza, helping the Palestinian people create an economically and politically viable state, taking generous steps to alleviate the humiliation and suffering of Palestinian refugees, and supporting Palestinian membership in the United Nations. Those steps, done with a spirit of openhearted generosity toward the Palestinian people and the people of all the surrounding states, is far more likely than military strikes against Iran or endless assaults on Hamas to provide a safe and secure future for Israel.

Similarly, if the United States were to apologize for its role in overthrowing the democratically elected government of Iran in 1953 and ushering in the Shah's dictatorial regime, it would strengthen the hands of those in Iran who seek an overthrow of the even worse Islamic fundamentalist regime that now terrorizes the people of Iran.

Why might this work better than military attacks? Some who have signed this ad believe that the best path to homeland security is through rejecting the old-fashioned "domination strategy" of exercising power against those whom we fear.

Domination strategies elicit fear, resentment at not being treated as a people who deserve respect, and then a desire to strike back. Instead we believe that what spiritual progressives call a "generosity strategy" based on caring for the other, compassion, and genuine respect for differences is likely to prove the most effective way to achieve long-term safety. The more the United States detaches from its previous role as the military champion of Western economic selfishness toward other countries in defense of their own global corporations, the more our influence will increase.

The Global Marshall Plan introduced to Congress as House Res. 157 by Hon. Keith Ellison (D-Minn.) – a plan developed by Tikkun magazine and the Network of Spiritual Progressives – offers a concrete vision for such a strategy of generosity. Please read it at www.tikkun.org/GMP. We offer this in a spirit of humility, knowing that no one can be sure of what is going to happen in the future, but certain that what has happened in the past with the domination approach to the world's problems has often led to worse disasters than whatever it was designed to forestall.

None of us who sign this statement accept as legitimate the denial of human rights in Iran, the pretense of democracy, the oppression of the Bahai, the denial of the Holocaust, or the right of Iran to verbally threaten the existence of the State of Israel. Our opposition to a war does not come from support for the Iranian regime.

The path of generosity outlined above will likely enhance, not weaken, Israeli, American, and global security, whereas an attack on Iran will make it hard for the democratic forces in Iran that oppose the current dictatorial regime to withstand nationalistic pressures to unite behind its current leaders against a foreign invader (Israel or the U.S.).

The signers of this ad do not agree on all of the statements above. Whatever the diversity of our perspectives, here's what we do all agree upon:

No war. No preemptive first strikes on Iran.

Memories of Holocaust Fuel Tensions with Iran

One reason some Israelis support a first strike is that they believe they are facing the current embodiment of Hitler in Iran and want to show that this time the Jews will defend themselves.

The Holocaust denial expressed by Iranian President Mahmoud Ahmadinejad and Iranian Supreme Leader Ali Khamenei is outrageous. Their verbal attacks on Israel often reflect a deep antagonism toward Jews. Their treatment of the Baha'i and their own domestic dissenters are crimes against humanity. We have no sympathy for them and hope to see their own people rise up against them. Yet not every oppressive regime is Hitler, and not every enemy of the State of Israel is the reincarntion of the Nazis. Many Israelis see Hitler everywhere. They detect him reincarnated in Nasser, in Arafat, in Hezbollah, in Hamas, in the Palestinian people, and now also in Iran.

I say this not to ridicule this Israeli perception so much as to acknowledge the ongoing post-traumatic stress disorder that shapes Israeli perceptions of the world and makes it difficult for them to make accurate interpretations of the intentions and dangers they face. I've discussed this in my new book, *Embracing Israel/Palestine*, where I explore in more detail how this reality has distorted daily life in Israel. The Israeli right-wingers tend to call anyone seeking peace with the Palestinians a Nazi or a Hitler. Some even called former Israeli Prime Minister Yitzhak Rabin a Hitler and thereby created the political climate in which he was assassinated by a religious Jew. It is this pervasive trauma that makes it so easy for Netanyahu, President Shimon Peres, and many Israeli people to feel justified in taking preemptive strikes against the variety of Hitlers they identify in their surroundings.

And of course, with that as their framework, the idea of nonviolence and "a strategy of generosity" that we've proposed seems absolutely insane. Hitler could not have been stopped by nonviolence in 1939, but a generosity strategy toward Germany and Eastern Europe in the 1920s from the victors of World War I could have eliminated the conditions that made possible the rise of fascism and anti-Semitism in the 1920s and 1930s. The New Deal's generosity toward the poor and middle class prevented the fascists and anti-Semites from attaining mass support in the United States. And the original Marshall Plan after World War II, aimed at giving aid to the countries that had been our enemies in the war, helped prevent a Stalinist distortion of communism from winning mass support in European countries devastated by the carnage of war.

A Strategy of Generosity as an Alternative to Militarism

So imagine if the United States were in fact to acknowledge its role in overthrowing the democratically elected government of Iran, imposing the Shah, and blocking support for the more moderate elements in the Islamic revolution that overturned the Shah at the end of the 1970s. And imagine if it apologized not only to Iran, but also to all the other countries where selfish elites have worked in concert with U.S. corporations to deplete local resources at bargain rates and impede the development or continuance of small-scale indigenous agriculture. Imagine if we changed our policies so that we no longer dumped products deemed unsafe for domestic use in the Third World. And imagine if we changed our economic treaties and institutions such as the IMF and the World Bank so that they enhance the development of Third World countries instead of impoverishing them. If such policies were accompanied by the Network of Spiritual Progressives' version of the Global Marshall Plan (including its careful attention to fostering a spirit of generosity – please download and read the full version at spiritualprogressives.org/GMP or ask our office to send you a copy), that approach could substantively undermine the anti-Americanism on which the Iranian fundamentalists depend to shift the attention of their own people away from the economic failures and suffering in their own society.

If Israel were to follow the steps outlined in my book *Embracing Israel/Palestine* for achieving a lasting reconciliation and peace with the Palestinian people, the situation with Iran would also change dramatically. Does that mean that if the United States and Israel were to actually embrace and act on a strategy of generosity, all extremists would suddenly throw up their arms, learn Hebrew, dance the hora, and embrace Israel and America? Certainly not! But what this approach to the world would accomplish in only a few short years would be a huge transformation in the way both Israel and the United States are perceived, and a huge reduction in the desperation experienced by people living in poverty and by people who have long been denied respect and the recognition of their dignity. In that context, the Iranian Green Movement, which sought to overthrow the rule of the mullahs after Iran's dishonest election in 2009, would no longer be marginalized by being portrayed as a tool of U.S. imperialism or Israeli expansionism. A Global Marshall Plan backed by the United States – and a generosity of spirit by Israel as it helped create an economically and politically viable Palestinian state – would undermine the ability of the oppressive regime in Iran to take advantage of fear and legitimate anger at Israel's policies toward Palestinians and U.S. policies that impose a global economic order with vast inequalities and vast suffering. Iran's leaders would no longer be able to deflect attention from the oppressive and distorted vision of Islam that has been imposed on the tens of millions of decent Iranians.

Indeed, fundamentalisms of every sort – Jewish, Christian, Islamic, Hindu, Buddhist, etc. – would have far less appeal, and their power to sway national elections would diminish. The use of nuclear weapons against the West would seem far less plausible, suicide would seem far less attractive, and hope would feel more available.

When presented with these arguments, many skeptics say, "Well, fine, but it's unlikely that our government would agree to move in that direction." This is a fundamentally different kind of objection – one based not on a problem with "the other" but on a problem with us and our own political structure.

And this brings into clearer focus what is so terribly dispiriting about the choices Obama has made while in office. He has been up against a contentious Republican party and disloyal Democrats in Congress, and there have been real limitations on what he might have accomplished even with a Democratic majority in Congress. But there was no constraint on his ability to use the presidency to challenge the worldview of materialism and militarism fostered by both parties since the ascent of Reagan in 1980. Instead, President Obama has pushed from public discourse progressive ideas he could have championed. This approach was evident when he refused to allow a national health plan with single-payer features to be considered in the gatherings he held to discuss health care reform. It was evident in his failure to explain to the American people what his good friend Rashid Khalidi had explained to him – the legitimacy of the Palestinian national movement, despite its many failures and distortions.

It was evident in his failure to challenge the role of banks and Wall Street. And it was manifest in his pandering year after year to AIPAC while ignoring the progressive Jews who were in the forefront of his efforts to be elected in 2008.

Some skeptics are willing to grant all of these points but still insist that it is too far-fetched to imagine a politics being built around this vision and that, in any event, such a strategy would take too long to address the "present emergency with Iran."

The short answer here is that *there is no present emergency* with Iran, except if the United States and Israel create it. Iran does not have nuclear weapons now, and if its leaders had nuclear weapons, there is little reason to believe that they would be willing to risk the virtually certain mass destruction that a nuclear Israel, backed by the United States, would inflict on Iran, ending not just the Islamic state but also burying the great history of the Persian people.

Given that there is no imminent emergency, we can focus instead on spreading a vision of politics that speaks to the deep human need for a society organized to facilitate love, caring, kindness, generosity, and ethical and ecological sensitivity. Until that vision wins majority support in the United States, we must work toward it with hope rather than wallow in depression or halfheartedly compromise with our leaders' militarist and fear-based assumptions. Progressives in November 2012 might reasonably decide to once again accept "lesser evil" politics in the November elections. But they should be organizing to push for a very different agenda than that likely to emerge from a possible second term for Obama, no matter how visionary he may present himself to be in the summer and fall of 2012 in an effort to attract our votes around election time. And we should certainly not rally around any military strike against Iran if Obama decides to covertly authorize Israel to make such a strike or similar military action in the months before the election to prove that he is "strong on defense."

It may take years to change the domination worldview in the United States and Israel, but this must be a high priority for spiritual progressives. Our strategy of generosity is far more realistic than the path of violence and wars.

Was Jesus Subversive?
Considering the 'other' reason Jesus died on the cross
by George Johnson

This article appeared in *The Lutheran*, a magazine of the Evangelical Lutheran Church in America prior to a Lenten season.

There is an aspect to Jesus' death that has been overlooked, or silenced even, because of the traditional emphasis on atonement. We focus on the sacrificial aspect of the cross: God sent Jesus to die for us so we can be forgiven.

But in recent years the word subversive emerges in the discussion in theological literature about Jesus' ministry. Questions abound:

- Why was Jesus executed as a criminal?

- Was there a legitimate reason for the Roman government to consider him a danger, a threat to national security?

- Did Jesus know the risks he was taking in his speech and actions?

- Was Jesus subversive?

Still, in most of our congregations the hymns we sing, the prayers we pray and the sermons we hear during Lent and into Holy Week lift up the death of Jesus as something he didn't deserve. He was innocent of all charges brought against him. He died so we might be saved. He paid the ransom. God was pleased with Jesus' sacrifice. "Worthy is Christ, the lamb who was slain, whose blood set us free to be people of God," I grew up with this liturgy.

Certainly some Bible verses do speak about the death of Jesus as payment for sin, as ransom, as atonement. But there also is strong evidence in the gospels that Jesus died because of what he said and did as a "subversive" Jewish teacher who was a danger to the status quo.

Religious leaders and Rome wanted him silenced because of the threat he posed to the established order. He had caused people to question some of their traditions and laws, and he showed that some things were more important than rules. These authorities didn't want to jeopardize their precarious standing with the superior authorities. So they turned Jesus over to be put to death.

Early in Jesus' ministry, as recorded in Mark, he questioned some laws regarding Sabbath observance. By his actions, he violated them. He didn't hesitate to heal the man with a withered hand. His disciples also broke the law by plucking grain on the Sabbath.

Jesus was accused of blasphemy because of his teaching about forgiveness. And the Pharisees conspired to destroy him (Mark 3:6). From the beginning of his ministry right up to the last week of his life, Jesus said and did things that brought conflict, leading to his death.

His cleansing of the temple took place just days before his crucifixion. It has important implications for why he was considered subversive. Jesus wasn't just criticizing the commercial use of the temple courtyard space but also confronting the domination system that violated God's intention.

The temple had become a cover for greed and exploitation. Jesus knew well the important role the temple played in the life of the Jewish community, yet he deliberately violated this sacred space to expose corruption in religion. That was subversion to some. He had to be stopped.

It can be helpful to read the gospels with a fresh perspective.

- What do the authors of the first four books of the New Testament, the gospel writers, tell us about the reasons Jesus was put to death?
- In what sense was Jesus executed because of what he said and did?
- Was atonement for sin the main reason? The only reason?
- How does subversion add to the concept of compassion in Jesus' death?

The gospels make it clear that Jesus was considered a threat to society by those who felt responsible to maintain peace and security; that he died because of what he said and did. It is also clear that he knew the possible consequences of his action.

These biblical insights don't take away from the sacrificial aspect of Jesus' death or diminish the love that led him to the cross. But they do encourage us to be more aware of the full meaning of the cross as a present reality as well as an event in Jesus' life.

When Jesus told his disciples to take up their cross and follow him, he was reminding us all that there will be times when our witness and actions will meet resistance from those in power. Yes, the cross can cause us to " . . . tremble, tremble, tremble" as we sing in the Negro spiritual.

The Jesus movement was, and is, countercultural. The proclamation of the gospel includes a declaration of God's justice: God's action to bring about an alternative to violence, greed, hunger and domination. We preach grace – but not only grace.

Old Testament scholar Walter Brueggemann writes: "A rereading of the gospel of grace and a reconsideration of the Enlightenment ideology will lead to a stunning and compelling fresh awareness: Our most serious relationships, including our relationship to the God of the gospel, are, at the same time, profoundly unconditional and massively conditional" (*The Covenanted Self*, Fortress Press, 1999).

Brueggemann goes on to suggest that it becomes a problem when we add the word "alone" to Paul's emphasis on grace. Could it be that our fixation on "grace alone" has left us deaf to God's call to "do justice, and to love kindness and to walk humbly with our God" (Micah 6:8)? When Jesus did exactly this, he was considered a subversive.

The sacrament of communion is centered on the cross and the presence of Jesus for us. Jesus' sacrifice is a strong element in our liturgy. Would we be as eager to gather at the table if we understood the full reason for Jesus' death? Is not the bread and wine also a reminder that Jesus died because he laid his life on the line by opposing the Roman Empire and religious traditions?

When we hear the words "do this for the remembrance of me," what are we invited to remember? God's forgiveness? Yes. But are we not also to remember that Jesus was considered subversive? …..and to realize that eating the bread and drinking the wine makes us part of his resistance movement?

When I was young, I was taught that God loves me and that Jesus died for me. I was reminded to be thankful that God sent Jesus to die for my sins. I accepted Jesus as my savior. I'm grateful for my early training. But something was missing: I don't remember being taught that the cross is also about confrontation, subversion and consequences.

Many Lenten hymns still move me. This season I will once again sing, with gusto, "Lift high the cross, the love of Christ proclaim." When I wear a cross around my neck, I don't do so because I think of it as "beautiful," nor do I slip it in the front pocket of my shirt because it's too heavy as one Bishop told me.

The cross is central to my faith.

But I am concerned for our church and for our witness to the world if the cross only stands for Jesus' sacrifice for our sins. As I read the Scriptures, I'm reminded that Jesus died because he was considered a threat to a society that neglected the poor and worshiped the sword.

Sometimes I even wish Jesus hadn't asked me to take up my cross.

Appendix

EXCERPTED FROM

The Shakertown Pledge

Some years ago a group of social justice advocates met for a gathering at a retreat center near Shakertown in Pennsylvania. Out of this gathering came this pledge that all the participants signed.

"Recognizing that the earth and the fullness thereof is a gift from our God, and that we are called to cherish, nurture and provide loving stewardship for the earth's resources, and recognizing that life itself is a gift, and a call to responsibility, joy and celebration, I make the following declaration:"

- I declare myself to be a world citizen.

- I commit myself to lead an ecologically sound life.

- I commit myself to lead a life of creative simplicity and to share my personal wealth with the world's poor.

- I commit myself to join with others in reshaping institutions in order to bring about a more just global society in which each person has full access to the needed resources for their physical, emotional, intellectual and spiritual growth.

- I commit myself to occupational accountability, and in so doing will seek to avoid the creation of products which cause harm.

- I affirm the gift of my body, and commit myself to its proper nourishment and physical well-being.

- I commit myself to examine continually my relations with others and to attempt to relate honestly, morally and lovingly to those around me.

- I commit myself to personal renewal through prayer, meditation and study.

- I commit myself to responsible participation in a community of faith.

EXCERPTED FROM

Don't Forget the Best

by Dorothee Soelle

◆◆◆

From *Against the Wind,* Copyright © 1990 used with permission of Fortress Press

Thirteen years ago, when I became a grandmother for the first time, I had the feeling that this new role – grown by now to include three grandchildren – would surely make growing older easier for me. And I became aware once again that I still wanted to hand on something of what was important for my generation. I do not want my people to forget fascism. Theodor W. Adorno once said, "The very first demand of education is that Auschwitz does not happen once again."

I don't want to let go of this basic feeling, and I cannot do so. To the last I resist that this German event be leveled out, as for example in the *Historiker-streit.* I resist people's now talking as if this event could be relativized through comparison with other peoples who behaved no differently. I find the whole white-washing of the event simply unbearable. It is in this sense that I really struggle against getting older, and I declare: There are things that must not be forgotten! Remembering, collective remembering, is not a luxury but the indispensable key to liberation.

This is something that I, as an older person, wish to pass one: Do not forget! Only they who remember have a future and hope. I see myself as a link in a chain, as a wave in a large wave-pattern; I am not the whole thing, I am a part. Not that I bear the root: The root bears me, as Paul writes in Romans 11:18. That calms me. There is a saying from the German Peasant Wars: "We go home beaten, the grandchildren will fare better." Ernst Bloch liked to quote these words. What is noted here is a connection between remembrance and the future; being beaten and seeing justice defeated are not in vain.

I remember an Irish fairy tale about the terrible trials a person must undergo when courting a prince or princess. "The king's son, who had just become my friend, must clean out a stable that has been manure-filled for 120 years.

Every time he throws out one shovelful, three shovelfuls of smelly manure come flying back in through each of the forty wide-open windows."

As I understand it, what is the origin of theology? I believe that it really does take its rise in a stable that reeks of historic injustice. And there we are with our far too small spades, talking to one another. Theology that is truly alive never arises outside of and apart from its situation; it does not drop straight from heaven as "God's Word." Rather, it constitutes itself in the solidarity of those affected.

I continue to understand faith as a mixture of trust and fear, hope and doubt – in the Gospels Jesus called it great or little faith – as life's intensity, the search for the true prince and for the reign of God. A conversation, in the full sense of the word, comes into being when people share together their hunger for spirit in leaden, spiritless times. The satiated have no need to talk to each other.

My life is that of a theological worker who tries to tell something of God's pain and God's joy. My language has perhaps become "more pious," but it was not my subjective development alone, as I have tried to describe it here, that has led to this. It was my participation in the worldwide Christian movement toward a Conciliar Process in which justice, peace, and the integrity of creation finally, clearly represent the heart of faith. Theologically speaking, I think I am less alone today than years ago. To be able to say so is a kind of bliss: *!Gracias a Dios!*

It was 1990 when a German radio station invited a contribution from me for one of its broadcast series; I was to compose a letter to my children and to state "what really counts in life." Grown-ups were to pass on what gave them comfort, what should not be forgotten or become lost. The following little text was my response.

Dear Children,

In the sagas and fairy tales I used to tell you years ago, there is a motif of a poor shepherd who one day is led far away by a little gray man, to a mysterious mountain. The mountain bursts open, and inside glisten the most precious treasures. But as the shepherd keeps stuffing his pockets, a voice calls out, "Don't forget the best!" The story goes on that the door crashes shut behind the shepherd, and the treasures in his pockets turn into dust.

I have never understood what "the best" was really supposed to be. Was it perhaps the clump of flowers at the gate of the mountain? Or a homely old lamp like that of Aladdin? Was it perhaps the key with which to get back in? Perhaps the wish to go back and not to forget?

Don't forget the best! All four of you know that the voice of a little gray man enticed me far away from ordinary life into religion, away from "its cultured despisers" and ever closer to something perhaps more Jewish than a dogmatic Christian faith.

Of all the things I would have liked to give you in the midst of the enmity that life shatters you with, this is the most difficult to explain. I can't simply sign my treasures over to you. To love God with the whole heart, with all one's strength, from one's entire soul – and that in a world that breaks with tradition – is something I cannot pass on like an inheritance.

My attempts to raise you as Christians had little chance of succeeding; the institution again and again attacked me from behind, the church was and is only rarely worthy of trust. But I am also very conscious of my own lack of credibly living out customs and symbols, of making hymn and prayer part of everyday life. It is as if we parents had no house of religion to offer you to live in but a derelict one.

A visible manifestation of the difficulty that children with vitality have with their parents today is the fact that you, Mirjam, as the youngest, did not become confirmed. Yet you live no farther away from the treasure mountain and perhaps also hear the voice of the little gray man. That may have been the reason why I held back from enticing you into Christianity – the word "educate" is surely quite out of place in this situation.

But – organized religion or not – I do wish that you all become a little bit pious. Don't forget the best! I mean, that you praise God sometimes, not always – only the chatterers and the courtiers of God do so – but on occasion, when you are very happy, so that happiness flows by itself into gratitude and you sing "hallelujah" or the great *om* of Indian religion.

On our trips we used to drag you into churches; on one occasion, the church we looked at was awful. I believe it was you, Caroline, who announced dryly, "No God in there." Precisely that is not to be said in your lives; God is to be "in there," at the sea and in the clouds, in the candle, in music, and, of course, in love.

Without grounding in the ground of life, this true joy is not there, and our joy is then focused always on occasions and things. True joy, the joy of life, the happiness of being alive is not the joy that arises because there are strawberries, because school was canceled, or a wonderful visitor had arrived. True joy is without a "why," or as my best friend from the Middle Ages, Meister Eckhart, used to say, *"sunder warumbe"* ("utterly devoid of why").

If I could give you only a little of this *sunder warumbe* joy, strong mother or not, it would already be very much. Then I would readily let go of my unwelcome extra-special wishes, those motherly demands, such as that once in your life you would read Meister Eckhart: I would gladly turn back again into the little gray man and sit in the blue cave among the glistening jewels and call out, "Don't forget the best!"

Your old Mama

Millenium Development Goals

Background

In September 2000, at the UN Millennium Summit, all the countries of the world, including the United States, affirmed a set of international development goals in the United Nations Millennium Declaration. Known as the Millennium Development Goals (MDGs), they have helped focus the energy and resources of the nations of the world on a common strategy to address the issues of poverty, hunger and health. Specific, achievable targets for the year 2015 have been set, and include:

The Millennium Development Goals: By 2015 . . .

- Eradicate extreme poverty and hunger
- Reduce by half the proportion of people living on less than one dollar a day
- Achieve universal primary education
- Promote gender equality and empower women
- Reduce by two-thirds the mortality rate among children under five
- Improve maternal health
- Combat HIV/AIDS, malaria and other diseases
- Ensure environmental sustainability
- Reduce by half the proportion of people without sustainable access to safe drinking water and basic sanitation
- Develop a global partnership for development
- Develop further an open trading and financial system that is rule-based, predictable and non-discriminatory
- Address the least-developed countries' special needs

From Words to the Word

by George Johnson

———◆◆◆———

This article is adapted from a chapter in *Beyond Guilt* by George S. Johnson.

We are discovering that the Bible says a great deal about the poor. It all seems askew, for while the poor do get a lot of attention in the Bible, the non-poor get a lot of attention in the church and usually end up running things. One reason for this is that the nonpoor have become the official interpreters of the Scriptures and have managed to take most of the sting out of the passages dealing with the poor.

Robert McAfee Brown

Many of us are so bombarded with words that we despair of reading anything more about the problems of the world. Our mailboxes are full of letters asking us to join this and that cause. Pleas are made for money to help alleviate human suffering. Magazines and newspapers are full of excellent articles that both enlighten and frighten. There is no lack of words to read or voices that cry for help.

There are times when we need to set aside spoken and written words in order to encounter the Word. Not that such words aren't important. But sometimes we reach a saturation point. More information is not what is lacking, but a time to reflect or time to be alone with God, a time of silence, a time to put our inner spirit in order. From our encounters with the Word we are strengthened and better equipped to handle the call for involvement and risk-taking.

There also are times when we need to return to the Word in order to listen to those parts of Scripture that we have neglected or ignored. Our listening is enriched by recalling not only how the Word comes to us but how the Word comes to others. For example, when we listen to the Word as encountered by the poor, we hear new things because of their unique experiences. Such a word is fresh, energizing and vital to our understanding.

In order for us to move beyond guilt and powerlessness we need to search the scriptures constantly. There we will find a God who listens to the cries of the poor, a promise of forgiveness that frees us from the burden of guilt, a Jesus who came to preach good news to the poor and set the oppressed free. In the Word we find a word of hope that sustains us when death and destruction surround us, and a young church that gave high priority to sharing with those in need. The Scriptures give us clear warnings about idolatry that causes human suffering and oppression. We are invited to participate in the kingdom where swords are beaten into plowshares and weeping is turned into songs of joy. The message within the Word dismantles the dominant consciousness of the privileged and energizes us with hope and courage to take one more step forward.

Shortly after I returned from a trip to Central America I planned my preaching for Advent and Christmas. Christians in Latin America had taught me how meaningful the Magnificat passage in Luke had been to them as they struggled to survive. I decided to use the Luke 1:46-55 passage as my text for Christmas Eve. It was a first for me.

In my sermon I talked about Mary's insight and confidence that the coming messianic age would include a reversal of things. The mighty would be brought down, the lowly exalted, the rich sent away empty and the hungry would be fed good things. When I applied this message to our current situation in an affluent society I asked, "Where is the good news for us as we listen to Mary's understanding of good news?" I then laid out some ways the coming of Jesus is good news to today's world.

During my sermon, a middle aged woman walked out. I didn't think much about it. Maybe she remembered the oven was left on or she needed a potty break. After the sermon the head usher came to me with these words: "Pastor George, for eight years I've tried to get my aunt to come back to church. Tonight she came. She walked out during your sermon and said to me on the way out that she didn't come to church on Christmas Eve to hear that. She said, "That's not the Gospel." I was crushed, hurt, embarrassed and bewildered. No doubt I could have said it better but I was reminded that sometimes the Word comes to us through the words of biblical characters and it may sound strange to us because we have been protected by a cultural screening of the biblical message.

The Power Monopoly

An article written by Walter Brueggemann for the *Hunger Times*, a tabloid used by the Hunger Program of the former American Lutheran Church.

Peace is the redistribution of power. Any talk about peace that does not face questions of power is unbiblical. I particularly want to call your attention to the work of Norman Gottwald who, for this sort of business, is the most important Old Testament scholar we have. Gottwald has helped us see that when we open the Bible, we do not find a bunch of innocent nomads dressed in burlap and bathrobes, but what we find is an empire.

In Genesis 12 it says that there wasn't any bread and they went to Egypt to get bread. Now social suspicion leads one to ask: "How come Egypt had so much bread?" *What the Bible knows is that we are born into a world with social monopolies.* And what Israel wants its boys and girls to learn from little on, is that there is something wrong with social monopolies.

Genesis 47 deals with the questions: "How did we get into this mess?" "How did we get into this monopoly where some people have so much and some people don't have anything?" And there it is said: We got into it because our brother, or our alienated brother, Joseph, was a smart guy and he bought up all the land for Pharaoh.

The first year, when the poor people came for bread, he said: "I'll give you some bread and I'll take your money." The second year they needed some bread and he said: "I've got your money: I'll take your cattle." (Call that the "means of production.") The third year, when they needed some bread, he said: "I don't think you have any collateral left." So he said, "Why don't we take your land? We'll take your land and your bodies."

And they said, "Take our land and our bodies. We just don't want to starve to death. We will gladly be your slaves!"

And that is how the monopoly got established.

One very telling little footnote in Genesis 47 says that *Pharaoh took all the land except the land of the priests. (Someone has to bless the empire!)*

Exodus starts out saying that we cried out and the Lord saw and the Lord knew and the Lord remembered and the Lord came down and saved – Exodus 2, Exodus 3.

This model of peace believes that the cries of those who are excluded from the monopoly mobilize the power of justice in heaven to rearrange things.

The exodus story is the liturgical reenactment that goes on and on in families and in schools and in business and in the world – the liturgical reenactment of the redistribution of goods and the power and the access.

You know where it ends. It ends in Exodus 15:20-21, where Miriam and her sisters take timbrels and dance. The liturgy invites the community of faith from Exodus 1 to Exodus 15 to start with the cry of oppression and end with the dance of liberation. And the narrative is the enactment of the redistribution of the goods which feels (to the Israelites) like liberation and gift and miracle – but which feels to Egypt and Pharaoh like terrorism and social revolution. It all depends on where you sit when you read.

Walter Brueggemann

BIBLICAL PASSAGES RELATED TO HUNGER, POVERTY AND JUSTICE

Genesis 1:29-30	God gives the world's food to Adam and Eve
Exodus 3:7-12	Moses asked to go to Pharaoh
Exodus 16:1-12	The manna life-style
Leviticus 19:9-11	Leave a portion of your harvest for the poor
Numbers 11:4-23	People greedy for meat
Deut. 14:28-15:11	A redistribution of wealth and law of tithe
1 Kings 21:1-20	Lust for land leads to deceit and oppression
Psalm 72:1-14	How to pray for government
Psalm 82	Justice to the weak and destitute
Psalm 146:5-9	The Lord is just and feeds the hungry
Proverbs 14:20-21	Happy are they who are kind to the poor
Proverbs 19:17	Who is kind to the poor lends to the Lord

Proverbs 21:13	Listen to the cry of the poor
Isaiah 1:17-18	Seek justice; correct oppression
Isaiah 3:13-15	Why do you grind the face of the poor?
Isaiah 5:1-7	I looked for justice but beheld bloodshed
Isaiah 58: 6-12	Pour yourself out for the hungry
Jeremiah 22:13-16	To know the Lord is to do justice
Ezekiel 16:49	Sodom destroyed because of neglect of the poor
Amos 4:1-3	Elite and wealthy women implicated in injustice
Amos 5:10-24	Let justice roll down like waters
Amos 8:4-7	The greedy buy the poor for silver
Micah 6:8	Do justice, love mercy, walk humbly
Matthew 5:23-24	First be reconciled, then offer your gifts
Matthew 6:25-34	Seek kingdom of God and justice first
Matthew 23:23	You have neglected justice, mercy and faith
Matthew 25:31-46	I was hungry and you gave me food
Mark 8:1-9	Feeding the multitude, also John 6:1-14
Luke 1:46-55	Mary's Magnificat, the great reversal
Luke 10:25-37	Good Samaritan
Luke 14:12-14	Invite the poor to your dinner
Luke 16:19-31	Rich man and Lazarus
Luke 19:1-10	Zacchaeus's radical generosity
John 6:25-35, 47-51	I am the bread of life
John 13:1-20	Jesus washing disciples' feet
Acts 2:42-47, 4:32-35	Sharing in the early church
Acts 6:1-7	First dispute in church over distribution of food
1 Cor. 11:17-34	Selfishness in the Christian assembly
1 Cor. 16:1-2	Put aside for the needy
2 Cor. 8:12-15	A question of equality and abundance
2 Cor. 9:6-15	God loves a cheerful giver
Galatians 2:10	Remember the poor
James 2:1-7	Rich, poor and God's bias
James 2:14, 17, 26	Faith without works is dead
1 John 3:17-18	Loving in deed, not just in word
1 John 4:19-21	Cannot love God without loving neighbor

Why Justice Is Not Secondary

The biblical term justice needs our attention. It has become a very popular word. We hear about racial justice, environmental justice, economic justice, gender justice, global justice, and creation justice to name a few. But what do we mean when we use the term? What do people think and feel when they hear the word justice? We need to unpack this concept.

A few questions may help us in our research and critique. Add your own questions.

1. A review of the context of Reformation theology reminds us that fear of God and eternal damnation were dominant themes in European society in the 16th century. Works righteousness was strong in medieval Christianity. Grace, the unmerited love of God, was welcome and became central in most Protestant teaching and preaching. Has our fixation on grace allowed justice to become secondary?

Our context is different today. Fear of damnation is not central. Perhaps inequality, injustice and violence are more dominant concerns rather than works righteousness. What is good news in our context? By elevating grace above justice have we missed something important in Biblical theology? This does not mean grace is secondary but neither is love of neighbor. How do we integrate them?

2. Was not love of neighbor central in the teachings of Jesus? Did Jesus ever suggest or act as though justice was secondary? Have we assumed that those who experience forgiveness will do justice? Is there a cause/effect relationship in our understanding of belief and ethics that needs reflection? Asking who is my neighbor is part of justice.

3. The biblical terms mispat and sedekah (justice and righteousness) almost always center on love of neighbor and correcting oppression. It is more than charity or relieving pain. It includes the elimination of the causes that bring inequality and pain. If we truly want justice it means a willingness to let go of privileges, systems and policies that contribute to the pain and suffering of our neighbors. Sister Marie Neal in her book, The Socio-Theology of Letting Go is helpful on this topic. In what ways does justice include the courage to let go? Nobody wants to lose one's job or friends or pension. How do we help people in danger of such loss?

4. In responding to the biblical summons to seek justice and correct oppression it is good to remember that it is not easy and can be dangerous. Shane Clai-

borne reminds us that charity can win awards and applause but joining the poor can get you killed. Dom Helder Camara of Brazil used to say when I help the hungry they call me a saint but when I ask why are they poor they call me a communist. Jesus reminded his audience of what happened to the prophets when they called for justice. "Blessed are those who are persecuted for doing right." How can we help people understand this dimension to doing justice?

5. Jose Miranda in his commentary on John (*Being and Messiah*) says that God is known only in love of neighbor. How do you respond to that comment? In I John we learn that whoever loves is born of God. How do we interpret and apply that?

6. Rolf Knierim, my Old Testament professor at Claremont School of Theology, reminded us that worship was the primary setting in which Israel experienced and celebrated justice. The advancement of justice and the proclamation of justice were the very function of worship. The Psalms document this clearly. What is the role of justice and proclamation of justice in our worship today? Music is important. How do our liturgies, anthems and hymns enable us to proclaim justice? Should an understanding of biblical justice be important in hiring a director of music?

7. What gives us hope? We hear a lot more about justice today than we used to. Church schools and seminaries have found ways to include justice in the curriculum. My seminary in St. Paul, MN has an endowed Chair for Justice and Christian Community. There is a strong effort to include experiential learning around social analysis and some form of social justice. Churches have committees assigned to help members connect their faith to current issues of justice. My personal library is full of books on justice. One is *Marx and the Bible,* which I had to read twice because it unsettled my Reformation theology. From that came the book, *Courage to Think Differently* that is going through a reprint as I write.

Where my wife Vivian and I worship, they sing every Sunday the Micah 6:8 song...."God has shown you O people what is good and what does the Lord require of you, but to do justice, love mercy and walk humbly with your God." What are some examples you can site that help us remember that justice is not secondary?

Rev. George S Johnson
Laguna Woods, CA
georgesjohnson@gmail.com

Irrelevant Religion –
Challenge for the Church

by George Johnson

◆◆◆

Five Giants are coming over the hill. They are: 1. Violence and war 2.Hunger and poverty 3.Greed and domination 4. Degradation of the environment 5. Irrelevant religion. It is # 5, irrelevant religion, that enables us to ignore the first four.

From Call to Action newsletter

1. **READING THE BIBLE AGAIN** . . . . Rethinking the scriptures

2. **FOOD, FARMING AND HOLY GROUND** . . . . . . Rediscovering creation

3. **GRACE YES, BUT NOT ONLY GRACE** Rethinking Reformation theology

4. **PERSONAL BUT NOT PRIVATE** . . . . .Revisioning Community

5. **JESUS OPENED THEIR MINDS** . . . . .Rethinking social analysis

6. **THE ORIGIN AND SIGNIFICANCE OF WEALTH** Rethinking inequality

7. **THE UNFINISHED REFORMATION** . . . . Rediscovering the laity

8. **UNLESS YOU ARE BORN AGAIN** . . . . Rediscovering conversion

9. **MAKING ROOM FOR PROPHETS** . . . . Rediscovering the prophetic

10. **DID JESUS DIE FOR OUR SINS?** . . . . Rethinking Atonement

11. **GOD AND THE EXCLUDED**. . . . . .Rediscovering the poor

12. **RELIGION VIOLENCE AND WAR**. . . . . . . .Rediscovering nonviolence

13. **WHAT DOES GOD REQUIRE?** . . . . Rediscovering justice

14. **NOT COUNTING WOMEN AND CHILDREN** Rethinking gender issues

15. **IN THE NAME OF NATIONAL SECURITY** . . . . Rethinking empire

16. **EXPERIENCING SACRED PRESENCE** . Rediscovering the sacramental

EXCERPTED FROM

How to Hang in There For the Long Haul

by Don Irish

◆◆◆

Young people who are committed to peace and justice sometimes ask their elders how they have been able to continue such efforts for so long. We need to gain and retain the talents, energies, and early commitment of these youth. What guidance can be given them? Here are some suggestions.

1. *Recognize that those who plant trees may not live to enjoy the fruit.* Others have preceded us; we can likewise serve those yet to come. Always take the long look, not expecting quick results.

2. *Everybody/everything is connected to everybody/everything.* A holistic approach to life is more effective, comprehensible, and satisfying.

3. *You can't do everything – but you always can do something.* To focus on effectiveness may often result in ineffectiveness. Do what you can, where you are, with what energies and talents you have, given other significant obligations.

4. *Remember that the world does not depend upon you alone for needed changes.* That's a burden lifted from your shoulders! Avoid burn-out: find respites fro continual, unceasing pressures. Life is to be lived!

5. *Redefine success in your endeavors for societal change.* To prevent a situation from becoming worse is success. To gain a portion of what is attempted, without retreat from one's goal, is success. To be among the first to initiate a movement for peace and justice that brings its achievements decades later is success. To keep hope alive during dark days is also success.

6. *Realize that courage is rarely manifested by persons who are alone.* You need to find others of like mind so you can provide support for each

other, enabling all to withstand the societal pressures that will be brought to bear against nonconformity.

7. *Develop a faith that can sustain you.* Avoid succumbing to despair or disseminating it, for that will immobilize you and others, making personal and collective action seem useless, hopeless.

8. *Adopt a nonviolent philosophy as a thoroughgoing way of life.* Try to make it applicable to all your behaviors and attitudes, not just a temporary tactic. Consistency to principle is essential for integrity and persistence.

9. *Find joy and satisfaction in small gains, because those are usually what you will get!* Appreciate the first words from an autistic child; a smile from a depressed individual; reconciliation with an opponent.

10. *Focus your challenges on issues/problems, not attacks on persons.* Avoid demonizing opponents, for hate will not resolve conflicts or reconcile the parties. People are what they are for reasons that need to be understood, though not necessarily excused.

11. *Know that a majority is not needed to bring significant changes.* A "critical mass," a minority of committed, informed, relentlessly persistent individuals, can accomplish wonders. One stone cannot make an arch. One drop of water cannot turn a mill wheel. But one plus one plus others make a million (or dozen) disciples!

12. *Believe that at times, "They also serve who only stand and wait."* We cannot always stop mounting tragedies midstream, especially if we are "outsiders." Ultimately, the parties in contention must be willing to resolve their problems together. Then we can assist.

13. *Know that there are many ways and means to bring change nonviolently, often with success.* Beware of those who argue either/or alternatives, or who contend that "we have no choice." There are always choices, even if unsatisfactory ones.

14. *Remember that means and ends are inextricably linked.* The means used predetermine the ends attained. "There is no way to peace. Peace is the way."

15. *Respond to those who question the efficacy of nonviolence.* Turn the question around: "How effective have violence and war been?" There is growing literature on the successful use of nonviolent means to resolve conflict and injustice.

16. *Observe that serious structural problems will not be resolved by "middle of the road" measures.* Radical changes may be needed for such conditions – dealing with the root causes, so as to move the action toward more basic solutions. "Extreme" and urgent proposals (if reasoned, civil, and nonviolent) can perform important social functions.

17. *Learn from the long experience of others.* For instance, indigenous peoples have much to teach and demonstrate to us about the nature of sustainable societies. Our current social system is not sustainable. It exists at the expense of others' welfare, depends on a fatal commitment to unlimited "growth," and is leading to the destruction of our earth and horrendous human problems.

18. *Retain a sense of humor.* Events often turn out better than you feared, though less well than you hoped. Humor can be a tool in struggles, as well as an antidote to despair. For example, in the South of the 1960s on one campus there were labels: "This tree for white dogs only!" "This tree for colored dogs only!" Or "Out of Order" signs appeared on only the "white" drinking fountains, bathrooms, elevators!

19. *Don't expect leadership for major, structural societal changes to come from the top.* Political courage is rare and tends to follow growing grassroots sentiment. Laws tend to follow societal changes in attitudes and conditions, not anticipate them. So the grassroots work has to precede, and build pressures for, change.

20. *Recognize that there really are no absolute dictators.* Even they must keep their ears to the ground, are affected by world opinion and actions, eventually must modify their positions to maintain control. Their legitimacy can be undercut by many nonviolent forms of resistance and non-cooperation, from within and without.

21. *Recognize that even when one has done all he or she has felt able to do, the human race may still collectively fail to change its ways sufficiently and in time to avoid its own created catastrophes.* Success is not guaranteed, but faithfulness is expected. However, one can still live with integrity, work for justice and peace, and feel secure with whatever reckoning the greater cosmos may render. If you, I, and others persist, we may even find that we have helped bring about a new, more humane, sustainable society!

EXCERPTED FROM

10 Reasons for Choosing a Simpler Lifestyle

by Jorgan Lisner

- As an act of faith performed for the sake of personal integrity and as an expression of personal commitment to a more equitable distribution of the earth's resources.

- As an act of self-defense against the mind and body-polluting effects of over-consumption.

- As an act of withdrawal from the achievement-neurosis of our high-pressure, materialistic society.

- As an act of solidarity with the majority of humankind, which has no choice of lifestyle.

- As an act of sharing with others what has been given to us, or of returning what was usurped by us through unjust social and economic structures.

- As an act of celebration with the riches found in creativity, spirituality, and community with others rather than in mindless consumerism.

- As an act of provocation (conspicuous underconsumption) to arouse curiosity leading to dialogue with others about affluence, alienation, poverty and social injustice.

- As an act of anticipation of the era when self-confidence and assertiveness of the underprivileged forces new power relationships and new patterns of resource allocation upon us.

- As an act of advocacy of legislated changes in present patterns of production and consumption in the direction of a new international economic order.

- As an excercise of purchasing power to redirect production away from the stisfaction of artificially created wants, towards the supplying of goods and services that meet genuine social needs.

Marx and the Bible

by George Johnson

⎯⎯ ❖ ⎯⎯

During our year of study in Sweden (1979-80) I read Jose Porfirio Miranda's book, *Marx and the Bible*. In fact I read it twice partly because it challenged my Protestant training in theology and partly because it opened my eyes to the meaning and use of the concept of justice in the Bible. I presented a paper on Miranda in a theology class at the University of Uppsala. A few years later was on a team that invited Miranda to come to the United States and speak at Augsburg College and Luther Theological Seminary in Minnesota.

While still in Sweden the challenge of Miranda's writing prompted me to write to some respected seminary professors and inquire how theologians are responding to Miranda's critique of Western theology. The only response I received was, "We aren't reading Miranda." I thought, "Why not?"

Walter Brueggemann has said this about *Marx and the Bible*: "Miranda combines radical social criticism with radical hermeneutical exploration in a way that requires a fresh hearing of the gospel...In his writings there is a kind of discernment that may reform and renew the study of scripture." When David Tiede, once president of Luther Seminary in St Paul, gave a review of Miranda' *Communism in the Bible* before the seminary community, he reminded us that Miranda engages us in an examination (argument) with the scriptures, not an argument with Miranda. Richard Mouw of Fuller Seminary in California says, "Jose Miranda's book (*Communism in the Bible*) is an extremely valuable statement, which advances the discussion of biblical economics to a new stage." I was disappointed to discover that the only people reading Miranda were those interested in liberation theology.

Jose Miranda is a Catholic from Mexico. He has studied economics at the University of Munich and Munster in Germany as well as Biblical sciences at the Biblical Institute in Rome. He has taught mathematics, economic theory, philosophy, law and exegesis. While teaching at a university in Mexico City he worked closely with student organizations, workers in the barrios and various groups living in poverty in Mexico.

Three books authored by Miranda that have formed my understanding of his theology are: *Marx and the Bible* (Orbis 1974), *Being and Messiah* (Orbis 1977) and *Communism in the Bible.* (Orbis 1982) A secondary source has been *Theology in a New Key* by Robert McAfee Brown.

Something caught my attention recently while reading Diana Butler Bass's book, *Christianity after Religion* (HarperCollins 2012) which reminded me of Miranda's contention that doing justice for the poor and oppressed is at the center of the biblical story of salvation. Bass calls for a reversal of accepted assumptions in both Protestant and Catholic theology. For centuries, she says, we have ordered faith in this way: first comes believing, next comes behaving and third comes belonging. This order she contends is neither scriptural nor effective. Instead of believing, behaving and belonging, she reverses the order to belonging, behaving and believing. An interesting thought.

I might debate the role of belonging as the first step; although she grounds this in the scripture. I do find some connection with her order in placing behavior before believing. Bass argues convincingly that we have placed correct doctrine (proclamation and beliefs) as the first step in evangelical outreach. Remember the first spiritual law, God loves you and has a wonderful plan for your life. That means what we believe produces behavior. As one pastor said to me, "When you preach grace enough it will result in loving one's neighbor." Both Miranda and Bass seem to suggest that we come to believe when we experience God in our neighbor and in the act of doing justice for our neighbor . . . not through correct doctrines or teaching. Following precedes believing. Am I reading Bass incorrectly? Check out chapter seven of *Christianity before Religion*.

My purpose in writing this for the appendix is to encourage people who are interested in social justice to read Miranda… with your Bible close at hand, and to have some conversation with Bass in her contention that behavior precedes believing. If you need some encouragement to think differently on this issue go back to chapter four of this volume and read Brueggemann's article called: Obedience That Is Not Legalism. Page 133.

Some things that Miranda thinks need our attention if we want to reform and renew Christianity are:

- Christianity has become an effective ally of the structures of economic and political oppression primarily because of a misunderstanding of mispat (justice) in both the Old and New Testaments.

- Western theology has too long been considered the norm by which all theology is judged and measured. There has been a theological captivity (of which it is not always aware), a mindset colored by situations of affluence, capitalistic assumptions and male dominance.

- Many interpretations of the Bible have been crystallized in the translation of the Bible. One example is the translation of the word mispat (justice) as righteousness. Psalm 72:1-2, Romans 1:17-18, Matthew 6:33, Phil. 3:9.

- Western theology has concentrated too much on individual sin and thereby missed Paul's understanding of sin. Miranda believes sin is to be abolished, not just forgiven. Otherwise the call to repentance is superfluous. The church needs to address structural sin.

- Exodus, not creation, is the primary and initial revelation of the God of the Bible. This is not a denial of God as creator of the world. But the elementary principle of hermeneutics is to understand that the moral imperative of justice is the primary revelatory intervention of God in human history in the Bible.

- To know God is to do justice and defend the cause of the poor and the needy. (Jer. 22:16) Nothing authorizes us to introduce a cause/effect relationship between to know Yahweh and to practice justice. The Bible does not introduce categories like "sign" or "manifestation of." It has been a mistake to differentiate between love and justice. Believing and loving our neighbor is the same thing. (I John 2:29, I John 4:7, I John 3:10, III John 11)

- The God of the Bible is not something to contemplate or thematize, but is rather found (experienced) in the moral imperative of justice. God is more concerned about inter-human justice than cultus, prayers and adoration.

- The message of scripture is crucial. The church needs to take the Bible seriously and understand that the message is subversive.

- Theology can be done only from the context of praxis. There is a need to "do theology". Theology is done out of one's experience, one's reality.

- Christ did not come to announce a list of truths to the world. He came to change the world. This is the mission of the church.

EXCERPTED FROM

Responses to World Hunger

Adapted from a Chart by Charles P. Lutz

	Response I	Response II
The Problem	Famine/Starvation	Underdevelopment
Visual Image	Starving Child	Floods, Parched Earth, Impure Water, Inadequate Technology
The Need	More Food Now	More Development
The Remedy	Relief Aid Hunger Appeal	Education, Self-Help Assistance, Wells-Seeds-Training
Typical Bible Text	Good Samaritan Joseph's Granary Matthew 25	Parable of Talents Law of Sabbath
Typical Object Of Study and Research	Food Deficits, Food Reserves, Population Growth	Sustainable Agriculture, Infra-Structures Appropriate Technology, Green Revolution
Motive Christian Value	Charity, Sympathy, Guilt	Sharing Service To Neighbor, Survival Interests
Lifestyle Response	Give Surplus Money and Food, Earn More-Give More	Give Money and Technical Aid, Seek to Understand "Underdeveloped"
Long-Term Consequence	Dependence	Self-Reliance For Some
Variation on Proverb	"Give the Hungry a Fish"	"Teach Hungry How to Fish"

Response III	Theological Understaning
Exploitation	Greed/Alienation
Wealthy Landowners, Western Extravagance-Consumption, Bloated Arms Budgets	Swords Into Plowshares, Great Wedding Banquet, Manna for Everyone
More Equity	Genuine Community A New World View
Fundamental Changes in the Socio-Economic Order, Internal and Global Conscientization	Conversion-Repentance At All Levels, Wholistic Sense of Mission
O.T. Prophets Beatitudes-Magnificat Luke 4	Shalom Jubilee, New Creation, The Eucharist-Lord's Prayer
Terms of Trade, Power of Rich, Commodity Prices, Role of Transnational Corporation, Christians as advocates	Visions of a Just Society, Political/Economic/ Social Theological Analysis, The Kingdom of God
Justice Interdependence Liberation	Identification with Our Lord, His Poverty-Option for the Poor, Creation-Centered Spirituality
Support People's Movement Abroad, Political Education, and Action at Home, Politics and Economics	Cooperative Living Voluntary Austerity Christian Stewardship
Shift of Power, Wealth	Both Rich and Poor Receive Their Humanity Again-Peace on Earth
"Give Fair Market Price For Fish", "Stop Polluting the Waters", "Make Room for Hungry to Fish"	

For Additional Discussion

1. List various programs of churches that would be described as social service or community action to help those in need. (In your church or others.)

   In which of the three responses in the chart do they fit?

2. There is nothing wrong with response #1. It is important. Why is it also important for churches and agencies to move into responses 2 an 3 or at least be supporters of those responses?

3. What can be done to help move us all into responses 2 and 3? How is courage to think differently involved?

4. What changes are needed in the socio-economic order (response 3) in order for there to be more justice in human relationships? In care of creation?

5. What would you change or add to this chart to improve it and why?

EXCERPTED FROM

Trapped

San Diego clergy small group

A group of clergy in the San Diego area gathered regularly to share, question, discuss and encourage each other. Someone was assigned a topic each time. They called themselves the agape group made up of a mix of gender, ages, perspectives and marital status. This article was written by one pastor in preparation for their discussion.

"As a young pastor, I must be honest and confess a spirit of fear and trembling when it comes to preaching about mishpat and zedekah (justice and righteousness). God siding with the poor, the hungry, the convicted, the undocumented – and calling us to do likewise – doesn't always set well with many in the pews. Even while I am convinced that this is what I am called to preach, in the interest of my job, my family, my pension, and my need to be liked and affirmed, sometimes I take a less confrontational approach. Here's where I might be rationalizing: In seminary we were constantly reminded of the importance of "meeting people where they are," and in my first call, I learned what happens when you don't. Walls go up, ears close, and people shut down with sarcasm or they just plain avoid you . . . or at least avoid any potentially sticky conversations with you. Achieving the kind of intimacy needed to grow a heart yearning for justice is halted dramatically.

So here are my questions:

To the "wisdom" in the group, those of you who have been out there in the church, preaching and acting for mishpat and zedekah for decades, can you relate to my fears? How did you cope? What did you do when/if people shut down? What mistakes did you make? And what has worked?

To the "energy" in the group, those of you who like me are in the early years of your ministry, passionate about peace and justice work, passionate about changing systems in the church and the world that entrap the marginalized, what do you say and do? Do you, like me, feel trapped?"

For Additional Discussion

• It is not just pastors who have felt trapped. Share a time when you felt trapped in the dilemma described by the author.

• How does this dilemma fit the mandate to speak the truth in love?

• Who has been a help to you in learning how to handle being trapped?

• Re-read and discuss Brueggemann's article, "Appearing Before the Authorities" on page 202 or Dorothee Soelle's article "Don't Forget the Best" on page 268.

• What can be done to help the church be more open to prophetic voices?

EXCERPTED FROM

Theological Root Causes

(From War on Want, London)

Theologians should stay out of politics.

Conflict in the church will cause our offering to decrease.

Jesus never got involved in politics.

Those who love the Lord will never go hungry.

It isn't just in the Third World we're fighting underdevelopment

Justification and Justice are two different things.

I want to feel good after a sermon.

I'm not responsible for systemic evil. It wasn't my decision.

Feeding the hungry is not as important as evangelism.

Jesus said "my kingdom is not of this world." So let's wait for Heaven.

JESUS SAID "THE POOR YOU ·WILL ALWAYS ·HAVE WITH YOU."

God has blessed us, therefore we are more advanced than other countries.

Please don't make me feel any more guilt.

Adapted by Erick Erickson from a poster by War on Want, a London, England organization

———— EXCERPTED FROM ————

Affirmation of Faith
by Joan Chittister

———— ❖❖❖ ————

Some liturgical churches still use the Apostles' creed, which dates back almost 2,000 years, in their worship services. Others are beginning to question this practice for various reasons. Alternative ways of affirming our faith have been created. (See *Banquet of Praise*, Bread for the World.) Below is an alternative affirmation of faith written by Joan Chittister, a Catholic sister, author, lecturer, church leader and retreat leader. Discuss what important things are left out of the Apostles' Creed. How does Chittister's affirmation offer a different way of thinking about what really matters? How would you say it differently?

Let us affirm our faith in the triune God, the God of our baptism.
    I believe in God,
        maker of an unfinished world,
        who calls us to participate in bringing about
        the fullness of Creation.

God, who created abundant resources to provide for all.
God, who has not divided people into rich and poor,
        owners and slaves,
        nor pitted us against each other because of race,
        color, social class or sex.

I believe in Jesus Christ
        who was ridiculed, tortured and executed
        for things he said and did.

He has overthrown the rule of evil and injustice
        and continues to judge and redeem
        the hatred and arrogance of human beings.

I believe in the Spirit of God
    whose flame comforts us with divine presence
    and causes our hearts to burn
    for righteousness and justice.

I believe in the reconciling power of God
    in our lives and in the world.

I believe that God, through people,
    can bring peace and hope,
    justice and equality,
    the relief of suffering and pain,
    and the final triumph of love and grace.

Amen

Letter To My Bishop

by George Johnson

◆◆◆

A letter sent to my Bishop in February, 2011 before a gathering of church leaders to discuss the future of the church after some fallout from a decision on gay/lesbian issues and the economic crisis.

I am sorry I could not be present for today's conversation. It is a great idea to gather and share our questions, our experiences and our vision for the future. My thoughts are not set in concrete but are part of my theological development and experience. They take the form of questions that invite further conversation. Thank you for this opportunity.

- As we think about the future and what opportunities present themselves to us as a church in this kairos moment, I wonder if it is time for us to **look at our theology**. We can examine our approach to leadership, our educational programs, needs and cultures of our neighbors, our worship and liturgies, current changes in our society and our resources and structures. This can be helpful. I wonder if it might also be a time to examine our theology and ask some critical questions. Has our theology become an escape from really addressing the crisis our world faces today? As Joerg Rieger says, "the problem of exclusion of so many people from the abundant life that Jesus talked about has become one of the most pressing theological problems today." From *God and the Excluded*

Douglas John Hall suggests that the real problem confronting churches today is its theology. He says, "We have all in some sense been seduced theologically by a history of intellectual and spiritual conditioning that is unbelievably hard to cast off . . . The real crisis of Christendom as it encounters its own demise lies precisely in the poverty and inappropriateness of its theology." *The Cross in our Context*, page 171

- I wonder if our **emphasis on grace** has created an imbalance in our preaching and teaching, and as a result the biblical call for loving our neighbors and obedience has been silenced. As Walter Brueggemann says, "The fearfulness and avoidance of obedience, as conventionally understood among us, has in my judgment two root causes, both of which are alive and powerful, even though not often frontally articulated. The first dimension of the problem is the Augustinian-Lutheran dichotomy of grace and law which runs very deep in Western theology." *The Covenanted Self* Page 35. Read on.

In our hymnal, *Evangelical Lutheran Worship*, in hymn #689, "Praise and Thanksgiving", we have taken out the phrase, "where all obey you" in verse 4 as it was in the *Lutheran Book of Worship* (Green) and replaced it with "where you are reigning." I wonder if we are too cautious about the word obey in our covenant theology. When last did I preach a series on the big Ten?

- Joerg Rieger in his book, *God and the Excluded*, suggests that our current theology has **failed to include the poor** in our interpretation of scripture, reflection, envisioning and planning. He says: "Closer listening to the traditions and texts of the church from the perspective of the marginalized in light of God's own work will be the major task ahead for theological reflection." Page 162. Reiger goes on to suggest that we need to become aware of our blind spots in theology and how we have been sucked into the powers that be (in our case the powers of exclusion). There will be need for courage to resist. Dorothee Soelle reminds us that the poor are our teachers and they are the ones that help the rich and educated be converted.

Robert McAfee Brown says rather bluntly: "We discover that the Bible says a great deal about the poor. It all seems askew, for while the poor do get a lot of attention in the Bible, the non-poor get a lot of attention in the church and usually end up running things. One reason for this is that the non-poor have become the official interpreters of the Scriptures and have managed to take most of the sting out of the passages dealing with the poor." *Evangelism and the Poor* by Ana de Garcia and George S. Johnson page 12

- I wonder if our theology has left us vulnerable to a kind of **individualism** (take a look at our sacraments) and **nationalism** that has promoted a piety that is divorced from politics. How easy it is to shy away from the political implications of Jesus' teaching and the sacraments for fear of being criticized for being too political. As a result the prophetic voice of the church has been silenced, not by any policy statement, movement of pastors, or careful selection of seminary seniors for our Synod, but by a theology that is careful to avoid the economic and political implications of Jesus' teaching. Maybe job security is another factor in this silence.

Sister Marie Augusta Neal sets out a warning for us: "The idea of civil religion is popular today because for any nation to assert its right to program the world economy in its interests, those in power need the assurance of a naïve, spontaneous, uncritical religion to mask the mass exploitation that such programs require. Religious enthusiasm uncritically expressed and charismatically released is one of the most effective ways of delaying the consequences." *A Socio-Theology of Letting Go* Page 38. Maybe this is what Hall means "seduced theologically."

• Do our theology and the proclamation of the gospel include the cost of discipleship? I don't think that Jesus waited until his listeners completely understood grace or had reached a certain level of maturity before he set before them that there is a cross ahead of those who follow him. Do we invite people to the table of bread and wine without any connection made to the call to share our bread with the hungry and the counterculture nature of our faith? Do our people understand that Jesus died because of what he said and did as well as for our salvation? What does the cross mean today?

Shane Claiborne describes his becoming a Christian in this way:
"I know there are people out there who say, 'My life was such a mess. I was drinking, partying, sleeping around...and then I met Jesus and my whole life came together.' God bless those people. But me, I had it together. I used to be cool. And then I met Jesus and he wrecked my life. The more I read the gospel, the more it messed me up, turning everything I believed in, valued, and hoped for upside down. I am still recovering from my conversion." Then

he goes on to say: "Charity wins awards and applause but joining the poor gets you killed. People are not crucified for helping poor people. They are crucified for joining them." *Irresistible Revolution* Page 41

P.S. This is not a call to abandon our Lutheran theology but as Luther said in his introduction to the 95 theses, the church always needs to rethink everything. Thank you for the invitation to share my thoughts in preparation for the discussion about the future of our church.

George S. Johnson
Laguna Woods, CA

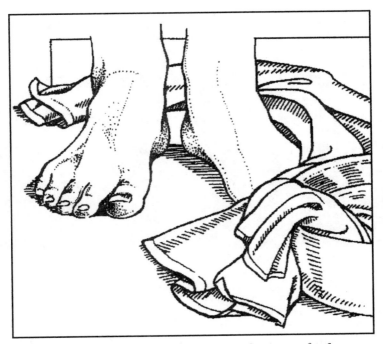

Now that I, your Lord and Teacher, have washed your feet, you also should wash one another's feet.

John 13:14

Cloud of Witnesses

JESUIT MARTYRS OF EL SALVADOR On Nov. 16, 1989 these priests and lay workers were gunned down by government forces because of their work for justice. Read about them and their lives in *Companions of Jesus* (Orbis 1990).

Original artwork by Stephen D. Kroeger, contact Stephen.Kroeger@uc.edu

Oscar Romero	Steve Biko	Ita Ford	Harvey Milk
1917-80	1946-77	1940-80	1930-78
El Salvador	South Africa	The Bronx	San Francisco

These four and countless other men and women have been brutally killed because they had the courage to think differently about justice and compassion. They, like Jesus, "became obedient unto death." Learn from them about courage.

Since we are surrounded by so great a cloud of witnesses. . .
Run with preserverance the race set before you.

Hebrews 12:1

About the Editor

GEORGE S. JOHNSON is a retired Lutheran Pastor who lives with his wife, Vivian, in Laguna Woods, California. He attended a Lutheran high school, Augustana College, a Lutheran Bible Institute, Luther Seminary and was ordained in 1962. Later he earned a M.Th from Luther Seminary in St. Paul and a D.Min. from Claremont School of Theology in California. Johnson has served parishes in California and Minnesota for thirty plus years as well as several interims.

The Johnsons took their daughters, Sonja and Joy, with them to Sweden in 1979 where both George and Vivian studied at the University of Uppsala. When they returned George became the Director of the Hunger Program for the former American Lutheran Church (1980-87). This involved extensive speaking, global travel and writting educational material.

George served as advisor to the Committee on Economic Justice at the 1984 Assembly of the Lutheran World Federation in Budapest, Hungary. After re-tirement he became the Director of Third World Opportunities where he took groups to Mexico for consciousness raising and service. Reading, writing, preaching, lecturing and travel have kept him connected and current on poverty, hunger, justice, and oppression issues. Liberation theology has been a special interest.

George has written and published material for small groups and adult classes. At San Marcos Lutheran he wrote and taught a 25-week class on Practicing the Faith and at Irvine United Congregational Church he wrote and taught a 6-week class on poverty issues. In 2013 he will write and teach on Food, Farming and Faith. His book *Beyond Guilt* has gone through five printings.

George's wife, Vivian, is the co-author of *Lifestories*, a conversation game of storytelling and has written four biographies and numerous articles on coping with loss. In Minnesota she worked as a parish worker, a school counselor, for the American Cancer Society and Director of ARC, an ecumenical retreat center in Minnesota. George and Vivian's son, Todd, died of cancer at the age of 15.

George has received DISTINGUISHED alumni awards from Augustana Academy and Claremont School of Theology. He is an ardent SF Giants fan and enjoys tennis, golf and reading.

Published works:

Beyond Guilt, Christian Response to Hunger/Poverty, Revised and Expanded

Critical Decisions in Following Jesus (CSS 1992)

How to Start Small Groups and Keep Them Going (Augsburg Fortress, 1995)

Following Jesus, a study guide for small groups (Augsburg/Fortress, 1995)

Evangelism and the Poor, with Ana DeGarcia (Augsburg Fortress, 1985)